The Labor Question
in America

The Labor Question in America

Economic Democracy in the Gilded Age

ROSANNE CURRARINO

UNIVERSITY OF ILLINOIS PRESS

Urbana, Chicago, and Springfield

Library of Congress Cataloging-in-Publication Data
Currarino, Rosanne.
The labor question in America : economic democracy
in the gilded age / Rosanne Currarino.
p.   cm. — (The working class in American history)
Includes bibliographical references and index.
ISBN-13: 978-0-252-03570-8 (hardcover: alk. paper)
ISBN-13: 978-0-252-07786-9 (pbk.: alk. paper)
1. Working class—United States—History—19th century.
2. Working class—United States—History—20th century.
3. Labor—United States—History.
4. United States—Social conditions—1865–1918.
5. Citizenship—United States.
6. Democracy—United States.
I. Title
HD8072 .C927   2010
323.60973'09034—dc22   2010047169

For C.C.W.

Contents

Acknowledgments

Annual income twenty pounds, annual expenditure
nineteen six, result happiness. Annual income
twenty pounds, annual expenditure twenty
pound ought and six, result misery.

Charles Dickens, *David Copperfield*

Mr. Micawber's famous equation of happiness with freedom from debt applies mainly to personal finance, for in many other aspects of life, debt may be a happy thing. The debts I have incurred while working on this project are many and great, and they remind me over and again of the pleasure of scholarly work, the real joys of engaged debate, and the sheer fun of historical research. I cannot possibly repay these debts but only gratefully and happily acknowledge them.

At Rutgers University, I had the privilege of working with Jim Livingston, Sue Cobble, Jan Lewis and Jackson Lears. I offer thanks for the enthusiasm with which they asked questions and proffered advice. Sue Cobble in particular pushed me to hone my framework and focus. She and Michael Merrill gave me many much-appreciated comments and editorial suggestions.

Librarians at the Bancroft Library at Berkeley, the Bentley Historical Library at the University of Michigan, the Kheel Center at Cornell, the Manuscript Division of the Library of Congress, the New York Public Library, Queen's, and Rutgers made my research both possible and enjoyable. I particularly thank David Kessler at the Bancroft, the late Stan Nash at Rutgers, and Harry Miller at the Wisconsin Historical Society. Funding from Rutgers University, Princeton University, and Queen's University made those research trips possible. A year as a Mellon Fellow at the Penn Humanities Forum, made all the more congenial by Jennifer Conway, Eugene Narmour, and my fellow fellows, helped me further conceptualize this project.

Jerry Friedman, Rich Schneirov, Robyn Muncy, Robert Johnston, Larry

Glickman, Kathy Peiss, and David Engerman slogged through a preliminary draft of the manuscript and offered invaluable feedback. Robert gave me one of the most detailed, helpful critiques of the project imaginable; it proved indispensable to revisions, even if I didn't follow absolutely all of his suggestions. Over the past few years, Jerry has skillfully edited my prose, improved my arguments, and cheered me on. At conferences, via e-mail, in the hallways, and over coffee, engaged, perceptive comments and suggestions from Leon Fink, Mary Furner, Lisa Fine, Jeff Sklansky, Shelton Stromquist, Thomas Winter, William Hagan, Jonathan Steinberg, Dan Bender, Andrew Isenberg, Petra Goedde, Sarah Wilson, and Alice Maurice have helped me clarify my arguments and think more broadly about the parameters of democracy in the United States.

I presented a draft of chapter 4 at the Penn Economic History Forum, skillfully run by Dan Raff. I thank the forum participants—in particular, Walter Licht and the late Alan Dawley—for their generous comments. I gave an early draft of chapter 5 at the UMass-Amherst Economic History and Development Workshop and benefited enormously from the skeptical questions and gentle proddings of the audience. I especially thank Jerry Friedman, Carole Heim, and Daniel MacDonald.

An earlier version of chapter 4 appeared as "The Politics of 'More': The AFL and the Idea of Economic Liberty," *Journal of American History* 93 (June 2006): 17–36. I again thank Sue Cobble, Grace Palladino, Larry Glickman, and Richard Oestreicher for their comments on that paper as well as David Nord and Susan Armeny. Parts of chapter 3 were published as "'The Revolution Now in Progress': Social Economics and the Labor Question," *Labor History* 50 (February 2009): 1–17. An earlier version of chapter 2 was published as "Meat vs. Rice: Working-Class Manhood and Anti-Chinese Hysteria," *Men and Masculinities* 9 (April 2007): 476–90.

In New Jersey, Philadelphia, and now Ontario, the worlds of work and leisure have blurred pleasurably thanks to Jonathan Nashel, Rebecca Brittenham, David Engerman, Peter Cohen, Jacqui Spadaro, Daisy Fried, Jim Quinn, Alex Gillespie, Richard Ogden, Jeannine Delombard, Dan White, Andrew DuBois, Ben Weiner, Jeremy Lopez, Sarah Wilson, Mark Stabile, Alice Maurice, and Mark Rigby. At Queen's, I'm delighted to count Sandra den Otter, Andrew Jainchill, Rebecca Manley, Jeff McNairn, and David Parker as friends and collaborators.

As readers for the University of Illinois Press, Rich Schneirov and Larry Lipin gave the manuscript sharp, sympathetic readings and offered precise and extremely helpful comments and suggestions, as did series editor Alice

Kessler-Harris. Ellen Goldlust-Gingrich skillfully copyedited the manuscript. Laurie Matheson has encouraged this project from the get-go. A more supportive, helpful editor I cannot imagine.

Matt Guterl reads almost everything I write, no matter how dreadful, and offers encouragement, criticism, and suggestions in equal measure, reminding me time and again that writing at its best is always a collaborative effort. Jim Livingston is the most relentlessly engaged historian I know. From his example, I have learned that narratives we create matter and that we write them every day, in the analysis of ideas and events both great and small. No lesson could be more important. Finally, my greatest debt is to Chris Warley, who, with endless patience and indefatigable enthusiasm, reads my drafts, refines my arguments, improves my prose, and keeps me on track.

The Labor Question
in America

The Labor Question in the Late Nineteenth Century

Could democracy survive in industrial America? This was, in essence, the labor question of the late nineteenth century. In earlier times, democracy's meaning—political equality among white men—had been clearer, or so thought Americans in the postbellum years. But by 1886, as J. L. Spalding, the bishop of Peoria, dishearteningly put it, "There is liberty of thought and expression. Every man has a right to vote, and still the golden age has not come."[1] What exactly that golden age might be was far from clear, but most Americans believed that it could not include desperate families crowding into New York City police stations begging for shelter from winter storms, or towns such as Amsterdam, New York, where almost the entire population stood on the brink of destitution. Nor should that golden age include an ever-growing class of men trapped permanently in the degrading dependency of industrial wage work.

What was the answer? Political rights, as Spalding noted, were no defense against severe economic distress, and they did nothing to ensure an independent citizenry. Breadlines stretched down city streets during the hard depressions of the 1870s and 1890s. Businesses failed, despite their owners' prudent efforts. Men who had dreamed of becoming shop owners like their fathers now faced a life of endless wage work. The contrast of the grim present with the imagined rosy past only heightened the sense of dismay. Labor journalist John Swinton fondly remembered that in antebellum America, "Everybody had a sense of manly independence; everybody was able to get along without anxiety; everybody had a pretty good time."[2] Now, however, men seemed fated to be nothing more than "bound dependents," without hope of either property or prosperity. The prospects for a democratic golden age did not look good.

All observers agreed that the culprit was the new industrial order, but the consensus went no further. At one point or another, the labor question seemed to include anything that could go wrong in industrial America. Labor questions per se were nothing new in the United States; in the 1820s, New York journeymen had taken to the streets to demand shorter hours; the 1850s witnessed a full-fledged "labor crisis" and a fight for a ten-hour day; in 1860, a "great strike" swept across New England, with close to a third of all workers in Massachusetts firms joining in. But the labor question of the Gilded Age and Progressive Era was different in size, scope, and significance. In the popular imagination, it was linked to the economic downturn between 1873 and 1897: wave after wave of business failures, seesawing unemployment, and repeated crises in banking. It was also tied to issues as disparate as the growing number of factories, the rising population of industrial wage workers, the staggering increase in manufacturing output, skyrocketing urban populations, the mounting availability of ever-cheaper consumer goods, and the explosive growth of immigration. Most of all, though, it was linked to the increasing number of permanent wage workers and declining number of independent, self-employed producers.

The breadth of the labor question meant that almost all Americans hotly contested its causes and effects and tried to provide answers; just what should or could constitute a democratic society was a problem Americans took very seriously. Workers, labor organizations, and employers, of course, were primary participants in the debate; industrialization touched them most immediately. But the labor question was a question for everyone, and just about everyone weighed in, offering an astounding array of contradictory answers ranging from the sublime to the ridiculous. Future secretary of state John Hay wrote *The Bread-Winners,* a serial novel demonizing labor organizations; playwright Henry Grimm insisted that the labor question could be answered by the simple phrase "The Chinese Must Go!" A Brooklyn plumber, testifying before one of the many congressional committees charged with investigating the "relations between capital and labor," argued that more free western land would end labor strife. Some, among them New York manufacturer Henry Rothschild, called for workers to be less extravagant with their wages. Bureau of Labor Statistics commissioner Carroll Davidson Wright blamed economic instability and subsequent labor unrest on underconsumption, and economists such as Simon Nelson Patten began to argue that workers' greatest contribution to economic growth should be as consumers rather than as producers. The American Federation of Labor demanded higher wages and shorter hours so that workers could enjoy the consumer products of the time, from sofas to newspapers. The Knights of Labor, conversely, saw the wage system itself as the root of social problems and called for employers and employees to share ownership of plants. Congress and state legislatures tried to improve workers' lives at work, passing laws limiting the number of hours of labor. The courts responded by ruling that such protective labor legislation stymied workers' individual right to decide their own terms of labor. Social reformers looked for ways to improve daily urban life for all citizens, suggesting everything from municipal ownership of utilities, which Henry Demarest Lloyd tirelessly advocated, to better playgrounds for New York children, one of the many local programs started by social gospel proponent Washington Gladden.

This book looks at the two overarching approaches to answering the labor question over the course of the late nineteenth century. The first effort drew on a proprietary-producerist model of citizenship and came out of antebellum understandings of republican citizenship. Like eighteenth-century republicanism, this approach equated social and political legitimacy with property ownership (whether in real property or skill) and individual virtue with productive labor. This citizen, assumed to be male (and usually white), was understood to be independent; property ownership ensured that unlike a slave, servant, wife, or child, he did not rely on the whims or will of another man. His independence and moral self-sufficiency were also guaranteed because he produced what he earned through his own effort. In direct contrast were such morally vacuous figures as speculators and gamblers, who, as mere parasitic robbers, fattened themselves on the toil of other men. Permanent wage work threatened the proprietary producer's independence because it made him dependent on the will of another for his survival; it ensured, in the rhetoric of the mid–nineteenth century, that his capitalist employer robbed him unceasingly of his rightful property in the full fruits of his labor. But just as wage work imperiled this model of citizenship, it also supplied an exceptionally elastic tool of protest against proletarianization. At times, the producerist citizen was used as a foil to heighten the problems faced by contemporary wage workers, as Swinton's nostalgic glance into his childhood showed. At other moments, as for the Knights of Labor, the producer-citizen appeared as a defiant alternative to the permanent proletariat, the center of a cooperative organization of the means of production that could eliminate the ignominy of wage work. The cooperative commonwealth, advocates hoped, could reinstate the republic and reaffirm the ideal of a nation of proprietary producers, each invested with the natural right to the fruits of his labor, no more and no less.

The second approach to the labor question grew out of the social and economic conditions of wage work itself. A specifically economic model of citizenship came to dominate both the emerging mainstream trade union movement and Progressive social thought and answered the question of what a modern democracy might look like by expanding the sites of democratic participation. Rather than exclusively a political issue, citizenship and democratic participation became an economic issue as well. In many ways, the economic citizenship of the late nineteenth century anticipated the social citizenship described by British sociologist T. H. Marshall in the 1940s—most notably, Marshall's emphasis on the citizen's entitlement to a range of social rights from "a modicum of economic welfare" to the right "to live the life of a civilized being according to the standards prevailing." Marshall understood these rights as social entitlements, specifically embodied within the legislation of the welfare state. Late-nineteenth- and early-twentieth-century conceptions of economic citizenship, however, did not rely on the state to the same extent but rather emphasized the economic power to act in society and the capacity to enjoy the abundance of economic life. This understanding of economic citizenship included more than the right to form labor unions, enact hours legislation, demand overtime pay, or claim unemployment insurance; it also counted the enjoyment of sofas, newspapers, and vacations as part of citizenship.[3] By the end of the Progressive Era, economic citizenship was imagined as the "demand of an individual for decency and comfort, for a chance to work and obtain the fullness of life," in Jane Addams's words, a means to an economic "socialized democracy."[4]

The model of economic citizenship and the economic democracy toward which it looked always existed in uneasy tension with the proprietary producer model of citizenship. And indeed, the history of the labor question is very much the story of how Americans negotiated and navigated between these two conceptions of citizenship and democracy. This book traces those tensions chronologically and in a wide variety of locales, for the labor question pulled in a diverse and sometimes unexpected range of Americans into the discussions. Chapter 1 begins with the economic collapse of 1873 and looks at the ways in which Americans invoked the language of proprietary producerism to explain and offer solutions to the social crisis of the 1870s. By the end of the depression and the beginning of the 1880s, the proprietary language on which both professional and lay commentators relied had come to seem inadequate to the facts of economic change. For many observers, a viable answer to question of the future survival of the American democratic experiment remained elusive. Chapter 2 moves into the 1880s, examining the debates regarding Chinese immigration, which gripped Americans regardless of class or region and which showed up, often quite suddenly, in many of the more general debates about the labor question. The vitriol poured out against the Chinese also helped redefine the producer-citizen as simultaneously a producer and a consumer. Chapter 3 turns to the 1880s and 1890s and looks at historical economists' efforts to describe a new basis for American democracy that could include wage earners as full citizens. Dismantling the wages-fund theory and the labor theory of value, these economists posited a social theory of value that expanded the labor question outside of the workshop to ask how workers could share in the social surplus of industrial production found in the world of leisure and consumption. Chapter 4 examines the American Federation of Labor's "pure and simple unionism" in the 1890s. Far from simple, demands for "more" constituted efforts to concretize claims to the social surplus through higher wages, shorter hours, and greater participation in social and economic life. At the center of this politics of more was an explicitly economic model of citizenship that included economic as well as political opportunities. Chapter 5 studies the early-twentieth-century expansion of economic citizenship into the concept of economic democracy, a socialized democracy that emphasized economic as much as political participation. The "new democracy," however, emerged in tandem with a new version of the self-sufficient citizen who was but a pale reflection of the proprietary producer and whose self-sufficiency and independence were based not on production but on the idea of freedom of choice.

The tensions between these conflicting understandings of citizenship have shaped arguments regarding the meaning of democracy and the nature of democratic life since the Progressive Era. Though Progressives offered new ideas of citizenship and democracy, they could not resolve the conflicts between competing understandings of industrialization, citizenship, civic participation, and democratic life. Consequently, the labor question has continued to animate historiographic debate, which, as Robert Johnston rightly points out, is as concerned with today as with the Gilded Age and Progressive Era. When historians ask, "How could democracy continue in an age of large-scale industrialization and incorporation?" they are also asking about the prospects for democratic life in contemporary America. For many historians, the course of the late nineteenth century made those prospects grim indeed.[5] Such narratives follow the general trajectory of historians such as Gabriel Kolko and James Weinstein, who argue that big business co-opted American democracy and effectively shut individual citizens out of the democratic process. Under the aegis of an increasingly centralized regulatory state that supported the interests of business over the common good, big business preached pluralism and sold a "false consciousness of the nature of American liberalism," effectively convincing (or hoodwinking) working-class leaders and reformers to work for the interests of the corporate elite. Kolko's and Weinstein's insistence that the Progressive Era moved the United States away from any democratic promise it might have had and into a period of profoundly antidemocratic conservatism has found significantly less strident but no less committed echoes in the recent works of historians similarly skeptical of the age of reform.[6] Nancy Cohen's *Reconstruction of American Liberalism,* for example, argues that Gilded Age reformers, particularly economists, sought not to expand democracy but to contract it. They increased the size of nonelected federal regulatory bodies over which citizens had no direct control and ceded more and more permanent power to corporations at the expense of direct democracy.[7] A chorus of works has bolstered this general argument. Some political histories have pointed to the emergence of a more complacent and less engaged citizenry. Others have noted the continuing absence of any significant challenge to the political status quo from a third party, such as those offered by the Populists, Greenbackers, or Socialists, while still others have focused on the rise of increasingly powerful special interest groups, which effectively pushed narrow and personal agendas onto state and national legislatures. Historians of race and immigration have highlighted the vigorous and successful efforts to exclude nonwhites from the democratic process.[8]

Perhaps the most damning indictments of the period follow from Christopher Lasch's wide-ranging and impassioned *True and Only Heaven.* Lasch, never one to spare the rod and spoil the reader, rebukes both contemporary and late-nineteenth-century Americans for turning their backs on proprietary democracy, based in a strong sense of community, in favor of the alluring mirage of "progress." For Lasch, the American belief that increasing material abundance and social progress were synonymous made it all too easy to replace participatory democracy with consumerism, resulting in an anomic society with little to no civic engagement. Thus, he reserves especially scathing words for Walter Weyl, who advocated "distribution, not participation" and replaced the "moral heroism" and civic spirit of proprietary democracy with mindless consumption by the "unnamed multitude."[9] Lasch here echoes the concerns of other cultural historians, particularly from the 1980s, who worry about the effects of mass consumption on civic engagement.[10] Efforts to substitute "attempts to achieve a redistribution of income, to equalize opportunity in various ways, to incorporate the working classes into a society of consumers, or to foster economic growth and overseas expansion" have not, he argues, "created the kind of active, enterprising citizenry envisioned by nineteenth-century democrats."[11] Instead, as political theorist Michael Sandel has argued, the Progressive Era move away from a republican, producerite model of citizenship and toward "a politics based on consumer identities" that pushed politics away from the question of "how to elevate or improve or restrain the people's preference" and toward merely asking "how best—more fully, or fairly, or efficiently—to satisfy them."[12]

Such interpretations feature a pervasive sense of loss—indeed, of a transition away from a better past to a more problematic and decidedly less virtuous present. This narrative may emphasize a particular moment in which an alternative to the present was forestalled (the decline of the Knights after Haymarket, for example, or the defeat and diminution of the Populists) or may emphasize a seismic change (away from a golden age of participatory democracy, often located in Jacksonian America, and toward the rise of consumer culture and political apathy, for example). But whether the virtuous, vigorous individual citizen of the past was done in by proletarianization, consumption, or the administrative state, the argument remains largely the same.[13] Underlying it is an assumption of the distinctness of "the economic" and "the moral" (or "the social"). The juxtaposition of uncommodified character and commodified personality—Tonnies's divide between *Gemeinschaft* and *Gesellschaft* in the American context—has become almost a commonplace in historiographic examinations of the "great transformation" of the nineteenth century. Before the market revolution of the early nineteenth century, writes one historian, "we had faces," but afterward we became merely "commodified identit[ies]," economic men without access to the moral world of personal relations, community, and sustained engagement in the political process.[14] In this new world, "personal autonomy" came to represent "self-expression rather than self-employment." Leisure activities that had once been celebrations of a "value-laden" participatory public life became instead "commercialized, sanitized," and "passive."[15]

Many of the late-nineteenth-century Americans in this book, however, might well have been surprised by this historiographic narrative. They understood themselves as very much committed to preserving and expanding the basis of American democracy. Whether politicians or economists, labor leaders or anti-Chinese activists, social reformers or writers, they sought to reimagine what democracy could be and to do so within the vocabulary and circumstances of their particular historical moment: wage work, incorporation, industrialization. They would have vigorously rejected the idea that any distinction could exist between "the economic" and "the social." Economic questions were social questions, and neither could be tackled separately. The stated goal of these individuals was not the creation a "moral community of self-governing citizens," predicated on the figure of the independent republican yeoman, but an economic as well as political democracy in which citizens' participation in social and economic life was at least as important as formal political involvement.[16] When George Gunton launched his magazine, the *Social Economist,* as an auxiliary to his New York–based Institute of Social Economics, he explained that the "subjects of the day" were no longer those of kings—diplomacy, battles, titles—but those of "general human well-being, the prosperity and modes of life of universal mankind. The subjects of the day are therefore not dynastic, esthetic, metaphysical or theological, they are mostly economical. They concern ways and means of living better, and being better, they are matters of wages, trades unions, and strikes, trusts, and finance, free trade and tariff, questions which . . . pertain to the welfare of all." For Gunton, democratic participation could not be imagined as separate from material or economic life. To say that economic activities, whether earning wages or consuming, was somehow less virtuous, less rigorous, and less important than political participation made no sense to him. Economic questions, he insisted, were always "questions of democracy . . . questions as to how the great good of the greatest number can be obtained, and the vast majority of men be made free, comfortable, and secure."[17] Or, as Addams repeatedly argued, it was necessary at last to "socialize democracy," "to make the entire social organism democratic, to extend democracy beyond its political expression."[18] Democracy, as Gunton and Addams made clear, was literally in the streets as well as at the ballot box, in all aspects of daily life—work, leisure, family life, politics, and consumption. None could be separated from the others.

Some recent historians have begun to reframe the historiographic debate along similar lines, suggesting that the most useful question might not be "Why did American democracy wither?" but rather "What did 'democracy' come to mean in an age of incorporation?" Indeed, as much of this historiography insists, civic and even political participation did not drastically decline, and Americans remained committed to democratic life, even as the terms they used and means they employed changed significantly. As Theda Skocpol, Robert Johnston, Elisabeth Clemens, and other historians of policy and politics have argued, popular political activity did not die back but instead found new venues and new participants at both the local and national levels.[19] Nor did the decline of organizations such as the Knights, the Populists, and antimonopolists or the limited successes of the Socialist Party portend a more constrained and limited democratic politics. In Chicago, for example, as Richard Schneirov demonstrates, workers and labor organizations forced a rethinking of urban political operations, market regulation, and the tenets of liberalism. Working within the Carter Harrison–run Democratic machine, these groups helped institute a cross-class social democratic movement.[20]

In a similar vein, historians have argued for a view of consumer culture as encompassing much more than buying and spending. James Livingston contends that consumer culture and corporate capitalism compelled rather than restrained new considerations of selfhood, politics, and social organization.[21] Lawrence Glickman has shown that consumerist concerns were often intensely political. Workers' demands for a living wage, set in accordance with the American standard of living, provided a means and legitimation for establishing and controlling market relations.[22] Kathy Peiss, Gary Cross, Nan Enstad, Leora Auslander, and other historians of consumer culture have argued that both the ability to consume and consumer goods themselves can have tangible political and social effects, propelling people previously excluded from public participation into active and engaged civic life.[23] Recent works in political economy, including Meg Jacobs's *Pocketbook Politics* and Lizabeth Cohen's *Consumer's Republic,* have traced the often obscured but very real connections between personal and private consumer behavior and public policy and politics.[24] Federal policies may have shaped American consumers' behavior, but the track ran both ways: consumers also demanded and received policies from the government, using consumption in ways that could be unexpected and deeply politically engaged.

Returning to the labor question in the twenty-first century entails reviving the questions of the relationship between democratic and economic life, between private and public life, between culture and politics, and between work and citizenship. The term *the labor question* has now vanished from our daily lexicon. Stores are no longer flooded by books with titles such as *A Momentous Question: The Respective Attitudes of Capital and Labor, The Labor Movement: The Problem of To-Day, Some Ethical Phases of the Labor Question,* or *Plain Talk on the Labor Question.*[25] But the central problem of the labor question—the basis of American democracy; the relationships among civil, political, and economic participation; the meanings of citizenship—remained vital in twentieth-century social and political thought and remain central still. In contemporary debates about mortgages, predatory lending, and home foreclosures, for example, we can see conflicting understandings of citizenship. Calls to save homeowners from bankruptcy and economic disenfranchisement, for example, are balanced by arguments that taxpayers not be responsible for individual acts of fiscal imprudence or interfere in an individual's right to borrow on any terms to which he or she and a lender agree. For every American who argues that "omitting relief for homeowners . . . would be like creating a post-Katrina program to provide relief for New Orleans lenders, but not the people displaced," another insists that individuals, not society or the government, must take responsibility for their actions: "I'm not in the mood to bailout some low credit score homeowner who is not working as hard as I am to make it in America," wrote John D. to the *New York Times*; "The problem here is a lack of personal responsibility."[26] The terms of these questions—the struggle over the essence of democratic citizenship—come out of the debates over the labor question of the nineteenth century.

1

The Cant of Economy

Narratives of Depression in the 1870s

The "labor question" became a question during the depression of the 1870s. It became a question in part because of the depression's effects on labor, because of workers' real and highly visible suffering, because of high unemployment, and because of the widespread distress of the manufacturing industry. But the labor question was more than just an endless series of economic hardships. It emerged as a social problem in the 1870s because it, like the depression itself, was an outward sign of seismic changes in American life. We now understand those changes as signaling the transition from proprietary to corporate capitalism, as the move from a social and political order defined by small property holders to one defined by permanent wage workers.[1] At the time, though, the economic collapse itself was the focus of national attention. It seemed to be the immediate and proximate cause of labor's and society's woes. It touched everyone where it mattered most, in the daily routines of working, buying, and selling, and its immediate and frequently catastrophic effects demanded explanations and solutions, which almost everyone living in the United States seemed more than willing to supply—at length.

When Americans—whether self-styled experts or hard-put bakers—tried to grapple with the causes of the depression, they generally presented a muddled picture. Yet however incoherent, contradictory, and even ridiculous their assessments of the crisis may seem in hindsight, they can and should be read as the beginnings of a decades-long effort to explain and make navigable the transition from proprietary to corporate capitalism. They were, in other words, early attempts to answer the labor question's central demand: Could democracy survive in industrial America, and, if so, would its meaning and manifestation change? The ways in which a wide range of Americans—from ordinary workers and businessmen to larger capitalists and financiers, from politicians and journalists to academics and clergymen—worked to define, explain, and solve the economic problems directly shaped how they would think and act in future moments of economic and social crisis. For them, specifically economic issues were inseparable from more general social concerns, and when they spoke of the depression, whether in terms of its impact financially or of the broader social suffering it had caused, they were always also engaged in a larger conversation about the future of America. The narratives of economic progress and disaster in turn reflected and molded people's ideas about what American democracy should and could be in the emerging but as yet undefined industrial world.

At first glance, the discussions of the causes of and remedies for the depression and the resultant social chaos seem to lack any sort of cohesion. So in 1878, when a House select committee assembled to investigate the "causes of the general depression in labor and business" heard testimony from invited witnesses and volunteers, the statements covered a dizzying range of topics. Some witnesses blamed drink. Several criticized the increasing employment of women and boys, who took jobs desperately needed by able-bodied men. Many participants condemned greedy railroad speculators and called for the government to assume ownership of the lines. Others pointed to excessive government regulation, with one witness even declaring that "Congress should go home and let the people manage themselves." Still other witnesses pinned the depression on the moral lethargy of individual Americans who simply refused to buckle down and work harder.[2] Newspapers, politicians, and recognized experts were hardly more consistent in their explanations or remedies, vacillating between insisting that nothing fundamental was wrong with the economy and proclaiming that everything was wrong with it.

It is possible, however, to distinguish patterns within the apparent cacophony of ideas. Almost all of the narratives of the depression relied on the language of producerism to assert mid-nineteenth-century ideals of citizenship and democracy and to mediate between proprietary capitalism and the emerging industrial order. But producerism was far from a coherent ideology, and many variations of it coexisted in postbellum America. Two in particular shaped discussions of the depression in the 1870s and 1880s: an older proprietary producerism and an emerging industrial producerism. Though the two were not distinct and indeed overlapped in myriad ways, we can roughly say that proprietary producerism, prevalent in the 1840s and

1850s, reflected the conditions of simple market society dominated by self-employed men or men who expected to become self-employed. Industrial producerism emerged in the 1870s, becoming more widespread in the 1880s. Its appearance was concomitant with the dominance of proprietary competitive capitalism and the realization that wage work was now a permanent condition for more workers.[3]

Proprietary producerism had its origins in eighteenth-century republicanism and a market economy largely though not exclusively defined by self-employment and simple commodity production.[4] Proprietary producerism emphasized the connections among social legitimacy, self-sufficiency, and the ownership of productive property. Property initially was understood narrowly, as real property, but in the first decade of the nineteenth century, it came to include property in skill as well. Thus, self-employed producers, whether yeoman farmers or urban artisans, could claim to be independent property owners, creating what Ronald Schultz has called "the small-producer tradition."[5] Property ownership of whatever kind remained a requirement for political participation, for it showed that a man was independent both economically and politically; his civic and political actions were his own and not another's. The opposite of the property-owning republican citizen was someone dependent on the will of another: a wage worker, a servant, a child, a woman, or a slave.

Proprietary producerism's stress on the importance of production stemmed in part from the Lockean emphasis on the improvement of property through labor as well as from the American version of the Protestant work ethic. Work not only created value, as Daniel Rodgers explains, but legitimated a man as a social being. Productive labor curbed the baser passions of lust and avarice and built character by demanding self-control, economic prudence, and continual striving. It also assured self-sufficiency, for a producer earned his rewards through the sweat of his brow, not off the labor of another. Success, then, was the reward for an individual's own work and as such displayed for all the inner virtues of the successful individual.[6] The ideals of proprietary producerism echoed in legislation such as the Homestead Act and public and legislative debates (which came to naught) about redistributing slaveholders' land to former slaves. In opposition to the hardworking productive proprietor stood the speculator or gambler, someone who took what others had labored to create, and the slave, servant, or wage worker, the fruits of whose labor belonged to their masters.[7] In the 1870s discussions of the depression, invocations of proprietary producerism usually emphasized the need for individual men to own property and were frequently tinged with nostalgia for a remembered past in which a man's hard work and self-restraint were rewarded with the combination of property, self-sufficiency, and a voice in civic life.

These uses of proprietary producerism were in many ways more a part of older debates (also framed as "labor question debates") than of the new labor question emerging in the 1870s. While the labor questions of the antebellum period, particularly in cities such as New York, had protested wage work and wage slavery, they had done so under the assumption that permanent wage labor was not the inevitable fate of the workingman. Even in the 1860s, David Montgomery argues, workers felt that they had "progressed but partway down the path from journeyman artisan to factory-wage labor," and they, along with most other Americans, still believed that they could avoid the stigma of permanent wage work. Workers, like employers, turned to the state to rectify the growing specter of permanent wage work, whether they appealed as individual voters, as middle-class reformer Wendell Phillips urged, or as a class, as Massachusetts politician (and former Union general) N. P. Banks claimed was necessary. In either case, they believed that it was "to the State, which represents the people, [that] the laboring classes should appeal."[8]

By the 1880s, however, the labor question was different precisely because wage labor had become the dominant form of social relations, as the growing public presence of labor organizations both recognized and demonstrated.[9] The other major variant of producerism, industrial producerism, constituted a response to the growing and troubling new permanence of wage work. Industrial producerism grew out of mid-nineteenth-century free labor ideology's understanding of independent men as those who were, in Abraham Lincoln's famous articulation, "neither *hirers* nor *hired*" but men who labored "for themselves, on their farms, in their houses, and in their shops, taking the whole product to themselves."[10] The question now was how to ensure that workers could again claim the fruits of their labor and simultaneously their status as independent men. For industrial producerism, the only way to achieve this goal seemed to be the abolition of the "wages system," which not only robbed workers of the fruits of their labor but forced them to sell themselves (that is, their labor power) rather than the products of their labor. Under this understanding of independence, the temporary inducements offered by rising real wages throughout the late nineteenth century could not forestall workers' slide into dependence.

In the labor movement, this variation of producerism was most often associated with the Knights of Labor and the "vernacular" socialism of Lawrence Gronlund, Daniel De Leon, and Eugene Debs, though it also found a voice in

Populism, the greenback movement, and antimonopoly movements.[11] Less committed to restoring the figure of the property-owning small producer, proponents of this view emphasized a broadly distributed democratic control of productive property as a means for workers to return to selling the products of their labor, not their labor power.[12] That control might take place through producers' cooperatives, such as those advocated by the Knights, or through public or government (whether federal or municipal) ownership of so-called natural monopolies such as utilities and railroads. Whatever their particular plans, advocates of this broader producerism spoke in the name of "the producing classes" and, like the Knights, stressed the virtues of membership in the brotherhood of producers. Like the variant of producerism centered on the small proprietary producer, the producerism of the Knights cast as villains those who took money they had not labored to earn. Small manufacturers or shopkeepers might thus count as producers; speculators and "monopolists" could not. The Knights' producerism could and often did use nostalgic language and images, reminding audiences that Americans had previously had alternative models of social and economic organization. But more often, this idea was grounded in the present and sought to find solutions to social problems—in particular, industrial problems—that could accommodate both the moral conviction that productive labor formed the bedrock of the American republic and the realities of life in an industrializing nation. As William Forbath has argued, adherents to producerism understood that "the redemption of the working class was inextricably caught up with the redemption of the republican tradition."[13]

During the 1880s, however, even as the Knights were at the height of their power, some observers of the economic landscape began to argue that the language and ideas of producerism failed to provide sufficient explanations or resolutions for either the depression or the labor question. The depression, proponents of this view claimed, had undermined producerism of all variations. As many Americans unconsciously admitted in their discussions of the depression, the economic crisis suggested that the social order of proprietary capitalism had been at best disrupted and at worst destroyed. Hard work and consistent production no longer ensured economic success; there could be no assumed relationship between inner virtue and outer achievement. More disturbingly, as the decade wore on, a few people cautiously suggested that production itself was the root cause of the depression and labor unrest: there was simply too much of it. Democratic control of the means of production might not, in the end, be sufficient to continue the American experiment.

Only a few observers in the late 1870s turned away from the framework of both producerism and overproduction and began to argue that the greater problem facing industrial America was underconsumption. Nevertheless, this explanatory shift would mark a move toward an understanding of American society and democracy in which consumption and consuming played a more central role. In the 1870s, however, that transition had barely begun. Instead, Americans used the common vocabulary of producerism to describe what kind of democracy the country should have and to worry about the possibility or impossibility of that hope. The narratives of blame and decline that emerged from the depression itself would shape the debates regarding the labor question throughout the rest of the century as well as define and constrain new ways of understanding social and economic transitions that emerged in the 1880s and 1890s.

The Economic Crisis of the 1870s

From the perspective of the twenty-first century, the economic and structural factors leading up to the depression are clearer than they were to nineteenth-century Americans: the unprecedented, explosive productive output of the United States (especially in the capital goods sector); the accompanying rise in investments in fixed plant rather than in materials or wages; and declining prices. The rise in productive output may have been the most astonishing and most significant economic change from the antebellum period. Thanks to the protective tariff, land grants to railroad companies, and monetary policy (particularly the expeditious repayment of the Civil War debt), manufacturing grew at an extraordinary rate following the war. Between 1860 and 1890, the United States overtook Great Britain, France, and Germany in industrial production. Though economic growth was uneven in the increasingly industrialized North, per capita income increased more than 50 percent between 1840 and 1880, despite recurring crises.[14]

Mass distribution and mass production, however, demanded immense investments in fixed plant—in railroads, in machinery, and in equipment. Industries became significantly more capital-intensive, operating with ever-tighter margins and diminished liquidity. And as businesses soon learned, an increase in output did not necessarily lead to an increase in profit, especially as the prices of many goods declined. The resulting pressure to find more profit in a deflationary environment while simultaneously investing heavily in fixed plant eventually led to the merger movement of the 1890s. More immediately, in the 1870s, this pressure led to efforts quickly to lower costs through wage freezes or sharp cuts.[15] These changes, in turn, triggered an economic retardation that made firms increasingly vulnerable to fluctuations in the economy. Overall, the low rate of economic growth in the postbellum period was "puzzling," in Simon Kuznets's words. Indeed, despite the fact that the United States was free from large wars during this period and despite the fact that it was now producing almost as much France, Germany, and Great Britain combined, the U.S. rate of growth was barely higher than the corresponding rates in these countries, and the U.S. growth rate was even lower than that of the significantly smaller Sweden.[16] All of these factors combined to make capital's position highly precarious.

For Americans in the 1870s, though, the immediate catalyst of the depression was much easier to pinpoint than its underlying causes and long-term origins. In the minds of most Americans, the depression began precisely on September 18, 1873, with the unexpected and previously unthinkable failure of Cooke and Company. When the venerable firm suspended payments on its bonds, its actions ushered in sixty-five months of "uninterrupted economic contraction," the longest such period in U.S. history.[17] Jay Cooke had achieved banking fame during the Civil War when he had pioneered the marketing and sale of government bonds to the average American, and he had emerged from the war with a sterling reputation for both patriotic fervor and financial savvy. Following the war, his bank had enthusiastically backed the Northern Pacific Railroad, which was building a second transcontinental line. But the railroad's bonds were at best of dubious value, and the investment house failed to sell enough to cover its investment. The Northern Pacific's incompetence compounded Cooke's problems: with barely five hundred miles of functioning track, the railroad had already spent more than fifteen million dollars. Cooke, running out of options, had used depositors' money as short-term loans, expecting an improvement in both the U.S. and European bond markets. That improvement did not materialize, and Cooke faced the impossible task of satisfying both the Northern Pacific and his depositors. Cooke and Company failed. Although two other investment houses, the New York Warehouse and Security Company and Kenyon, Cox, and Company, had folded just days earlier, Cooke's demise pushed investors over the edge. The bank's collapse precipitated a rush on New York banks by depositors, and banks began to call in their loans. Another major investment house, Fisk and Hatch, failed the next day. Despite the New York Clearinghouse's best efforts to prevent a run on the banks, demands for cash payments from outside New York led the Clearinghouse itself briefly to suspend payments.[18] Alarmed, the Board of Governors closed the New York Stock Exchange on September 20. The *New York Times,* along with many other papers, sanguinely predicted that "trade is not likely to feel [the collapse] appreciably, unless it should take a much more serious turn than present appearances lead us to anticipate." The banks' interest in railway speculation, the *Times* continued, was not a substantial part of "the ordinary channel of business" and would have limited effect.[19] But the same issue of the paper also hinted at what was to come: the First National Bank in Washington, D.C., had "gone down" soon after news of Cooke and Company's failure reached the city.[20]

The initial crisis was specifically financial, stemming from Cooke and Company's disaster, and quickly infected the nation's banking centers. New York, which had an exceptionally large concentration of investment houses as a consequence of its advantageous interest rates, suffered most. In the days following Cooke and Company's collapse, papers reported further financial calamities, and by October the United States had settled into a depression almost as severe as those that would come in 1893–97 and 1929–32.[21] Newspaper headlines reported the diminishing prospects for business and labor, and reporters felt "obliged to report general depression, and not very cheering prospects."[22] Economic historian Samuel Reznick has estimated that between 1873 and 1879 there was an overall economic decline of 32 percent. Indexes of railroad stock prices plummeted by almost 60 percent; wholesale commodity prices fell about 30 percent; and net capital imports declined sharply. The more general financial downturn lasted until 1897; the period between 1879 and 1881, which appeared to be one of economic recovery, merely represented a temporary lull.[23] The United States was not alone in this crisis, however local Cooke's speculative indiscretions might have seemed. In May 1873, Austria and Germany also plunged into financial crisis, further constricting the European market for American investment and worsening the U.S. panic even more.[24]

For most Americans, the quickly skyrocketing unemployment, plummeting wages, and widespread business failures were more noteworthy than the declines in European investment in railroad bonds. The financial crisis quickly became a wholesale social disaster. In 1873 alone, 5,183 businesses declared bankruptcy. Matters did not improve over time: in 1878, 10,478 businesses failed.[25] Newspapers throughout the country noted that wages had quickly fallen as capitalists tried to hold onto whatever profit they could.[26] During the first winter of the depression, the New York Society for Improving the Condition of the Poor estimated that a quarter of the workforce was unemployed. By the following winter, the Society guessed that between seventy-five thousand and one hundred thousand workers, or approximately a third of the workforce, had no jobs. The number of families who registered with the Society jumped from five thousand in 1873 to twenty-four thousand in 1874. In small towns, such as Olneyville, Rhode Island, too, papers grimly reported that "soup houses" had opened, "where a hot dinner [was] served to needy families, many of whom have to make this one meal last through the twenty-four hours." For the first time, government agencies felt it necessary to count and track the number of unemployed in urban areas, especially in more industrialized states such Massachusetts, where more than 30 percent of the workforce was unemployed for more than four months during the mid-1870s.[27]

Plunging wages were accompanied by a staggering drop in prices, but few workers could take advantage of deflation, and businesses' distress intensified with each month. The Senate Finance Committee's 1893 report on wholesale prices estimated that the cost of most household goods had dropped about 20 percent during the 1870s. Luxury goods manufacturers survived, if indeed they did survive at all, by dropping prices, often below the cost of production, and accepting payment by installment. In the Philadelphia market, pig iron, a good indicator of the health of railroads and heavy industry, dropped from $53.00 a ton in 1872 to a mere $16.50 in 1878. For the few fortunate businesses that could continue to limp along, transactions were limited to what the *Philadelphia Inquirer* called "hand-to-mouth transactions"—that is, "no trading, buying, and no . . . ordering more of any article than is necessary to meet the absolute requirements of the hour."[28]

Locating the "Real Cause of Suffering"

While most observers in the winter of 1873–74 could agree that Cooke and Company had brought the economy to its knees, the larger forces at work were very much up for debate. If the ideals of midcentury democracy had emerged from the belief that America "was to be characterized by an unprecedented degree of social equality, whereby even the poorest man would at least be secure, economically competent, and independent," as Drew McCoy has described the republican vision, then the explanations for the depression gradually began to call that vision of democracy into serious and troubling question.[29] Initial assessments insisted that the crash was limited to the railroad industry and did not suggest that the economic downturn offered any profound challenge to the republic vision. Subsequent appraisals that stressed the role that individual corruption and speculation had played also continued to insist that the basic assumptions about American democratic life remained sound. But by the late 1870s, as testimony before a House subcommittee shows, some ordinary Americans feared that the era of the small proprietary producer was ending and that they were now fated permanently to live as wage workers. The growing sense that the problems facing the economy were systemic and not easily remedied only heightened this sense of despair. For many members of both the elites and the working classes, such conclusions seemed to foretell the decline of the republic itself.

Immediately following the crash, many professional observers maintained that the collapse of a few investment houses represented nothing more than a local problem within the relatively small sector of the economy that speculated in railroads. There was, they insisted, no larger or systemic problem with the economy. National publications such as the *Nation* and the *Commercial and Financial Chronicle* initially maintained that the depression was merely a temporary dip in the railroad bond market, soon to be righted by the invisible hand of the market. But even amid such hearty optimism for a speedy economic recovery, these publications conceded that greed, mismanagement, and individual malfeasance had helped precipitate the crash. After all, admitted the *Nation,* the English market was now closed to American railroad securities as a consequence of "repeated cases of American rascality." Although the *Nation* continued to believe that most roads would eventually turn a profit, it also acknowledged a long litany of problems with railroads and railroad securities. In the summer of 1873, for example, the Brooklyn Trust Company had failed, thanks largely to the "plundering" of the New Haven and Willimantic railroad by its managers. The Mercantile Warehouse and Security Company had also succumbed to poor management, having advanced too much to the Missouri, Kansas, and Texas Railroad, and a similar fate met Kenyon Cox and Company, which had unwisely loaned money to the Canada Southern. "All this," explained the *Nation,* with a certain understatement, "produced a high degree of nervousness and distrust," even if, as the paper hastened to add, "it does not follow from this . . . that there is anything nefarious about railroad-building" or that "there are no good railroad bonds."[30] Such accounts suggested that the nation's economic troubles were unfortunate and that they probably could have been prevented by less aggressive speculation in railroads and better management of the roads themselves; nevertheless, they maintained, the downturn did not indicate any profound or deep-seated problems.

Even if, as some observers thought, nothing was fundamentally wrong with the American economy, some explanation had to be found for the emergence of such widespread distrust. From the relative hindsight of 1877, Indiana congressman Morton C. Hunter placed the blame squarely on the government's "unnatural" renunciation of the gold standard during the Civil War, a move that had created a tempting speculative environment few men were strong enough to resist. The "seductive charms of speculation," enhanced by the "surplus money" circulating for several years before 1873, had irrationally raised the expectations of investors, who then behaved irresponsibly—lured, Hunter suggested, by the irresistible scent of excessive profits. But as soon as capitalists "realize[d] the true condition" of these speculative ventures—mainly dubiously conceived railroad expansions—which provided no "security for their money," business leaders returned to their usual prudent and sensible selves. Hunter lauded this return to reason but acknowledged that businessmen's sudden reversal of action had had dire and immediate consequences for the economy as a whole. In an effort to reinstate reasonable parameters for investment, they abruptly "refused to invest their means in the bonds issued to build and complete these works, preferring to lose what they had invested in them instead of risking more and then losing all." The result was a full-scale liquidity crisis, as capitalists hoarded rather than invested their monies: "The works had to stop and tens of thousands of laborers . . . were thrown out of employment," explained Hunter. Such "wild and speculative enterprises" ultimately brought "a great whirlpool of ruin and bankruptcy . . . upon the country."[31] Though Hunter certainly held the capitalists at fault for their irrational and excessive speculation, he more aggressively faulted the monetary policy that had, like a siren, turned previously good businessmen away from their generally virtuous course. Returning to the moral high road would no doubt be painful, as the current refusal to lend or invest suggested, but in the end, the economy would be stronger, more stable, and morally upright.

If Hunter blamed a flawed federal policy, others blamed not just the act of speculation but the larger and more alarming speculative mentality adopted by some powerful businessmen. New York Democratic congressman Dwight Townsend, for example, held that some entrepreneurs' moral failings had destroyed the financial markets. Greedy speculators, he explained, had diverted money from "the usual channels of active trade and commerce where it is most needed" and to the "largely unremunerative" western railroads. The result of such an "unnatural" imbalance in investment was the "artificial" stimulation of other industries, leading to a demand for immigrant labor, higher wages, and excessive production of dry goods and staples needed to support a burgeoning workforce.[32] However disturbing the results of the speculation had been, Townsend insisted that the real blame lay in a few individual businessmen's willful quest for excessive and immediate profit, to the grave detriment of American industry and trade. Similarly, William

Graham Sumner, unflagging advocate of laissez-faire, pointed to business-men's irresponsible behavior before the crash. "Everybody's confidence in the market was such that he did not want to pay his debt," explained Sumner to a congressional committee headed by Abram Hewitt and the crowds who had come to hear Sumner pontificate. "Everybody wanted to renew his ob-ligations, to extend his operations, because he expected a rise in the market still further." So with the collapse of Cooke and Company, the groundless confidence in the market vanished, and the market contracted sharply, the result of actions by unscrupulous individuals.[33]

Oxford professor Bonamy Price went much further, telling the New York Chamber of Commerce in 1874 that the problem extended beyond individual behavior to the overall mentality of business and banking. According to Price, the current panic had been caused not by a specific calamity such as war or even the failure of Cooke and Company but rather by a newly opaque and de-ceitful world of speculative investment. Panics, Price held, were acute psycho-logical "agonies of the market" in which "every man frightened his neighbor and every one caught a contagion which was the more alarming that it had no definite cause," brought on by "borrowing from banks on discount." Such borrowing on limited collateral was a symptom of a more disturbing problem than individual fiscal irresponsibility. Incessant demand for money led holders of bills to discount them and exchange them for cash or commodities. These discounted bills circulated freely, disembodied and uncoupled from any real form of collateral. And therein lay the root cause of the current economic distress, claimed Price; nothing real or tangible was ever exchanged by people or by banks. The problem was so pervasive that no one, he argued, could even tell what banks actually did. Banks, he said, should lend their money more judiciously, resisting the temptations of facile profit and supporting proprietors who wished to improve their property or expand their industrial productive capacity.[34] While he suggested that a systemic problem might have existed, in the end he instead merely called for a return to a recent past in which exces-sive speculation and ill-advised banking policies were neither tolerated nor encouraged and virtuous behavior was rewarded.

But by 1878 not everyone agreed that just a few bad businessmen had spoiled the economic apple barrel. When Hewitt's congressional committee allowed volunteer witnesses to talk about the depression for a few days before Sumner and other invited notables arrived, the speakers offered a more com-prehensive if sometimes less coherent critique of recent changes in American society. Though they shared Sumner's belief that economic success should reflect an individual's effort and virtue, these citizens were increasingly worried that individual effort made little if any difference in a man's life. They described their efforts to work and save, to become self-employed, and to buy or hold onto property but tempered these descriptions with details of their failure or keenly anticipated failure to save or become self-employed or own property. They vividly imagined that the world of proprietary producerism was slipping away. They presented the committee with clear and often moving pleas for help in reclaiming their moral and social importance as proprietors. These volunteers (mainly small businessmen and workers) had come from all over the Northeast.[35] The *Philadelphia Inquirer* crankily dismissed them as nothing more than a lot of "queer witnesses" whose ideas were disorganized and ludicrous at best. The *New York Times* mocked them as ignorant bumpkins. Given the wide range of explanations and solutions they proposed, perhaps the papers' disdain is understandable. Several witnesses suggested the abolition of the wage system. Others called for temperance or the elimination of machinery. One man suggested that the government provide a grant of fifty-eight dollars to "everybody."[36] Cigar maker William Wagner asserted that the solution to the economic depression had to be less competition, while watch repairer William Hanson claimed that the problem was too little competition, a result of the protective tariff. Exporter A. Mervin held that there was "an excess of nearly everything" caused by too much "parsimony," though his exact meaning was not at all clear.[37]

But their testimony was hardly as jumbled or disparate as the newspapers suggested. Almost all the witnesses, whatever their particular argument, talked about their desire to become proprietary producers and their increasing fear that this goal was no longer achievable. Before the depression, many either had owned property and been self-employed or felt they had a realistic expectation that they would soon become property owners. Above all else, they wanted to reclaim their status as property owners, and they wanted the government to help them do so. This desire for land united men of vastly different political perspectives. Brooklyn plumber Alexander R. Robb, a member of the Socialistic Labor Party, argued that "the real cause of . . . suffering" was a "Government which had fostered the growth of an emasculated religion," in which man's sacred right to land was ignored. Robb's proposed solution included an immediate halt to government grants of public land to corporations, the nationalization of railroads and the telegraph, free travel, and the leveling of competition between "one man's labor" and that of "a man like Vanderbilt, who controlled the joint earnings of 14,000 men."[38]

Jeremiah E. Thomas, "a colored man, a waiter by occupation," did not seem to share Robb's political philosophy but "wanted the Government or anybody to send him to the country, where he might have a chance to settle and make himself a home." Though Thomas hoped the federal government would provide land and transportation, he clearly envisioned making himself a home through his hard work. An engineer named Clarke agreed with Thomas but felt that the government should ensure each hardworking man's success with a grant of five hundred dollars, funded perhaps by a tax on "the products of machinery."[39] Even those who opposed direct relief or employment assistance from the government, a group that included E. Herbert Graham, secretary of the Working Men's Union of New York, argued that access to public land was the only solution to the problem of high unemployment in New York. Without guaranteed land, witnesses argued, the twenty thousand or thirty thousand men then out of work could never become proper (and property-owning) citizens of the republic.[40] In their collective statements before Hewitt's committee, these individuals held up the Jeffersonian ideal of the small property owner as the moral center of the republic and as their best hope for competency and security. Their failure to fulfill their hopes of becoming or remaining small holders did not reflect an individual lack of ambition or hard work but a widespread absence of opportunity that was the result of railroad and bank malfeasance rather than systemic changes in the economic and social structure. And while their calls for government assistance did prefigure the Populists' more forceful demands for government intervention in the economy, these witnesses envisioned a limited role for the government. The government would provide them with or help them acquire land, but they did not call for significant social change. Instead, they sought ways to reassert their positions as proprietary producers, to reestablish past ideals in the turbulent present.

A small number of the witnesses, however, suggested that these hopes were no longer tenable in American society. In this view, the depression was not the fault of individual or collective greed and could not be corrected by a return to moral behavior on the part of businessmen and bankers. Rather, the depression was the outward sign of systemic economic changes that made the particular kind of individual, independent smallholder that Thomas had hoped to become increasingly incongruous. As shorter hours agitator George McNeill, along with cooper Valentine Becker and publisher William Wittick, argued, the economic situation could improve and unemployment lessen only if manufacturers curtailed and controlled production.[41] However inadvertently, they suggested that the simple market economy that lay (theoretically at least) at the heart of the Jeffersonian vision no longer existed in the United States and, more to the point, was no longer desirable. The market relations of industrial America precluded it, demanding instead some kind of more comprehensive control. It is difficult to imagine that McNeill saw his argument as a rejection or repudiation of producerism more generally, even if its implications should have quelled Thomas's hopes. Rather, it makes more sense to see his concerns about overproduction as a forerunner of efforts to reassert the moral and economic position of the producer collectively, through cooperatives in particular, rather than individually, through land grants and subsistence farming. Indeed, in the 1880s, various industrial cooperatives sought to ensure economic stability and more general prosperity through control of productive output. Similarly, in bituminous coal regions, miners urged restriction of output as a way to stabilize the market and ensure higher prices.[42]

These later efforts echoed the growing call in the 1870s to treat overproduction as a root cause of the current economic and social crisis. By 1877, the concept of overproduction was sufficiently commonplace in the editorial pages of *Scribner's Monthly* that the magazine could confidently assert that there appeared to be no alternative to "regulated production." The laws of supply and demand did not lead to any kind of equilibrium and did not necessarily "work with the requisite nicety or sensitiveness" that one might desire. Instead, a specific demand generated a glut of production, which led to a sharp and sudden reduction in wages, layoffs, and closing. Consequently, workers "cease to be consumers of anything but the bare necessaries of life, and thus every interest with which they hold relations is made to suffer with them. . . . The demand brought the supply, but the supply for a year was produced in six months." If production were to remain high, new foreign markets appeared the only solution, "but nobody knows anything about this," the editors glumly concluded. Instead, manufacturers would have to decrease production in combination with each other and learn "contentment with modest profits." For a columnist in a trade paper, the *Manufacturer and Builder,* restriction was an equally obvious solution: after all, he asserted, price deflation was caused by overproduction, though some people refused to accept what he saw as an obvious truth. "An article is going the rounds of the papers," he said, "stating that if any product of the farm brings a low price in the market, all that the farmers have to do is to increase their production of that very article" to generate the same gross income. "It does not appear to enter . . . the head" of this foolish author "that the main cause of all variations of prices lays in the balance of consumption and production." The solution, according to the *Manufacturer and Builder,* was to restrict production, thus raising prices. Employment opportunities would then adjust themselves "as people are naturally inclined to abandon less profitable occupations for those promising more liberal returns." As the *Atlantic Monthly* noted, some observers still contended that overproduction was the sole result of "false or erroneous thinking" on the part of manufacturers, who made "excessive and abnormal investments of capital . . . because [they] depended upon imaginary markets" and were blinded by simple greed.[43] But as the commonsense attitude of *Scribner's* and the *Manufacturer and Builder* suggested, the orthodox belief that supply and demand could never be systemically imbalanced was dwindling rapidly.

Less commonly, contemporary explanations of the depression moved away from considering production as the most salient factor in precipitating the downturn and began to focus instead on the problem of insufficient consumption. Such arguments, which prefigured those of historical economists in the 1880s and 1890s, departed even further from the world of proprietary producerism that so many of the volunteer witnesses had hoped to salvage. Whereas arguments about overproduction made productive work problematic rather than virtuous, arguments that placed greater emphasis on consumption than production challenged the basis of producerism's moral suasion. Underlying the former arguments was a conception of the economy as an arena for containment and self-control, whether of individual spending or of manufacturing output. Arguments that stressed the role of underconsumption, in contrast, moved away from such views of the economy and individual economic behavior, suggesting that self-control (or control of productive output) was not only not necessary but also actively harmful. As "P.P." explained in a stinging letter to the editor of the *New York Times,* those who urged the poor to "economize" and the "man of limited means . . . to consume less and make sure he lives within his income" were fools. That might be "very good advice" for some individuals, this author believed, but it was disastrous advice for society as a whole: if such "economy" were to be "generally observed, its effect [would be] general stagnation." "The only possible remedy," P.P. argued, lay "in creating new wants that can be supplied only by the employment of labor."[44] The *Times's* editors impishly ran this letter under the headline "The Cant of Economy," using the term *cant* (the peculiar language or jargon of a class) to refer to the language of those who urged restraint for those who could least afford it. The title thus gently mocked those who, like manufacturer Henry Rothschild, blamed workers' woes on their moral weaknesses, their "improvidence," and their "careless" refusal to save money.[45] But *cant* also means "a whining manner of speaking, especially a beggar's whine," and the use of the word suggested that perhaps those calling for restraint—especially the restraint of others—were perhaps more morally petulant than anything else. And finally, of course, *cant* plays on the contraction *can't:* individual restraint and the control of production, the title suggested, could not resolve the economic and social crisis.

But the calls for higher levels of consumption did not sway everyone, and many Americans saw arguments like P.P.'s as direct attacks on the moral world of the work ethic. Responding to P.P.'s letter, one irate reader crankily insisted that the nation had to return as quickly as possible to prewar business methods, to the "slow and sure" economy practiced by the prudent individual merchant. Those who had wallowed too long in the unproductive and immoral world of the speculative market—the "briefless lawyer, the broken tradesman, the idle clerk and laborer"—would find both livelihood and redemption on western lands, the "millions of fertile acres" waiting for cultivation. "Of course," admitted the writer, each new homesteader "must expect some hardships, but they are more fancied than real, and nothing to an industrious man when compared with the demoralizing and enervating effects of enforced idleness." But with hard work, settlers would find, as the letter's title read, that "economy was yet a virtue" in a double sense: to economize, to limit and control spending, was indeed a virtue, but the title also suggested that the economy itself could (and should) still reflect and reward the virtuous behavior of individuals.[46]

Still, those who held onto "gloomy" Malthusian ideas about the dangers of overproduction were merely perpetuating "the delusion" that persisted in "watching production to the forgetfulness of consumption." "The stupendous and far-reaching fact," argued the *Times,* "is that consumption per head is an expanding quantity. Economists and laborers fall into a common error when they look upon increased efficiency of labor as having any tendency to permanently throw out the laborer, for this is equivalent to the delusion that human wants are capable of being satisfied." Far from being a sign of greed or moral turpitude, such insatiability offered the hope of economic and social progress. Just as the labor movement would argue with increasing vigor in the 1880s and 1890s, the paper suggested that the "cheapness and abundance of consumable things can never be a calamity." Rather, increased demand could translate to demand for more labor as well as the continued improvement of daily life. "If this were otherwise," claimed the article, "it would be wisdom to put back the clock and return to cultivating the soil with the pointed stick." The choice it presented, then, was between civilization and comfort and what the article imagined as a primitive and highly inefficient past.[47]

By the mid-1880s and the 1890s, underconsumption appeared to be a far greater problem than overproduction, at least much of the time, and economists came to link economic fluctuations with systemic causes rather than with individual virtues or vices. Earlier in the century, as Karen Halttunen has argued, "The traditional association of personal virtue and material prosperity had been held together by a supernaturalistic cosmology, the Protestant faith in an ordered universe presided over by a benevolent deity who actively guided the affairs of men to ensure the material rewards of ascetic self-discipline."[48] By the end of the century, such assumptions had been turned upside down. Individuals' personal decisions were less important than aggregate behavior, productive capacity seemed less important than consistent consumer demand, and fears of scarcity had been replaced by the terrors of a perplexing abundance. Indeed, as George Basil Dixwell, an American diplomat and trade representative to China, argued, the problem was precisely that production had outstripped effective demand. Faced with a glut of products and insufficient demand, manufacturers had suddenly and drastically decreased production below the level necessary for profit, thereby laying off workers and furthering the depression. Sustained production accompanied by lowered prices (another common reaction by manufacturers) could have similar deleterious results, as economist David A. Wells pointed out. Heavy investment in fixed plant, he explained, compelled large-scale manufacturers to continue producing goods even as prices dropped, further flooding the market.[49] As the railroads' experiments with such measures in the 1870s showed, lowered prices did little to increase consumption or lift the depression; instead, price drops merely increased the general rate of business failures and raised unemployment even higher, fueling the general sense of social crisis.

As Dixwell and Wells implied, the most troubling explanations of the depression suggested that the industrial economy's successes were also its undoing. Productive capacity, increasing each year, seemed to spell doom, the editors of *Scribner's* likewise concluded. Supply and demand might well still regulate the market, they wrote in 1877, toward the end of the initial economic downturn, but when demand sprang up, "immediately hundreds of mills start into action, each anxious to do its utmost to meet that demand with supply. They are operated night and day, and before they can feel the subsidence of the demand, the market is glutted."[50] *Scribner's* editors seemed to suggest that greater sensitivity to market saturation might prevent or at least lessen such gluts. As Bureau of Labor Statistics commissioner Carroll Davidson Wright explained in an 1886 *Forum* article that synthesized most of the dominant explanations for the depression, the depression of 1873–77 had been a "crisis in production." "This crisis," he argued, "exists in each nation given to mechanical production. . . . [T]hey have vast resources, vast territory, vast population. Nevertheless, they have a limited consuming power and a super-abundance of productive power." Faced with the question of what "social conditions" were "necessary to make increasing returns . . . in production *economically* possible," Wright argued that long-term increased consumption offered the immediate solution to the linked problems of overproduction, cyclical depressions, and fluctuating wages.[51] Diminished production was impossible considering the high level of capital investment in fixed plant, meaning that the capital could neither circulate nor be reinvested. For such capital investments to pay, production had to increase continually, but such increases could return the investment and create profit only if the products themselves were consumed consistently.

By the mid-1880s, New York's Hearn's Department Store on West Fourteenth Street was confident enough in the public's acceptance of the dangers of underconsumption to use that idea to exhort potential customers to buy more clothing: "Overproduction, so economists say, / Is the cause of all troubles and bane of the day. / Under consumption, it seemeth to me, / Is more to be feared in the land of the free."[52] At a meeting of New York's Anti-Poverty Society on July 25, 1887, held at Rheinwald's River View Casino on Eighty-sixth Street, socialist Englebert Bruckmann argued that Henry George's land theory "spoke glibly of overproduction as the cause of . . . poverty." "Would it not," Bruckmann asked, "be more logical to call it 'compelled underconsumption'?"[53] By the end of the century, F. Spencer Baldwin, a professor of economics at Boston University, could confidently argue, "If we spent more and saved less, the industrial system would be improved," for the "wealth of society is not a fixed fund [but] rather a variable mass." The expenditure of that wealth, he argued, "does more substantial good to society" than "indiscriminate" giving to charity. The Puritan condemnation of luxury no longer held indisputable sway in America, and, in Baldwin's mind at least, the country had turned away from the world the 1881 *Times* article characterized as "cultivation with a stick" to one that celebrated—and enjoyed—the "cheapness and abundance of consumable things."[54] And for Baldwin, this transition from scarcity to abundance, and from a producerist to a consumerist society, was a very good change indeed.

Transition Questions

In the 1870s, however, the lessons of the depression seemed much grimmer than they did by the 1880s, painting a dire picture for a democratic society based on proprietary, republican principles. If overproduction were indeed a systemic root cause of depression, then individual virtue—indeed, individual action of any kind—could have little effect on the course of economic development. If property ownership and self-employment were as difficult to achieve as the volunteers testifying before the congressional committee believed, then it was difficult for Americans in the midst of the depression to imagine that the American experiment could continue. Few could yet envision a democracy that included wage workers, mass production, and mass consumption. Instead, people saw a diminution of the existing economic and social order but had no clear sense of what kind of world would or could replace it.

A deep, melancholic sense of loss suffused discussions of the fate of the nation. Wells noted dismally that "heretofore, . . . there has been no country in which a man, through industry and economy, could so rapidly and easily raise himself from the position of laborer, dependent on others for employment, to the position of a capitalist, himself controlling employment, as in the United States." But from the vantage point of 1877, that era seemed to have passed away forever, and he saw little hope of regaining it. Unlike many of the eager witnesses before Hewitt's committee, Wells saw little hope in the West, where he believed the lands were now all "exhausted," with the possible but hardly useful exception of the "arid regions of the plains." More crucially, the common man had no access to the large amounts of capital now necessary to start up a business, especially in manufacturing. No amount of hard work or vigilant saving could overcome this problem; from now on, only the rich had a reasonable chance of success. This fact marked a significant and troubling change in American society, for it meant that the United States had "entered upon a new social order of things; an order of things," Wells observed grimly, "similar to what exists in . . . the Old World, in which the tendency is for a man born a laborer, working for hire, to never be anything but a laborer."[55] In the future, Wells feared, the United States would more closely resemble Europe, plagued by social stratification, class warfare, and ever-growing inequality. In Wells's assessment, the republican experiment, the era of social mobility, seemed finished.

The political and social consequences of this melancholy frankly terrified the *Nation,* which saw in the demise of the proprietary past a disturbing "softening" of the nation's moral fiber. Previously, "almost every American voter in the Northern States used to bring to the transaction of all business a fund of common sense which never failed him, and he did not separate political business from other business. He did not attend the town meeting with one set of ideas about the way money ought to be made and spent, and then go to his store or farm with another set." Town meetings brought together equal proprietary citizens whose civic duty governed their private actions as well as public decisions. Most important, individuals' decisions had real impact on both politics and economics. This republican society was, the *Nation* implied, small, local, and individual.[56] But by the late 1870s, it seemed, "a great change has taken place in the character of a considerable portion of the population." No longer "shrewd and intelligent" or as "familiar with business as [they] used to be," the American people had dulled and were now neither "as prudent [n]or calculating" as formerly. As a result, the American population had "less of the qualities by which laborers grow into capitalists, or, in other words, it has less providence. With it, therefore, times are always hard." No doubt, suggested the *Nation,* increasing immigration, crowded cities, and scarce resources contributed to the general mental lethargy—how else could one explain the "idiocy" that Americans proposed to the congressional committee in place of more sensible political economy?—but the change resulted from more than an influx of less-than-desirable migrants. Now permanently separated from the world of business and no longer in charge of their own work, American men had lost the sharp edge that had made them worthy republican citizens; they had been made stupid by the new economy. Consequently, the *Nation* warned its readers, "it is as well to remember that in a certain sense, which may be called the American sense, the times will probably never be as good again as they have been." Trade and production would no doubt resume, but "the distribution of wealth is never likely to be as satisfactory hereafter as it has been."[57]

Some northerners as well as southerners turned to the myth of the harmonious plantation South as the antidote to current social crisis. In that invented past, class conflict had not troubled the socially stable and contented world of the slave South.[58] Others for whom slavery could offer no idyllic respite from the present turned instead to the myth of a republican past, which similarly offered a vision of social harmony and stability. The contrast with the present could not have been more striking or more disheartening. As Lyman Abbott, a lawyer turned Congregationalist minister and editor of the *Outlook,* explained, the new world of industrial capitalism not only had provoked depression and social unrest but also had irrevocably destroyed the republican past. Now, Abbott explained, "politically America is a democracy; industrially America is an aristocracy. The community which allows the laborer to determine the destinies of the nation, allows him no voice in determining the nature or the profits of his own industry. He *makes* political laws; he is *under* industrial laws. At the ballot box he is a king; in the factory he is a servant, sometimes a slave."[59] As a result, America was now divided into classes, and the lines of division seemed to harden with each passing day, as Abbott was hardly alone in noting. Even as congressmen held that "the formation of classes is to be deprecated," many recognized that as recently as 1868, "labor was in demand and wages ris[ing]." Now, however, "capital nowhere in Christendom can find safe and profitable investment . . . , and labor everywhere is suffering."[60]

The labor upheavals of 1877 confirmed Abbott's sense that an age had passed. At the beginning of August, following the chaotic violence in Pittsburgh that had ended with federal troops in the streets, at least twenty-five people dead, and millions of dollars in property destroyed, many Americans perceived the "events of the last fortnight" as constituting "a national disgrace." The "uprising" was not against a specific oppression but unnervingly "against society itself."[61] That sense of willful social self-destruction ultimately proved more troubling than the descriptions of burned engines or accounts of looters madly carting off "hams, flitch, soap, butter, eggs, cheese, hardware, bedding, cushions, sleeping car furniture, whips, high wine."[62] The depression seemed to have revealed or perhaps created fissures in the American republic that neither military force nor a return to prosperity would overcome. In light of this disturbing break with the past, the *Boston Herald* declared emphatically, "A worse danger to our institutions than Mississippi or South Carolina could show now stares us in the face, and can no longer be laughed at or ignored. The whole labor question now demands, as never before, the consideration of our wisest men."[63]

Everywhere there were signs that European revolutions had come to the New World, and Americans particularly feared the bloodshed of the 1871 Paris Commune, in which Communards attacked politicians, employers, and clergy before being brutally suppressed by French troops.[64] The *New York Times* spoke ominously of "the socialistic spectre of Europe," where workingmen hear "of the new gospel of communism and social equality, but they behold around them vast inequalities of property and a distribution of the good things of life which seems to them unjust and unequal." It would not have been hard to conclude that such a statement might now apply to the United States as well.[65] Journalist James Dacus, in his history of the "great strikes," worried that in Pittsburgh, "the Commune has risen in its dangerous might, and threatened a deluge of blood."[66] The unexpectedly harsh depression and the equally unanticipated violence doused the "the optimism in which most Americans [had been] carefully trained and which the experience of life" had previously seemed to justify "to the industrious, energetic, and provident."[67] As Eric Hobsbawm has argued, 1873 seemed to mark the beginning of a new era in both European and American history, a dividing point between a period in which "economic expansion and liberalism seemed irresistible" and a period in which "they were so no longer."[68]

What was to be done? The most likely option for those who, like John Hay, looked on with dismay at the chaos and conflict around them was a forceful and immediate reassertion of law and social order. Hay presented his argument for social order in a serialized novel for *Century* written in direct response to the labor violence of the summer of 1877. As art, *The Bread-Winners* has not stood the test of time well at all; at its best, it is an overwrought screed against labor grafted onto two mawkish love stories. It remains, however, a forceful (and at the time quite popular) call for a return to social stability. Its plot is straightforward enough. Under the spell of a silver-tongued charlatan, Andrew Jackson Offitt, the working men and women of Buffland form a union, the Brotherhood of Bread-Winners. Goaded by Offitt's excessively revolutionary rhetoric, they first strike and then gleefully move on to ransack the houses of the city's elite. At the last possible moment, the rioters are thwarted by a civilian police force hastily assembled by the novel's hero, Captain Arthur Farnham, a dashing former Civil War officer. Thanks to Farnham's quick thinking and ready pistol, *The Bread-Winners* ends with both property and the social order assured. The upheavals in Buffland appear to have ended, and civic calm returns. The workmen go back to their jobs, once more pliable and content. Domestic tranquility reigns as well, with two weddings (one Farnham's and the other one a former Bread-Winner's).

Hay intended his novel to be, as Vernon Parrington has put it, a vigorous "defense of the old economic order against the increasing claims of labor."[69] But the novel itself makes such a straightforward reading all but impossible. If social stability here is to be guaranteed by the twinned triumphs of the "better sort" and the domesticating influences of marriage, then the prospects for civil accord in Buffland look grim indeed. The riots are not likely to produce any soul-searching among the city elites who, Hay notes acerbically, respond to their close call by foolishly "congratulat[ing] themselves on their escape" and failing to give any "thought to the questions which had come so near to an issue of fire and blood." Farnham and his compatriots may represent restrained civic virtue in the face of mobocracy, but their militia's great triumph over the motley mob is tempered by their inability to fight base popular politics even at the low level of public library administration. Nor can Hay guarantee an end to dangerous working-class radicalism with the marriage of Maud Matchin and former Bread-Winner Sam Sleeny. Their union ostensibly represents the triumph of social order, with Maud's acceptance of her social status (which she spends much of the book farcically trying to escape) and the end of Sleeny's flirtation with violence and unionism. But Hay's constant description of Sleeny as a "sullen" man of "limited" intelligence, angry and easily manipulated, makes it seem likely that he will rejoin labor radicals. Even the narrator must admit that he cannot predict either domestic tranquility or social stability in a marriage "between two natures so ill-regulated and untrained, where the woman brought into the partnership the wreck of ignoble ambitions and the man the memory of a crime."[70] By the end of *The Bread-Winners,* Hay unwittingly finds himself almost exactly where he started. He leaves his readers merely with an agitated indictment of contemporary America's corrupt politics, labor unions, and demagogues. Despite Hay's best efforts to resolve the crisis in Buffland, he ultimately lacks the imagination to offer any kind of substantive solution; he can manage only the shallow, unsatisfying resolution of marriage.

In contrast to Hay's desperate effort to control and stop social transformation, the ideals of producerism provided a more comprehensive starting point that could look simultaneously backward and forward, as *Progress and Poverty,* Henry George's response to the depression, showed. He called for the abolition of parasitic landlords who robbed honest workers (whether laborers or manufacturers) of the wealth they toiled to create. Like many of the witnesses before Congress, George wanted each man to have the opportunity to labor for himself and to enjoy the fruits of his labor: "This, and this alone I contend for," he said, "that he who makes should have; that he who saves should enjoy."[71] George was not blind to historical circumstances, however. He knew full well that the Jeffersonian past, the world of the self-sufficient yeoman, had been replaced by a "new forced social interdependence." A direct return to a simple market economy of small producers was now impossible. But his utopian idea of the single tax insisted on the possibility of returning to that era's cherished principle, the natural right of each man to enjoy the fruits of his labor in a society defined by small holders, limited government, low crime, and no extremes of wealth or poverty.[72]

As George's work and the voluntary testimony before Congress attested, moving into the future while retaining the ideals of the past was a difficult task at best. Efforts to do so simultaneously demonstrated both the continued power of the first principles of proprietary producerism and the new structural obstacles to the re-creation of a decentralized economy of smallholders. Few people were either willing or able to abandon a model of democracy rooted in the tenets of proprietary capitalism and an ideal of independent citizenship based on control of productive property. By the 1880s, though, proprietary producerism often seemed to offer an incomplete vision of democracy, even if it was still a prominent lens through which to imagine social justice or to critique American society. For if workers recognized themselves as the guardians of producerite virtues against the nonproducing parasitic classes, these workers as well as other Americans also understood that the world of proprietary capitalism, in which the proprietary producer was valorized above all, was slowly vanishing. The lessons of the 1870s, which would shape discussions as seemingly far afield as the anti-Chinese movement, revealed that the relationships among self-determination, property ownership, and production were no longer self-evident, though how that relationship would be reimagined had yet to be determined.

2

Meat versus Rice

Anti-Chinese Rhetoric and the Problem of Wage Work

On December 11, 1878, Isaac Cohen, an unemployed machinist and labor agitator from Washington, D.C., volunteered to give his views on the "current depression in business and labor" before New York Democrat Abram Hewitt's investigating committee, now returned from New York. The depression, Cohen insisted, could not be understood without addressing the "Chinese Question." "The Chinese," he explained to the committee, "are a barbarous, debased, demoralized people. If they come here, and are detrimental to the interests of the workingmen, then I say, in the language of Dennis [*sic*] Kearney [the leader of the anti-Chinese Workingman's Party of California], 'They ought to go.'" A very puzzled Hewitt asked for clarification: "Would you limit that view to the Chinese, or would you include all other degraded and demoralized people?" Cohen, himself a German immigrant, replied, "I would limit it to the Chinese." Hewitt reiterated, "Then you would not exclude all degraded and demoralized people from this country, but only the Chinese?" "Only the Chinese," persisted Cohen.[1]

Why was Cohen so convinced that ending Chinese immigration would restore the United States to economic health? Few Chinese immigrants lived east of the Rocky Mountains, and they offered almost no competition for jobs in the industrial Northeast and Midwest. It is quite likely, too, that Cohen had never actually seen a Chinese worker, much less lost a job to one. Yet for Cohen, the "Chinese problem" was inseparable from the financial and labor crisis of the 1870s, and he was hardly alone in making this seemingly unlikely connection. The United States certainly had had a long history of

Orientalist ideology that cast the Chinese as a malevolent and threatening force, irrevocably alien and unknowable, but the anti-Chinese movement itself came to flourish in the decades after the Civil War, thriving even in places where there were few Chinese workers.[2] In Duluth, Minnesota, and Omaha, Nebraska, local residents worried about "driv[ing] back" the "filthy Chinese." The *Baltimore Sun* feared that "idol worship" would soon prevail in Baltimore. The *Chicago Inter-Ocean* followed the fate of the "almond-eyed immigrants" in California with rapt attention. Politicians from states such as Maine with no "Chinese problem" whatsoever enthusiastically leapt into the fray, demanding that the "Chinese Must Go."[3] Long speeches supporting exclusion fill pages of the *Congressional Record,* as congressmen outdid one another detailing the faults and defects of Chinese workers. Anti-Chinese diatribes turned up in popular culture, too, punctuating literary and visual culture with references to "the Yellow Peril" and "the menace from the east." Writers on the labor question, whether working-class activists or middle-class reformers, consistently included elaborate tirades against the Chinese in discussions of industrial labor and economic instability; George McNeill's *The Labor Movement: The Problem of To-Day* sandwiched a rant against Chinese labor between a "History of the Knights of Labor" and a central chapter on "The Problem of To-Day."[4]

How did Chinese workers become so central to national discussions of the labor question in the 1870s and 1880s? In California, as Alexander Saxton has shown, hatred of the Chinese served as the catalyst for the formation of a white working-class culture and for working-class political action.[5] But nationally, anti-Chinese rhetoric was not the purview only of workers, politicians, social scientists, or magazine illustrators. It offered a common language in which diverse regions, classes, and occupations could argue about the implications of industrialization and proletarianization for American democracy; such rhetoric provided, in other words, a racialized and gendered language with which to continue the debates about the depression of the 1870s—in particular, concerns regarding the fate of American democracy.[6] Three factors made the Chinese particularly useful vehicles for such discussions. First, they were racial and national outsiders, excluded from the American polity by the color of their skin and by their national origin. Second, few Chinese lived outside of the western states; for many participants in these discussions, therefore, the Chinese remained an abstraction, divorced from the specificities of local concerns about immigration, job competition, and race. And third, the anti-Chinese rhetoric of the 1870s and 1880s made the Chinese into the most exemplary of workers. Politicians and labor advocates alike agreed that the Chinese worked extraordinarily hard; they were rarely if ever extravagant in their personal expenditures; and they saved their wages.

The Chinese, in other words, reflected many of the most admirable aspects of the producer—self-control, thrift, hard work—but did so in such an exaggerated form that they seemed to distort and mock these central traits of productive labor, challenging the abstract ideal of the producer-citizen with its own warped image. According to exclusionists, the Chinese perverted these virtues: they worked too hard and for too little money; they denied themselves basic quantities of food and rest; and they produced too much, too cheaply. In an era defined by overproduction of industrial goods, the consequences of such imagined behavior could not be taken lightly.

In depicting the Chinese as both the ideal and perverted version of the worker, anti-Chinese rhetoric reflected white American anxieties about the decline of property ownership and the increase of wage work. However, this rhetoric also reflected the continued significance of producer to American political and social thought, and as the 1870s and 1880s wore on, Americans used the racialized and gendered language of the anti-Chinese movement to work out new understandings of producerism. Gradually and unevenly, anti-Chinese rhetoric came to imagine the producer-citizen as a wage-earning breadwinner rather than a proprietor, a man whose wages allowed his family to enjoy the comforts produced cheaply and efficiently by industry. In contrast to the Chinese, whose excessive productivity was not accompanied by vigorous consumption, white male workers were increasingly lauded as both producers and consumers.

The Changing Nature of Work

This shift in the possible understanding of the producer-citizen reflected the magnitude of changes in work and the workplace after the Civil War. Before the war, most workers labored in small shops, and even in 1860, the average shop employed only six workers. As many as 90 percent of white men owned their farms or shops, and among the 10 percent who were wage earners, half worked with ten or fewer fellow employees. Economic transactions were often personal in nature. Individuals might well know who had made their shoes or who sold them grain. Even if they did not personally know the specific cordwainer or merchant, as was increasingly likely during the antebellum period, they could easily imagine him as a distinct individual, much like themselves, who owned capital in land or tools, capital that was tied to production itself.[7]

Despite severe economic downturns in the antebellum period, many Americans remembered that time as filled with opportunities for hardworking men. Labor journalist John Swinton, for example, recalled that he had been "told by a very old and horn-handed Yankee acquaintance that the American workingmen of those times were 'pretty tolerable independent,' as they 'were sure of getting a job somewhere or somehow, and they had the right to take up land out West, if they wanted to.'"[8] Such opportunities—or at least the belief in such opportunities—reinforced the conviction that any white man worth his salt, willing to work hard and to avoid squandering his earnings, could be assured of claiming political and social independence in a producers' republic. As Ronald Schultz and others have explained, the "moral vision of the producers' republic" rested on four central tenets: pride in individual work; the belief that ownership of skill and knowledge made an artisan the equal to any man; the possibility of social mobility through the ranks of a trade culminating in self-employment and property ownership; and the idea that hard work and self-control would result in both a moderate prosperity and community respect.[9] During the early republic, skilled workers understood themselves as the moral bedrock of American society, the physical embodiment of the idea of the "heroic artisan," whose physique and skill reflected his work ethic, frugality, and personal independence. He was most commonly depicted as a tall, square-jawed man, legs spread in a resolute stance and muscular arms crossed, accompanied by the tools of his trade. His claim to republican citizenship was visualized doubly, first through his self-contained pose (he was not a man easily swayed) and second through his status as a self-employed property owner, implicit in the ownership of his tools. As such images declared, he controlled both the means of production and his person.[10] This model of artisanal citizenship seemed within the reach of many men in the years before the war. Thus, when Daniel Webster asked in 1857, "Who are the laboring people of the north?" he promptly answered his own question: "They are the whole North. They are the people who till their own farms with their own hands; freeholders, educated men, independent men."[11] Wage work, though not uncommon, was seen as "the school period of practical life," and "while working for wages, the young man was looking forward to the time when he should work for himself."[12]

By the end of the Civil War, as industrial workplaces steadily increased in size and immigration swelled, the number of wage workers surpassed that of self-employed men; there were now 2.5 wage workers for every self-employed man.[13] After 1870, the number of industrial wage workers began to grow dramatically, rising steadily from 27 percent of the labor force in 1870 to 42.4 percent by 1920.[14] At the same time, the average size of industrial firms more than tripled between 1860 and 1890; in technologically advanced industries such as textiles and metal, that increase was much greater.[15] The labor force in all manufacturing increased 5.4 times between 1860 and 1910, and by 1899, manufacturing represented 53 percent of the total national income.[16] This change had overwhelming implications. Whereas the heroic artisan had relied on his knowledge and ingenuity to finish a job, an industrial wage worker seemed likely to need only the ability to follow orders and the stamina to repeat a task over and over again.[17] Instead of providing and assuring his own competency, as the heroic artisan had done, the wage worker depended on his employer's goodwill and success for wages and consistent employment. Unemployment, especially during the economic downturns that plagued the postbellum period, confirmed the industrial worker's precarious position.[18] The emergence of a class of permanent wage workers overtly mocked the republican hopes for America. Economic self-sufficiency, property ownership, and self-employment now seemed unreasonable goals, no matter how hard an individual might strive.[19] An industrial wage worker, as the minister D. O. Kellog mournfully noted before the 1879 Social Science Association meeting, could "no longer hope to become a capitalist and employer himself. The little shop of his ancestors he could aspire to emulate, but the gigantic factory with its larger resources is beyond his hope." Now, it seemed, he was fated to be nothing more than a "bound dependent."[20] Kellog's narrative of decline pervaded much of the commentary on the labor question. C. M. Morse, writing in the *Forum* at the end of the 1880s, explained that "in the first half of the century, men were independent," owners of both real property and their own labor. But now, "their little shops are dismantled; they have nothing but their labor to exchange for the necessaries of life; they must accept what wages are offered or starve." As a result, Morse concluded, with an appalling but completely commonplace myopia, "they have fallen, by a simple train of events, from a position of independence into a condition of wage slavery which, in some respects, is worse than that of the black man in *ante-bellum* days."[21]

Morse's use of the term *wage slavery* linked his assessment of labor's condition in the 1880s with workers' protests of the 1850s, when white workers compared their wage work to the enslavement of African Americans, both to protest wage work as immoral and to reinforce their whiteness and status as free men.[22] After the Civil War, such comparisons continued, using the specter of slavery and blackness to condemn the ignominy of wage work. In a truly astonishing reorientation of Harriet Beecher Stowe's *Uncle Tom's Cabin,* for example, novelist Alice Wellington Rollins proclaimed the "new cabin is now at the North, instead of the South." Uncle Tom had become "white, not colored."[23] By the 1870s and 1880s, however, white labor's comparison was more likely to be with Chinese "coolie" labor than with black slaves.[24] Just as in the antebellum contrasts of white workers and African American slaves, these comparisons reflected efforts to distinguish white workers from nonwhite workers; and just as in the antebellum period, these comparisons sought to reinforce native-born workers' whiteness and positions as citizens of the republic.[25] But at the same time, these newer comparisons accepted that white workers were likely to be wage workers. But what would it mean to have a nation of wage workers rather than producers? For many, the example of the Chinese in California provided some sobering answers.

The Threat of "John Chinaman"

Anti-Chinese literature was quick to point out that the Chinese had seemed harmless at first. The earliest immigrants, almost all male, came to the United States in the 1840s and 1850s to try their luck in mining, but as the mines yielded less and less, they gradually drifted into railroad work until the construction of the Central Pacific Railroad.[26] After the road's completion, many Chinese moved to San Francisco and other cities, taking jobs in manufacturing and low-skilled service sectors and, according to opponents, beginning to drive white workers out of well-paying jobs. By 1877, local sources estimated that about eighteen thousand Chinese were employed in factories in San Francisco. Although that number was probably exaggerated for effect, it nevertheless suggests that the Chinese comprised a sizable portion of the city's population. In the early 1870s, about one in seven hirable men in California was Chinese.[27] White workers increasingly found themselves competing with the Chinese for jobs, and agitation against the Chinese, couched in moral as well as economic terms, grew exponentially.[28]

White Californians were swift to counteract the growing "menace," as they labeled Chinese workers. Legislators passed a wide variety of measures aimed at protecting white workers, and residents staunchly supported Kearney's newly formed Workingman's Party of California, whose platform was simply "The Chinese Must Go."[29] Newspapers and magazines depicted westerners struggling futilely against the "Mongol menace," and most people seemed to agree with enthusiastic opponent of Chinese immigration James Whitney when he insisted that "the results of the cheap labor of the Pacific coast have not been limited to that region, but have come in direct competition with the labor of the eastern portion of our country."[30] Quite quickly, demands for the exclusion of Chinese immigrants became increasingly popular among easterners as well. Some Americans, including abolitionist William Lloyd Garrison and writer Mark Twain, opposed restrictions on the Chinese, but such individuals were the exception and not the rule. By the 1880s, anti-Chinese sentiments were shared enthusiastically by organized labor, financiers, Democrats, Republicans, easterners, westerners, and midwesterners. Numerous tracts denouncing Chinese labor appeared in East Coast newspapers as well as in national magazines such as the *North American Review* and the *Forum. Frank Leslie's Illustrated Weekly, Harper's Weekly,* and *Puck* frequently ran spreads detailing the dangers of Chinese immigration. In 1881, the *Sacramento Bee* reported with some satisfaction that in New York, Brooklyn's Board of Aldermen had seen the danger posed by the Chinese and had consequently "passed an ordinance prohibiting the issuance of laundry licenses to any but citizens of the United States, which action was induced by a desire to break up the Chinese wash-house business in that city." With the specter of unlimited immigration from China to New York and Massachusetts looming, Congress debated the merits of exclusion throughout the 1870s and in 1882, under the guidance of ardent exclusionists Benjamin Butler of Massachusetts and James Blaine of Maine, passed the first law severely restricting immigration from China. The law was renewed and strengthened in 1892 and in 1902.[31]

Congressional debate and later legislation, however, did nothing to diminish widespread fear of Chinese labor. Images and descriptions of the Chinese in California, whether published for a popular audience or offered as testimony to Congress, combined hatred of the Chinese themselves as racial threats with a palpable fear that American workers might become like the Chinese. Most discussions of the "Chinese menace" began with vivid and quite lengthy descriptions of Chinatown's housing. These descriptions not only dehumanized the Chinese but also warned all Americans, working-class and middle-class alike, what wage work might do to the pillars of the republic. In a nationally publicized 1880 report, inspectors from the San Francisco Board of Health repeatedly described their perilous descents into Chinese basement housing, where large cooking fires raged.[32] The same year, the Workingman's Committee of California issued a pamphlet, *Chinatown Declared a Nuisance!,* noting that during a board of health inspection of Chinatown, officials found the "walls of the rooms . . . thick with dirt, slime, and sickening filth." Horrifyingly, "the odor from some of the rooms compelled even one of the doctors to cry 'enough.'"[33] Foul smells, sewage, and garbage repeatedly appeared in other descriptions of Chinatown as well. Kentucky representative Albert Willis told Congress in 1878 that in Chinatowns, "neatness and cleanliness is the exception. The air in their apartments is filled with noisome smells and pestilential vapors, threatening disease and death. Property occupied by them is consequently lessened in value."[34] *The Chinese in California,* intended as a lavishly illustrated exposé of the true effects of Chinese immigration, described Chinatowns as filled with the "germs of disease . . . produced by the decay of animal and vegetable matter" as well as by the "exhalation of the withered inhabitants," whose very breaths "robbed" the air of oxygen. Even evidence of "careful personal hygiene" was used to show that the Chinese were inherently dirty: "They often wash their feet and legs in the same bucket they bring water for drinking and cooking in," noted *The Chinese in California* with a mixture of horror and satisfaction.[35] Similarly, in a paper read before the 1877 Social Science Association of America, Edwin Meade explained that "their personal habits [can be] described as disgustingly filthy. Nothing can exceed the noisome odors which exhale from their proximity. . . . [N]ot only by the cheapness of their labor, but by the offensiveness of their personal habits, they drive the white laborer before them."[36] One San Francisco doctor simply told a House committee, "I have no language to describe the horrors of Chinatown."[37]

Lurking beneath such descriptions of Chinatowns was an alarming inversion of some of the most deeply held tenets of producerite ideology. The Chinese were not rotting in slums because they were lazy or unwilling to work or because they otherwise failed to engage in hard work. They were there precisely because they embraced the producerist work ethic without reservation. For without a doubt, even the anti-Chinese agitators agreed, Chinese immigrants worked harder and longer than anyone else. L. T. Townsend, a theologian who opposed exclusion but was no supporter of Chinese immigration, warned his readers that Chinese laborers "work patiently, expeditiously, and skillfully from daylight until dark. They accomplish more for a day's work than either a Negro, Irishman, or than the average American laborer."[38] Willis admitted to the House that the "Chinese laborer, in some respects, is desirable. He is frugal, thrifty, patient, cheerful and obedient. He readily learns his trade and expertly performs any species of light work."[39] But such vigorous work did not make the Chinese self-possessing individuals or heroic artisans. It made them inhuman, mere machines. As James Whitney explained, "What the Chinaman has once seen he can do himself with refinements of execution due to his close perception and habits of work. Once taught, he works as an automaton."[40] Hard work, it seemed, ensured not manhood, virtue, or self-sufficiency but rather the opposite.

This paradox lay at the center of anti-Chinese thought in the United States in the 1870s and 1880s. The Chinese possessed all the qualities that defined the heroic artisan and that were lauded by the Protestant work ethic, but they somehow distorted and inverted these values. According to Congressman Charles N. Felton, the Chinese "are more to be feared for their virtues than their vices."[41] Behavior or actions that one might think would be praised—thrift, for example, or diligence or productivity—became signs that the Chinese were dangerous and malevolent. In a chronicle of "China's Menace to the World" in the *Forum,* Thomas Magee marveled at the intensity of agriculture in China, but he would not applaud it. Instead, he described rich rice fields, fertile farms, and abundant harvests as if they were San Francisco's Chinatown. "Fertilizers undreamed of in Europe are used there," he informed readers, "and the nostrils of the European or an American are assailed with all sorts of odors at every turn in city and country." These fertilizers were then "applied directly to the roots of the plants, and not placed on the surface of the land, as with us, for in the latter process is evaporation and waste." Such thrift—including the careful use of human waste as fertilizer—and painstaking plant husbandry were depicted not as examples of careful farming but as signs that China was somehow unnatural. "There are," he marveled, "practically no plant weeds to be seen. . . . There is no room for them, and they are completely extirpated in a land where agriculture is so minute that the roots of the plants are examined to expel or to kill an insect or grub." Nothing was wasted, he explained, not even rainwater, which was captured in "ponds or in water holes for irrigation, and in all cases fish are grown in these reservoirs."[42]

Although Magee suggested—in passing—that American farmers might learn something from Chinese agricultural practices, he spent much more time dwelling on what he clearly saw as the excessive and abnormal intensity of Chinese agriculture. Magee's rendition painted something malevolent and unnatural about such productivity. Even if American farmers adopted some of the techniques of their Chinese counterparts, he suggested, such intensive agriculture would be beyond Americans precisely because they were not unnatural. For Magee, the most obvious sign that all was not quite right in China was what he identified as the Chinese desire for discomfort, which no proper man could or would stand. "Fresh air and sunshine the Chinaman can come nearer to doing wholly without than any other human being," he claimed. "Both seem to be superfluities to him." Perhaps, he worried, they even enjoyed physical discomfort: "I have seen a Chinaman, while waiting at a railway station, lift himself upon an empty, headless, sharp-edged barrel, sit down upon the edge, and, with his feet as a brace across the barrel fall asleep." Such suffering, willingly endured, coupled with a determination to increase production no matter the means, suggested to Magee that Chinese immigrants threatened to overtake American workers. There was no way an American could suffer as much or endure such privations. What might be "exceedingly trying to an American," explained Magee, "would not inconvenience a China-man in the least." The Chinese innately possessed an unimaginable capacity for work and suffering, but such traits were hardly laudable.[43]

Instead, the anti-Chinese movement used Chinese hard work, productiv-ity, and willingness to endure hardship to highlight the distinctions between Chinese workers and American heroic artisans. Hard work frequently was explained as the result of centuries of servility. Adolph Strasser, president of the Cigar Makers' International Union, assured Hewitt's subcommittee that Chinese labor could never be anything but "coolie labor." For "the Chinaman," claimed Strasser, "his religion and his habits are law."[44] McNeill similarly went to great lengths to show that Chinese workers were inherently servile and dependent. "From his cradle," McNeill explained, "the Chinese serf is disciplined in the doctrine of nonentity. He was born under a government having a spiritual and temporal head and he is, therefore, mangled body and soul."[45] Even without a master or labor enforcer, the Chinese worker was still enslaved, as his puzzlingly ceaseless work demonstrated. And as a result of his "nonentity," the Chinese worker was willing to labor without any goal beyond that of the physical work itself, according to his opponents. James Whitney described "John Chinaman" as inevitably "stunted in figure, and with the dull and animalized visage peculiar to his race," "devoid of the wants, the aspirations, the high humanity with all its attendant needs which ages of intellectual, emotional, and physical advancement have given the races with which time and circumstance have brought him face to face."[46] Californian W. W. Stone explained that "the laborer, naturally, *per contra,* views the Chi-naman as a mere labor-machine, devoid of intelligence, utterly destitute of ambition and reason."[47]

In all of these descriptions, the authors are torn between horror at the conditions that the Chinese "willingly" endure and the conviction that the Chinese did not want anything else. Because they had no wants, no desires, nothing to give their work purpose, the Chinese could survive on very little. And indeed, anti-Chinese rhetoric fixated on the poverty of Chinese possessions, not with the goal of alleviating suffering but to catalog the differences between white Americans and the Chinese. Meade carefully explained that a Chinese worker needed only a "little rice" and was willing, if necessary, to supplement that rice with "the meanest kind of food, including vermin." Just as Magee had noted an unusual tolerance of discomfort, Meade described dank and hellacious living quarters: "He occupies a small room in common with twenty to fifty others. . . . Coolie lodgings literally resemble a box filled with herring." Even in his clothes, the Chinese worker showed himself more willing to endure hardship than his white counterpart. "His dress," Meade confided, "consists of the cheapest quality, without undergarments."[48] American workers did not and could not live in such a manner, Meade and others insisted. They were neither slaves nor automatons but independent, freethinking men with desires and wants. McNeill, horrified at the idea that white workers should emulate the Chinese, explained that "the Caucasian must add to his own individual needs the cost of maintaining a wife and family. There is rent to pay, clothing to provide, books to buy, and, added to all of that, the many little wants that arise out of the conditions of a Christian civilization." The "Mongolian" could work for less because he "is not burdened with the cares and expenses of a family." Without others to think of, "he is content with a little shelf in a barrack-structure, fashioned after the forecastle of a sea-going vessel."[49]

But such insistences rang increasingly hollow by the 1880s as the American worker came to resemble more closely the image of the Chinese worker. Like the Chinese, American workers became more like "mere labor machines," with little control over their work or workplaces. Photographs of men leaving ever-larger factories showed small figures, barely distinguishable from one another, pouring out of the gates. Were these men now similar to the Chinese, who were, as their opponents often claimed, so many bees, drones serving a distant queen?[50] And if white workingmen came to look too much like the Chinese, what would that mean for the heroic artisan? This question weighed on the minds of workers, of course, but was asked more widely as well. As William Corlett, a Republican from Wyoming, explained to the House, "No calamity can befall this country and its institutions so serious as the degradation of the laborer." For Corlett, competition from Chinese workers posed a far more serious threat to white men than did the dependence of wage work. If the current situation were not changed, the United States would cease to be a republic and would instead be characterized by the "grossly unequal distribution of wealth [that] is always observed where low wages prevail as the reward of the toiling millions."[51]

Just what kind of threat the Chinese and wage work posed to the heroic artisan lay at the center of Henry Grimm's short, strange 1879 play, *The Chinese Must Go!*[52] The play tells the story of a white man and his family who have been utterly ruined by the onslaught of Chinese immigrants. The father, William Blaine, had been an honest and prosperous tailor but lost his clients and his shop to cheaper, if less skilled, Chinese tailors. His status as a proprietary craftsman destroyed, he is unable to support his family. His son, Frank, cannot find employment and has resorted to a life of gambling and general hoodlumism. William's wife, Dora, has abdicated control of her household and kitchen garden to Chinese "servants," who do little but supply her daughter, Lizzie, with opium. From the beginning, the play makes it clear that William has lost his status as a producer, a proprietor, a husband, and a father. He cannot provide for his family. He cannot pass his trade and shop onto his son. He has lost moral control of his children and wife. He has even lost his common sense as a respectable citizen, so much so that at one point he is easily duped by a scheming minister who convinces him that the Chinese are a benign presence. He has been, in other words, utterly unmanned.

Having established the white craftsman's complete humiliation, the play then sets about reasserting the social and familial position of the "true American" workingman as the steady provider and rightful head of household, but not in the way that William expects. Despite his financial, social, familial, and intellectual decline, William still believes in the values of the heroic artisan. If Frank could find a real job as a craftsman, William muses, then the boy would immediately grow up, stop gambling and carousing, and settle down as a family breadwinner. But William is deluded: producerite virtues cannot save the day in *The Chinese Must Go!* The family's economic and moral salvation comes from ne'er-do-well Frank's very nonproductive and decidedly unmanly activities. Instead of assuming the qualities of the heroic artisan, Frank embraces both feminine wiles and female dress. Slipping into his sister's dress, he admires himself before a mirror ("Ain't I a lovely girl? Lady Nature, why didn't you make me a girl so I could kiss all the boys in town?") before mincing off to swindle his sister's inexplicably rich suitor, Julian Turtlesnap. The illusion is so convincing that Turtlesnap cannot tell Frank from Lizzie, and Frank makes off with Turtlesnap's money. Frank has transformed himself into precisely what his father most fears Frank will become: feminized—or worse, a woman. The heroic artisan cannot redeem the Blaines, but the feminine trickster can. At the end of the play, Frank assumes not only another gender but also another race, dressing as a Chinese woman, an imported bride in a box, to steal money from the family's thieving servant, Sam Gin.

Frank has no qualms about assuming the appearance and manners of a woman and even a Chinese woman; in fact, he enjoys his actions as part of a "lark." But although Frank's enjoyment of his role as a woman is a driving comic force in the play, it is also a continual source of anxiety. Why must he dress like a woman to prevent disaster? Does he really want to "kiss all the boys?" Would he really have preferred that "Lady Nature" have made him a girl? The play never resolves these questions. It is clear, however, that though Frank's success comes through his assumption of female dress, behavior, and desire, it does not ever completely subvert his manhood. His escapade as a Chinese woman is closely monitored by another white working-class man, the hardy Jack Flint, who continually offers reminders that Frank is "really" a white man. And when a policeman asks Frank-as-Lizzie where Frank Blaine is, he quickly snaps back, "In his pants," which Frank is wearing underneath Lizzie's dress. By the end of the play, all is well: the family is solvent, Frank is a hero, Lizzie is in the kitchen, and the Chinese have, for the moment at least, been vanquished. At the same time, however, none of the major problems in the play have really been resolved. William remains without employment as an artisan tailor. He cannot assure his family of a consistent and reliable source of income. Frank's pranks have staved off imminent disaster, but Frank has not become an upstanding producer or even a wage worker. Even his gender is sufficiently questionable, so that other characters in the play and the audience need frequent assurances of his manliness. He remains "frankly" at loose ends, looking for the next lark, but there is no guarantee that he will ever assume his duties as a producer and family provider. In the end, the play's only firm conclusion is that "the Chinese Must Go!"

The play's inability to resolve any of the Blaines' substantive problems reflects Frank's ambiguous future as a worker in American society. Though the play lauds producerite values, they ultimately seem to have little effect on the Blaines' lives. Frank's pranks are funny, but they do not offer a viable alternative to producerite ideology. Underneath the jokes and shenanigans, the final message of *The Chinese Must Go!* is that the twinned problems of wage work and the Chinese are likely to destroy men such as William Blaine. As prolific historian J. N. Larned explained in 1876, "The real essence of slavery . . . is the coercing of a man to yield the labor of his hands, or the service of his faculties to the benefit of another man, without freedom or power to exact an equivalent return; because, with some few exceptions, that is all which renders the enslaving of one man by another an object of desire."[53] In the anti-Chinese movement, the Chinese workers, described as willing—even eager—to accept wage slavery, received the blame for dragging white American workers down as well. Just as in the antebellum period, the term *wage slavery* helped reinforce the whiteness of the workers protesting it, but now, in addition to distinguishing themselves from African Americans, whites also distinguished themselves from the Chinese. In California, James Ayers insisted that Chinese exclusion was the only way to protect the United States from "the inconveniences and evils of a slave population." Without exclusion, "the toiling masses" of white American workers would "find themselves outcasts at home to make room for the conquering strangers."[54]

Fixing the Bread-and-Beef Standard

Could this decline—of both workingmen and the republic—be prevented? And was wage work itself the root cause of such debased conditions? For some, the answer to both questions was, thankfully, yes. If the republic were to be salvaged, they argued, workers had to have some assurance that they could rise to the ranks of property-owning producers. In such arguments, the Chinese became doubly symptomatic of the problems facing skilled white laborers. First, large manufacturers, committed to paying as little as possible for labor, hired Chinese workers; their presence in the United States and their low wages thus exposed forces aligned (even conspiring) against virtuous workers. And second, thanks to their lower wages and innate ability to withstand discomfort, the Chinese lived in appalling conditions, raising the dreadful question of whether white workers would face similar lives if the conspiracies against them were not stopped. Such concerns were central to an allegorical pamphlet (published in California under the pen name "Iota"), *The Raid of the Dragons into Eagle-Land.* In this tale, workers ("Working Bees," an inversion of more common depiction of the Chinese as menacing swarms) stood to lose everything to the Dragons (the Chinese) unless the Big-Bug president of the United States and congressional Grizzlibars stopped the invaders. Though the prompt removal of the dangerous Dragons is the immediate goal of this "plague(y) pamphlet," its larger goal is a return to a more just past. Previously, explains a beleaguered Working Bee, "in [our] homes (or hives) . . . there was comfort, plenty and hope for the future." Now, there is "poverty, sadness, and despair, and the cause of this alteration in the condition of the Working Bees, can be easily traced to the actions of our enemies, the Dragons."[55]

But the Working Bee also acknowledges that the problems of his fellow bees are larger than the Chinese Dragons. The eviction of the Dragons will not change the behavior of the industrialist Hogs or bring about a return to the more comfortable and plentiful past. While Iota blames the Dragons "for having as [their] principal object the acquisition of all the h(m)oney in the State," the Hogs seem more committed to that goal than do the Dragons. In either case, of course, the result is "the total destruction of the Working Bees, who should be [the state's] principal prop and pillar."[56] Similarly, in 1888, the "workingmen of San Francisco," furious over the Republican nomination of Benjamin Harrison, told their "brothers throughout the Pacific Coast" that "our *all* is at stake. That *all* means the opportunity to work at some honest avocation which will insure us a respectable living and the support of our families in the reasonable comforts of life." By the end of the document, however, San Francisco's workingmen have shifted their ire from the Chinese to the trusts, which "are melting the fat out of every housekeeper who burns coal; they are melting the fat out of every poor man who has to buy lumber to build a house for his family; they are melting the fat out of every farmer who has to buy sacks to put his grain in; they are melting the fat out of every fruit-grower who has to get his fruit canned for market, and in a thousand other ways they are melting the fat in an unseen way out of all of us."[57]

The Working Bees' condemnation of the trusts and the Chinese in virtually the same breath is not as discordant as might initially seem to be the case. Carlos Schwantes, for example, has noted that white workers in mid-1880s Washington state linked together the evils of the Chinese and the Northern Pacific railroad through a language of disinheritance. The disinherited in Washington were, like the Working Bees, white men who saw the linked forces of greedy capital and cheap nonwhite labor conspiring to deprive them of their social and political status as producers.[58] Politicians such as Oregon gubernatorial candidate Sylvester Pennoyer gained popularity by effectively exploiting the perceived links between Chinese labor and monopolies. Pennoyer, whose Harvard law degree suggests that he was not among the disinherited, rallied Oregonians by declaring that "to-day the great producing and labor classes are being ground down between the upper and nether millstones of corporate power and cheap servile labor. Without an end to Chinese immigration, it will only be a few years until the Willamette valley will be the home of only rich capitalists and Chinese serfs."[59]

The producerist language of Iota and Pennoyer tapped directly into both antebellum traditions and producerite protests of the late nineteenth century, particularly that strain of producerism that emphasized producers' right to enjoy the full fruits of their labor, condemned the degradation that accompanied wage work, and denounced parasitic nonproducers who lived off the labor of others. The Knights of Labor as well as the Populists also based many of their platforms, including their shared interest in the possibilities of co-operative ownership, on this school of thought. The successes of the Knights and the Populists, however brief, clearly showed the power of such language at both the local and national levels. As Saxton has argued, in such contexts, "anti-coolieism . . . became a means of product differentiation in which small producers could cling to a toe-hold in the market."[60] But anti-Chinese rhetoric also protested wage work and working conditions in another fashion, again initially drawn largely from antebellum producerite traditions. Instead of fo-cusing on saving the small property owner or employer—a man like William Blaine—however, such rhetoric cited the goals of competency and moderate prosperity.[61] As the century drew to a close, anti-Chinese writing increasingly emphasized the effects of wage work on the private life of the family and the position of the male worker within it. Such arguments accepted wage work as the permanent condition for workingmen in an industrial society and did not yearn for a return to independent proprietorship. But these argu-ments protested quite vigorously against low wages as detrimental to both the individual and the nation. Without high wages, white workingmen would experience neither competency nor prosperity. They would look a lot like the Chinese, and the fate of the nation would hang in the balance.

Anxiety regarding the perceived threat to white workers' economic com-petence, then, undergirded most anti-Chinese pronouncements in the 1870s. Willis explained to the House in 1879 that no matter how cheap the Chi-nese were to hire, no matter how well they performed their appointed tasks, "the material advantages of this kind of labor . . . sink into insignificance when compared with the personal considerations at stake—the comfort, the self-respect, the decent, honorable living of the laborer himself." In the end, argued Willis, "the Chinese laborer does not come up to the American standard of industry. The central idea of our system is that the laborer shall possess courage, self-respect and independence." But Willis did not then insist that the laborer should be self-employed. Instead he focused on the home, that "mold in which society is cast." Low wages, depressed by cheap Chinese workers (who supposedly had no families to support), were not sufficient to "secure homes or comfortably support white labor." The social consequences of poorly equipped white working-class homes were dire: "the loss of the homes, the comforts and the appliances of personal civilization, which [have] always been enjoyed by the laboring classes of America, and from which springs that spirit of self-respect and manly independence which is the highest result and best security of our political system." Willis was un-concerned with the self-employed or even with property ownership. Rather, he located the source of republican citizenship and "free institutions" in a well-stocked home.[62]

Without high wages, however, the male head of household would not be able to provide that well-stocked home for his family and, like William Blaine, would be stripped of "self-respect and independence." Just how low he might sink was made abundantly clear in an 1884 front-page article in *Swinton's Paper* that described, in great detail, the moral and material debasement of poorly paid "Hun" miners in western Pennsylvania. Given few choices by the mining companies, family heads pushed not only sons but wives, daughters, and small children into the mines, where they faced brutal physical labor. Even with every family member working, these people still lived in abject poverty: author Simon Lullaby noted with disgust that "when night comes, they sleep about promiscuously on the floor, or perhaps in bunks," not in proper beds, and "their utter inability to elevate themselves above the animal stage does not suggest even the drawing of curtains between portions of the house occupied by the members of one family." Even worse, Lullaby confided to his readers, "I have been told of their eating the flesh of animals raw, and I have no doubt of its truth." But even more troubling than the Huns' supposed preference for raw meat was the inversion of the proper family structure. Forcing women into the mines had made them stronger and more masculine than the men. Lullaby recalled "seeing a Hungarian woman carrying from the store a good-sized stove, while her lord and master walked beside her, carrying a loaf of bread."[63] Here then, was William Blaine's worst nightmare: unable to provide even the most basic comforts for his family, he (and then Frank) would be unmanned completely. Blaine's fear reflected the significant social and economic changes wrought by the emergence of industrial capitalism. As Corlett explained to the House, "The laborer's wages in this country have heretofore been such as to admit him to the enjoyment of all the more important social advantages which enable him to develop his intellectual faculties" and provide for his family.[64] Now, however, those wages were in jeopardy, in no small part thanks to fierce competition for jobs.

The depression, however, ensured that any declining standard of living for white skilled labor could not be blamed entirely on the Chinese, since wage drops and unemployment constituted national problems and the Chinese lived primarily on the West Coast. Nor could the Chinese be blamed for the decline of the small producer; as Iota had noted, increasingly large corporations producing ever-cheaper goods made it difficult if not impossible for independent producers to compete. More than anything else, the Chinese served a largely symbolic role, acting as a metonym for the social transformations of work under large-scale industrialization. But many Americans had no trouble directly blaming the Chinese for willfully injuring the American economy, and by the 1880s, increasing numbers of anti-Chinese advocates accused the Chinese of being economic parasites. Though they had long been seen as an "Asiatic herd of grasshoppers," funneling earnings back to China, a more urgent tone emerged in the 1880s.[65] McNeill noted in disgust that a Chinese shoemaker would refuse to buy even his own products but would instead insist on "send[ing] to China for his shuffling slipper."[66]

As economic instability came to be seen as a result or at least a reflection of underconsumption, Chinese immigrants' apparent refusal to consume American goods, which these workers were paid to produce, seemed especially malevolent. "The Chinese lives on Chinese products as the least expense possible wherever he goes, and gives nothing back to the communities of other nationalities on which he fattens. Money paid to him for his labor or his products ceases to be a circulating medium. He breaks the circuit of exchange and the money disappears. He is a parasite on the body politic."[67] Moreover, the Chinese seemed uninterested in even the most basic comforts. In 1902, former California governor George Perkins argued in the Senate that the Chinese, by nature, were "satisfied with bare roofs. . . . Their wants are simple and do not increase when their earnings increase." Chinese labor consequently could never "add materially to the wealth and prosperity of the country," even in the unlikely event that the Chinese ceased both "religiously" to send their wages home and to import "the merchandise of most of [their] wants" from China.[68] Moreover, as James Whitney had argued several years earlier, China could provide no market for U.S. goods because "we cannot sell flour to a population that prefers rice to wheat and which raises rice in kind and quantity unexcelled anywhere in the world." Nor could Americans sell machinery to a country that seemed to reject out of hand the advantages of mechanization.[69] Many observers argued that the Chinese refusal to consume American products was so complete that it included American cemeteries. Grumbled Perkins, "scarcely a steamer leaves a Pacific port for China that does not have on board hundreds of boxes containing the carefully-cleaned bones of deceased Chinamen."[70]

Such behavior evoked the specter not only of economic disaster but also of national decline, as Perkins was quick to note. "In the contest of survival between the Anglo-Saxon and the Chinese," he warned ominously, "the latter has an overpowering advantage." The Chinese historically "have been compelled to live on the scantiest of means and the result is a race—the fittest only surviving—which is probably capable of sustaining more hardships, of living on cheaper food, of needing less clothing and shelter, of having fewer wants, and the lowest estimate of life, as a whole, of any civilized people."[71] Similar arguments, increasingly common by the turn of the century, relied on an inversion of traditional American beliefs. Endurance in the face of hardship, privation, self-control, and determination no longer signified the pioneer spirit but rather indicated a "regressive" civilization. Precisely the traits that had made the Chinese dangerous competition for white workers now made Chinese civilization both a threat and an anathema. A history of privation had created a nation of desireless drones; the effect of their invasion on the United States could be deadly.

In contrast to John Chinaman, whose willingness to work for low wages ensured the economic degradation of the white workingman and whose refusal to spend money in America threatened the country, anti-Chinese rhetoric held up the white worker whose high wages provided his family with all of the comforts of industrial life. This argument offered a partial solution to the question in *The Chinese Must Go!*—What hope existed for the Blaines? As William Blaine had learned, tailors were being replaced not only by Chinese workers but also by larger factories, churning out cheap, ready-to-wear clothing. Against such forces, the small producer had little hope if his goal was to remain self-employed and prosperous. But if his goal was to achieve comfort and economic security, he had a chance. Indeed, in a just world, he should have every reasonable expectation of achieving those goals.

Underlying all these arguments was a set of shared if unarticulated assumptions about what these commentators meant when they used the terms *civilized* and *uncivilized*. To be civilized meant, above all else, two things. First, it meant having a desire for a life beyond mere subsistence. Vermin, Meade would no doubt have acknowledged, could keep a man alive, but rats were no fit food for civilized men, and civilized desires might well stretch beyond the dinner plate. Decent clothes and a private home were construed as signs of civilized life just as clearly as their opposites—the Chinese's cheap clothes (with nothing underneath!) and herring-like living quarters—denoted an uncivilized, primitive existence. Second, to be civilized meant providing similar comforts for a family and protecting dependent family members from want and privation. Indeed, the "Mongolian's" primitive nature is both assured and created by his status as a lone man, without family to provide for and protect.

The equation of white workingmen and civilization and that of Chinese workingmen with the primitive or barbaric demonstrated that white men were more evolved than Chinese. By emphasizing white wage-earning men's civilized status, anti-Chinese rhetoric attempted to insist that superior racial status trumped the position of dependent wage earner, an argument that succeeded only partially. More successful and more enduring was the equation of civilization with a man's ability to provide for his family. A civilized man not only ensured that his family members could survive but provided them with access to books, papers, nice clothes, and leisure activities—in short, with a comfortable standard of living. The male breadwinner and his housebound wife and children here became the epitome of civilization. Primitive or barbaric peoples failed in these most basic of tasks, and their failure was visible by their confusion of gender roles. Chinese men wore suspiciously feminine garments and unmanly "slippers." They took on women's work such as cooking and cleaning, seemingly without complaint. The fact that Chinese men's housekeeping was seen to be of such poor quality merely confirmed that they were neither true men nor good women; white Americans found Chinese men's gender confusing, often describing them as simultaneously masculine and feminine and seemingly as disturbed by the apparent gender ambiguity of Chinese workers as by their acceptance of feminized clothing and tasks. The equation of civilization (and civilized races) with the male breadwinner norm provided a yardstick by which to judge other immigrant groups as well. The failure of Eastern European "Hun" men to provide for their families, for example, was understood as merely an outward sign of their inward barbarity. Their racial inferiority was made visible to all by the meanness of their lodgings (the lack of "proper beds") and food (their consumption of raw meat) as well as the hypermasculinity of Hun women, whose superhuman strength was matched only by their inability properly to cook and clean. These languages of race and gender, linked through the evolutionary concept of "civilization," made the white male wage earner's position as family breadwinner, able to assure his dependents' comfort, the sign that he was a legitimate part of American civilization. In turn, "civilized" tastes for comfort and moderate leisure assured U.S. prosperity.[72]

By the 1890s, such arguments had become commonplace. In 1902, Charles Litchman told the Senate Committee on Immigration that unlike the Chinese, the white workingman, regardless of background or even ethnicity, "must have . . . the necessities of life; he expects the comforts, and would like occasionally to get within telescopic distance of the luxuries." Such "necessities," "comforts," and "luxuries" formed the "standard of American citizenship and American civilization" and the foundation of distinctions between American and Chinese workers.[73] And indeed, explained Edward Livernash before the same committee, the American man "cannot go without less of sunshine, less of beef, less of care for his race and his country" without courting almost certain death.[74] No European immigrant group filled this role of desireless machine; even southern African Americans were more like white Americans than were the Chinese, argued James Whitney, precisely because African Americans worked with goals beyond work itself: "The negro, although his wants are few, has been unused to privation. . . . The negro can no more subsist on what would content the Chinaman than the buffalo could exist on wayside thistles."[75]

Whitney was hardly proposing that African Americans were the equal of white laborers, but his decision favorably to compare African Americans to Chinese workers suggests a great deal about the importance he placed on desire. Common equations of black and lazy or indolent relied on stereotypes of African Americans as individuals who craved unearned luxuries. Here, Whitney made this desire a positive attribute, at least in contrast to the Chinese, whose lack of desire signified their innate depravity. As Elias Merriman explained in the pages of the *Social Economist,* white workers earned higher wages than the Chinese "simply because the standard of living of the whole class is higher." For the nation as a whole, workers' desire meant consistently high consumption, so that, as Merriam maintained, "flying shuttles and spindles all over the land cannot work fast enough to speed our industrial prosperity, the prosperity of toilers as well as capitalists."[76] White workers' desires assured individual happiness and national economic prosperity; Chinese workers' desirelessness had the inverse effect.

Such ideas resonated for the American Federation of Labor (AFL), established in 1886. The AFL—particularly its nearly perennial president, Samuel Gompers—stressed the connection between economic competency (expressed through the male breadwinner norm and the assurance of family comfort) and citizenship. In part, Gompers followed the ideas of eight-hour prophet Ira Steward, who had used the image of desireless Chinese as the counterexample to his insistence that workers' aspirations helped determine wages. "A peasant of the Celestial Empire can live on rats, and his wages are gauged accordingly; but a Man accustomed to beefsteak, succeeds in getting work enough to buy it," Steward explained.[77] By the 1890s, though, the AFL saw exclusion as more than merely an issue of wages. It was as much an issue "of the quality of American citizenship."[78] The Chinese could never, in Gompers's eyes, claim that citizenship. Testifying for the renewal of the Chinese exclusion laws in 1902, Gompers explained before a Senate subcommittee, "We cannot say that [the Chinaman] can not do the work. The fact is that he does it, and if not to the same extent, if not to exactly the same productivity, yet he does it." Gompers objected to the Chinese laborer because he was "unnatural" and unlike any other man; he had no wants. "He stands alone of all the men in the world defying all sociological influence. He stands as a contradiction to all economic definitions and explanations that have ever been given to the world." Gompers continued, "He lives as no other man in the world can live. He lives upon less than any other man in the world can live, and seems to thrive and prosper."[79] In the hands of the Chinese, then, thrift and frugality were not virtues but detriments and even perhaps perversions.

The AFL's most vigorous exposition of the comparison between Chinese and American workers was surely a 1902 pamphlet, *Meat vs. Rice.* Written to encourage the renewal of the Exclusion Act, the document was first presented to the Senate and then reprinted and widely distributed in 1908 by the California-based Asiatic Exclusion League to encourage further limitations on Chinese and Japanese immigrants.[80] Relying on testimonials, commissions, and other publications from the West Coast, *Meat vs. Rice* exposed the differences between the Chinese and American workers, using the faults of the former to define the strengths of the latter. When the Chinese first arrived in California to work in factories, the pamphlet explained, they worked for far less than any white worker, male or female, would work. As a result, families like the Blaines found themselves pushed out of trades and jobs and with no prospects for future employment. *Meat vs. Rice,* however, insisted that the Chinese willingness to work for low wages was part of a larger plan "to gain control" of American jobs. General Arthur MacArthur, leader of the U.S. troops in the Philippines, had observed as much, the AFL pamphlet noted. "Individually," MacArthur was quoted as saying, "the Chinaman represents a unit of excellence that must always command respect and win admiration, but in their organized capacity in the Philippines the Chinese represent an economical army. . . . [T]hey are bent on commercial conquest." As a commercial army, though, the Chinese accomplished more than merely pushing white women and men out of their jobs. The Chinese also set in motion the downfall of the republic. To compete with Chinese, *Meat vs. Rice* argued, white workers would have to "not only pursue the same kind of life" but also "abdicate [their] individuality," with consequences that "would be lamentable. . . . We would in that even have a labor class without homes, without families, and without any of the restraining influences of society." The ultimate result of this "degradation" would inevitably be danger to "the State" from the white worker "kept in a perpetual state of anger, exasperation and discontent, always bordering on sedition, thus jeopardizing the general peace and creating a state of chronic uneasiness, distrust and apprehension through the entire community." The AFL explained this state of affairs with Senator Blaine's words: "You cannot work a man who must have beef and bread, alongside of a man who can live on rice. In all such conflicts, and in all such struggles, the result is not to bring up the man who lives on rice to the beef-and-bread standard, but it is to bring down the beef-and-bread man to the rice standard."[81] Of course, industrial workers argued along the same lines throughout the postbellum period. Wage cuts by capitalists had deprived them of homes, families, and social standing, and many incidents of labor unrest were directly linked to plummeting wages. In *Meat vs. Rice,* however, the threat of warfare between capital and labor was recast as a conflict between white and yellow, between consumer desire and excessive frugality. The solution to the labor question, at least as articulated within anti-Chinese rhetoric, did not involve siding with either capital or labor but rather siding with the desiring worker over the frugal, Chinese worker. Therein lay the crux of the AFL's argument: the beef-and-bread standard must be maintained.

The beef-and-bread standard was not just a xenophobic reaction to foreign, nonwhite labor. Nor was it only an articulation of a working-class program based on shared whiteness and an equally shared Sinophobia.[82] It was also a clear vision of the new worker-citizen: a man who worked, probably permanently, for a wage rather than for himself but earned enough to keep himself and his family in comfort, able to participate in consumer and leisure cultures. Such a well-dressed, well-housed man would have achieved everything that William Blaine was losing except property ownership and self-employment. And like the property-owning artisan of old, he was a responsible citizen, the backbone of the republic. What made him equally responsible, equally worthy of being a citizen was, the AFL suggested, his competency, derived from a high wage and access to what Gompers called "the civilization of our time."[83] The threat of the Chinese—of the rice diet—was ultimately the threat of having that competency taken away, of losing any claim to a certain standard of living.[84] This is not to say that the AFL's position was not at its heart based on racism or on assumptions that the worker-citizen should be (indeed, must be) white; rather, *Meat vs. Rice* also represented an articulation of a new model of working-class citizenship that meshed easily with Americans' racialized and gendered understandings of civilization.

Under such a rubric, the AFL pursued its "pure and simple" "practical" unionism, demanding shorter hours and higher wages as the just rewards of virtuous citizens committed to the well-being of the nation. The low wages ensured by Chinese labor would not, Gompers argued, benefit the nation.

Any resulting profit would be "a profit only for a time, because producing, say, $2 worth and consuming 15 cents worth, the difference contributes to what is popularly known as overproduction, but in truth is in its more accurate economic term known as underconsumption." At the same time, depressed wages would make white workers unable to satisfy their desires or consume, thereby depressing demand and eventually production. "People who live on little consume little," Gompers warned, "and give employment to an exceedingly small number of people."[85] Gompers's argument closely followed that put forward by Carroll Davidson Wright in the 1886 Bureau of Labor Statistics report on the 1870s depression. But, in case anyone had forgotten the traumas of the 1870s, Gompers explained to an enthusiastic audience of fifteen hundred people (among them "a sprinkling of women") the consequences of having an underpaid and undesirous labor force: "You will find that people get wages just enough to buy things they consent to live on. It is so in this country. In China they get wages just enough to buy rice. . . . Let the American people decide next week or next year to wear blue jeans and eat red herrings and crackers and you'll find that they would get just enough to buy blue jeans, red herrings and crackers. So the reverse is true; let the people demand an extra room with all that goes with it, and they will get wages enough to buy it."[86]

The ideals of citizenship that came from within the anti-Chinese movement became increasingly important answers to the labor question in the 1890s and 1900s. The stress on the male breadwinner norm, the importance of consumption, and the centrality of attainable desires helped shape a new and emerging understanding of economic participation as a vital component of American citizenship. For the AFL in particular, claims for the necessity of private comfort, consumption, and desire became central to arguments for workers' rights in industrial America. And in the field of economics, similar ideas also appeared in response to the economic and social crises of the 1870s and 1880s as a new generation of young economists, raised in a robust tradition of reform and trained in historical economics, reconceptualized the position and role of wages in production, consumption, and capital investment.

3

The Value of Wages

Historical Economics and the Meanings of Value

In the mid-1880s, economist Henry Carter Adams received a nervous letter from his mother. She worried that with so much being written on the labor question, "all would be said" before her son's book came out. Adams replied teasingly, "What a foolish little mother you are! This question we are rapidly coming on to is as big as the Reformation, or the English Revolution." There was yet, he assured her, "great opportunity for *thinking*, and some opportunity for writing."[1]

Much like other Americans, the young Turk economists who came of professional age in the 1870s and 1880s recognized the labor question as raising fundamental concerns about the nature of American democracy in an age of mass industrialization. Trained in German historical economics during the immediate postwar period, these men went on to create the academic discipline of economics and to found its professional society, the American Economic Association (AEA). They consequently understood the labor question as a particularly and peculiarly economic matter and saw themselves as especially well placed to answer it. Indeed, many young economists began to study economics precisely to continue the kind of social reform in which their abolitionist parents had engaged. Their understanding of economics as an arena for the kind of social reform we associate with abolition may seem jarring if not absurd to present-day Americans. Everyday contemporary usage of *economic* stresses the bottom line and profit margins, while references to the academic discipline of economics presuppose a reliance on abstract models and assumptions about predictable market behavior. Both current uses of the word are narrow, focused on account books and assuming a cast of rational, self-interested actors. The young economists of the 1880s, however, had a much more capacious view of *economic* that stretched beyond financial transactions and took into account the word's origin in the Greek *oikonomia,* the art of household management. In early modern usage of the term *economic,* household management included not only control of goods and trade but also the maintenance of domestic harmony. The art of household management, of course, was as much as about social relations as about account books. For late-nineteenth-century economists, it was an easy step from the individual household to society, the household writ large. As Columbia's Edwin R. A. Seligman explained, economists had finished with the "old, old commercial questions." Economics could not be reduced to mere "matters of dollars and cents" but represented the larger and more important study of "the struggle for manhood and true civilization."[2] In the 1870s and 1880s, no struggle seemed more crucial to these young men, and with society as their subject of study, the young Turks turned to answering the labor question. Class discord and potential class warfare threatened the American republic much as slavery had a generation earlier, and this generation of economists tackled the threat with all the zeal their parents had brought to their struggle.

The economists began their inquiry by confronting the vexing problem of wages. Wages were, Adams explained to his mother, "the right end of the problem." As workers realized, demands for higher wages and shorter hours were less crucial than demands "for a way to determine wages and hours."[3] What was needed, in other words, was a reassessment of the social position of wage workers. Here the economists had much to contribute. The questions at hand concerned not only specific and individual compensation or work conditions but also the nature of the social order of industrial capitalism more broadly. What was the basis of wages? How were they determined? Who paid them, and from where? What did wages represent? The expenditure of capital? The efforts of labor? Such questions demanded a specific, detailed accounting of the workings of an industrial economy as well as an extensive rethinking of the social meanings of the wage and the social roles that wage earners could claim. The problem facing the economists then could be distilled into one weighty and formidable question: Could there be a democracy without Jeffersonian republicanism? If they could not find a way to ensure the continuation of democratic life without the proprietary producer, then, as Adams's fellow economist Richard Ely put it, "our future downfall will be inevitable."[4]

These economists, the founders of the academic discipline in the United

States, have been roundly lambasted for asking such a question. Many historians have criticized this focus on wages (and eventually on consumption) rather than on reversing the ongoing process of proletarianization. These economists have been depicted as crass apologists for corporate capitalism and enthusiastic proponents of a decidedly antidemocratic, bureaucratic state run by experts (themselves most definitely included) who determined what was best for capital and by extension for everyone else. Critics have acknowledged that some economists (especially Adams, John Bates Clark, and Ely) had clearly felt youthful twinges of radical politics, but those stirrings were crushed by the vicious backlash against anticapitalist radicalism following the 1886 Haymarket bombing. They subsequently were either cowed by fear of job loss or bribed by jobs in the new regulatory agencies. (Adams lost his job at Cornell and almost failed to secure an appointment at the University of Michigan. Soon thereafter, when his tone had moderated somewhat, Adams was appointed chief statistician of the new Interstate Commerce Commission.) By and large, this portrait suggests that these economists were most loyal to their own middle-class backgrounds, which, coupled with the post-1886 pressures to foment no revolution, propelled them toward an acceptance of the industrial corporate order at the direct expense of the alternatives proposed by Populists, Socialists, and the Knights of Labor. The young Turks may have understood the older meanings of *economic,* but they paid more attention to its emphasis on household *management* than to the self-sufficiency and independence implied by the household as a socioeconomic unit. In the end, this narrative argues, all that labor—and the democratic project more generally—received from the "ethical economists" was disengagement from any meaningful political decision and the rather disappointing consolation prize of vacuous mass consumption.[5]

The economists, not surprisingly, understood their efforts quite differently. They were not revolutionaries, but they did see themselves as self-consciously building on reform traditions, most notably the abolitionist politics with which many of them had grown up, and participating in conscientious efforts to transform the specific society in which they lived.[6] They also understood themselves as specifically *historical* economists, and their methodology of historical inquiry shaped their approach to the labor question. Careful studies of the labor movement in the 1870s and 1800s, of the economic instability of the decades, and most importantly of the workings of industrial capitalism led them to two conclusions. First, the financial and social organization of the United States (excluding the South) was now irrevocably based on large-scale manufacturing, national distribution, and wage work. Any solution to the labor question, whether espoused by socialists, labor unions, or capitalists, would have to begin with an acceptance of that fact. For this reason, they began with the question of wages rather than with an effort to end wage work or reassert the priority of the proprietary producer. Second, capital was at least as important a factor as labor in ensuring economic stability and prosperity. With those two conclusions in mind, then, the young economists approached what Adams had suggested was the crux of the labor question: What would "democracy" now mean in an industrial society? The answer to that question meant, as Adams understood, rethinking the meaning of the wage itself.

The Young Economists

Though the postbellum economists differed, sometimes quite substantially, among themselves, they were motivated by two factors that almost all of them shared to some degree: many came from evangelical, often abolitionist families, and most had studied the new discipline of historical economics in Germany. These two factors gave a general coherence to their approaches to the labor question, convincing them that as economists they could solve it and that as Americans they had a moral obligation to do so.[7] Francis Amasa Walker (1840–97), who had a distinguished career in the Bureau of Statistics before becoming president of the Massachusetts Institute of Technology, learned to combine economics with social reform from his father, Amasa Walker, an economist, reformer, and leader of the Free Soil Party in Massachusetts. John Bates Clark (1847–1938), like Walker a New Englander, had been raised in a strict Congregationalist household with daily prayers. Clark had hoped to enter seminary after graduation from Amherst College but turned instead to economics as a more immediate means of social transformation.[8] Like others of his generation, he self-consciously understood himself as participating in the New England tradition of active reform. He remembered traveling as a five-year-old from Rhode Island to Boston to see his great-grandfather, who had helped drive the British from Boston in 1775 and had fought in the Continental Army for the duration of the war. Clark saw the secondhand memory of the revolution as connecting him to an American reform tradition that provided a model for social action during the economic turbulence of the postbellum period.[9] Although Richard Theodore Ely (1854–1943) grew up in western New York, the son of a deeply religious civil engineer and art teacher, he also identified with the New England reform tradition. The atmosphere of fervent belief and reformatory zeal in Fredonia led Ely to declare it a transplanted New England town and himself "a son of New England, a Connecticut Yankee."[10] Edmund Janes James (1855–1925), head of the University of Pennsylvania's Wharton Business School in the 1890s, was the son of a circuit-riding Methodist minister whose religious faith was matched by his loyalty to the party of Lincoln. And Simon Nelson Patten (1852–1922), who grew up in Sandwich, Illinois, was raised as a strict Presbyterian, an opponent of slavery, and a staunch proponent of the Union.[11]

Even those economists raised in less ostensibly religious households had been instilled with a sense of social responsibility that transferred itself to their economic work. Edwin R. A. Seligman (1861–1939), one of the few Jewish economists to rise to prominence in this period, came from an urbane German Jewish family that had settled in New York. Seligman's father was "public-spirited banker" who proudly named his son after Robert Anderson, the stalwart defeated commander of Fort Sumter. Frank Taussig (1859–1940) and his friend, Arthur Twining Hadley (1859–1930), came from families less overtly committed to social reform; nonetheless, the war provided a model of social action for both men. Taussig's father, a well-to-do St. Louis doctor known for his extensive work with visually impaired children, had been an ardent Union supporter and taught his son a sense of public duty. Hadley grew up in Connecticut, where his father was a professor of Greek at Yale. Though his family was less directly touched by the fervor of the war, Hadley shared Taussig's commitment to practical social reform and saw economics as well suited to lead the way.[12] "I believe," he announced in his 1898 presidential address before the AEA, that economists' "largest opportunity in the immediate future lies not in theories but in practice."[13]

Hadley's call for practical social action came in no small part from the German school of historical economics most closely identified with the Verein für Sozialpolitik and Adolph Wagner, Gustav Schmoller, and Karl Knies. The Verein and its economists emphasized the need to understand economic behavior (at both the macro and micro levels) within particular historical contexts and thus privileged empirical investigations over abstract and static theories. For Schmoller and others, this methodology was inseparable from social reform in imperial Germany; as economic historian Erik Grimmer-Solem has argued, empirical research "seemed to provide insights into the dramatic urban and industrial changes of the 1860s and 1870s, and held the promise of solutions to problems for which theory had no ready answers."[14] Though the practitioners of historical economics adhered to dramatically different political doctrines, they shared a firm belief in the value of social scientific research to social reform. The generation of American economists who came of age after the Civil War—whether they were "younger traditionalists," as Joseph Dorfman has labeled Hadley and Taussig, or more liberal historical economists such as Ely and Adams—shared this belief.[15] The lessons of Wagner, Schmoller, and Knies resonated among the Americans, even those who, like Taussig, were less enthusiastic about the Germans' advocacy of "state socialism."[16] To the end of his life, the German school's influence on him was clear, and he "always acknowledged the influence of, and to the end retained his feelings of sympathy and respect for" Wagner. Joseph Schumpeter later maintained that Taussig's "ability to see problems in their sociological settings and in their historical perspective" showed the German school's influence on him.[17] For Patten, whose embrace of the German school was more wholehearted, studying in Germany proved an intellectual turning point, and he recalled to Ely, "I had little notion of what I was to see in Germany when I went but I had very definite notions when I returned. I was tired of American politics and traditional religion, and even more disliked classical studies. It was a craving for a broader view that lured me to Germany, and while there I learned to base my thought on the world's experience instead of on conventional English ideas. The study of history did even more for me than that of economics. . . . I found the narrow self-satisfied attitude of the American very trying."[18]

That dissatisfaction with American and classical economics shaped the 1885 constitution of the AEA, formed by Ely, Adams, and others to bring the lessons of historical economics to bear on America's social problems. Economists, the organization's charter proclaimed, should look "not so much to speculation as to the historical and statistical study of actual conditions of economic life." Like Patten, the members of the new group wanted to base their economics on "the world's experience." They saw themselves reacting against the tired assumptions of classical economics and inciting radical reform, if not exactly wholesale revolution. "We were," Ely later remembered, "rebels fighting for our place in the sun."[19] Even after the Haymarket riots, when general sentiment turned against activist economics and universities sought to purge any and all economists who seemed too radical or sympathetic with the labor movement, the younger generation of economists continued to ask what conditions constituted democracy in an industrial society. More frequently couched in terms of specific investigations into taxation or the tariff, railroad regulation or monetary policy, a quest for social justice remained lurking within (sometimes well within) their works. Even Clark, whose economics came to be increasingly static through the 1890s and who more and more viewed capitalism as a "historic constant," continued his commitment to establishing a less economically divided society.[20]

Dismantling the Wages-Fund Theory

By the 1880s, many economists saw the question of wages as the linchpin to any solution of the labor question. They had lived through the depression of the 1870s, with its astronomical unemployment; they had witnessed desperate workers unable to buy basic necessities for their families; and they had seen the widespread disastrous effects of underconsumption. Echoing the testimony of the volunteer witnesses before Abram Hewitt's select committee, the young economists understood these financial and social catastrophes as signs of some kind of social transformation, a seismic shift in the ordering of society. Much like the American Federation of Labor (AFL) in the 1890s, they sought practical solutions to these problems, and, again like the AFL, they understood these practical solutions to have broader implications about wage workers' position in American society. So they tackled the question of wages with a great sense of urgency.

Since the Jacksonian period, most American economists and businessmen had adhered to David Ricardo's "wages-fund" theory. Laborers' wages, argued Ricardo, were an advance from capital, paid prior to any profit from production. Since workers had to be paid long before a product's sale, wages did not represent any part of the employer's profit but rather a potentially risky investment. The wages-fund theory assumed, then, that a finite amount of capital existed for wages, no matter the number of laborers, and that the amount was not immediately affected by increases in production or consumption. Although the fund could vary in size over time, increasing slowly as profits grew or contracting sharply during a depression, at any given moment "the amount of it cannot be increased by force of law or of public opinion, or through sympathy and compassion on the part of employers, or as the result of appeals or efforts on the part of the working classes."[21] Consequently, if the wages fund decreased, as it would have to do during a depression, wages would also have to decrease, no matter what hardship the decline brought to workers. According to the wages-fund theory, no alternative existed; neither striking workers nor sympathetic employers could increase the fund itself. At the same time, any increase in the total number of workers would inevitably decrease the amount each could earn, since the total now had to be divided among a larger pool. During good times, more workers could find employment without lowering the wages of all. During a depression, however, each additional wage earner sucked profit from his employer and wages from his fellow workers. For most Americans, the wages-fund theory made intuitive sense, and they believed it whether they attributed it to Ricardo or just to common sense.

By the 1870s, however, the seemingly endless economic contraction, the increasing anxiety about overproduction and underconsumption, and the social effects of unemployment and poverty combined to throw the wages-fund theory into question. Wage cuts certainly were a quick and effective way for employers to temporarily raise profits (or lower debt); as employers insisted, "higher wages cannot be paid because the wage-fund is not greater than it is."[22] But as underconsumption came more commonly to be seen as a major cause of industrial depression, lower wages seemed more likely to exacerbate business failures than to solidify employers' economic positions. Furthermore, of course, plummeting wages and escalating unemployment created previously unimaginable levels of misery, particularly in such urban centers as New York and Chicago. Wage cuts increasingly seemed to make neither economic nor social sense.

Walker was the most prominent early opponent of the wages-fund theory. Although he was not the first to attempt to discredit the popular theory (he cited his father as an important predecessor in this effort), his fellow economists saw Walker as the undisputed leader of the opposition to the wages-fund theory. Walker's commitment to the Union cause (he had signed up for the army almost immediately and served with distinction) had suggested to him that social problems could be solved through unified action without necessarily radically altering the basic tenets of American society.[23] After the Civil War ended, David Ames Wells, then special commissioner of the revenue, persuaded Walker to accept the position of chief of the Bureau of Statistics. With military efficiency, he reorganized the bureau and revamped the Census, pushing for the inclusion of a broad-ranging questionnaire within the census in order to document the variations in Americans' lives across the country. As a result, the 1870 Census, explained Harvard political economist Charles F. Dunbar, showed "the social and economic changes wrought by four years of prodigal expenditure both of life and of resources, and by the unparalleled revolution in the industrial organization of the former slave States."[24] Though Walker remained committed to some of the ideals associated with laissez-faire, particularly the belief "in the virtue of freedom, in the power of individual effort," his postwar experience as a statistician and director of the U.S. Census taught him that the new industrial society would need substantial interference if class warfare and social collapse were to be avoided.[25] His work on both the 1870 and 1880 Censuses earned him an international reputation as a statistician. As Dorfman has argued, this work made Walker "more aware of the vast complexities of the American economic organism; consequently he had less of the dogmatic assurance of his contemporaries in the academic world."[26] Fellow Civil War veteran and statistician Carroll Davidson Wright, eulogizing Walker at the 1897 American Statistical Association quarterly meeting, explained that "he placed manhood at the centre of his economic system." While "he upheld the theorist's views, . . . he understood the pressing influence of environment, of the constitution of human nature, in affecting human economic conditions."[27] For Walker, economics was no mere abstract calculation; it was the study of human life.

His investigation into the specific realities of daily life in industrial America compelled Walker to consider that wages were not paid out of a preexisting fund but from the product of labor. Proponents of the wages-fund theory, like British classical economist John E. Cairnes, "made no account of the increase of the wage-fund through increased production resulting from increased labor," scolded Walker. "On the contrary," he continued, "the wage-fund (the aggregate of wages, let it be observed, not the average rate of wages) is, according to [Cairnes,] diminished by an increase of labor." While Cairnes held that more workers simply meant that the fixed fund would have to be divided up into more and smaller parts, Walker pointed out that a larger workforce should increase production and consequently profit. Furthermore, Walker fumed, Cairnes and others had failed to take into account increases in efficiency or productive capacity. Increased productive power had to become "a reason for immediate advance of real wages." Thus, "the economical right of the working classes to an advance of wages corresponding to any and every increase in their own efficiency as laborers" could not be denied, either ethically or economically. But for Walker, an increase in the productive capacity or efficiency of work could be accomplished only through the moral fortitude of the workers themselves: improvement in "intelligence, sobriety, and diligence," watchwords of the self-reliant individual, were essential to obtaining higher wages. Workers' economic fate ultimately lay in their own hands.[28]

This belief represented a marked departure from the assumptions of earlier economists. In the past, explained Walker to the alumni association of Lehigh University in June 1887, "the accepted philosophy . . . declared that the manual laboring class were not called upon to make any efforts, on their part, in order to secure their just distributive share of the product of industry. . . . The laborer was not called upon to seek his interest; his interest would seek him and would unfailingly find him." The worker had been seen as someone who lacked all agency, the very personification of the dependent wage worker. By the 1880s, however, Walker argued that it was clear that "competition must be imperfect, and, in the result, more or less injurious, unless the laborers, on their side, are alert and active in pursuing their economic advantage." Now, he insisted, "economists and the general public . . . see, what the working classes long ago saw, that each man is the proper trustee of his own earnings, and that these are only safe when paid into his own hands."[29] No longer the wards of benevolent employers, wage workers were themselves independent economic actors whose wages represented their earning and striving rather than a gracious loan from an employer.

But for what part of the increase in productivity might sober, diligent workers hope? In his 1883 magnum opus, *Political Economy,* Walker turned to the problem of distribution, or how the relative profits of investor, entrepreneur, manufacturer, and worker were determined. Keeping in mind his earlier conclusion that labor could control its own wage levels through hard work and, if that approach failed to increase wages, through direct demands and strikes, Walker concluded that labor's share of the profit was the "residue" left over after the capitalist, the employer, and the entrepreneur had taken their shares (determined by rates of rent, interest, and profits). Labor was, in Walker's phrase, the "residual claimant." If workers increased productivity without a simultaneous increase in investment, then they would see a corresponding rise in wages. Walker's theory of the residual claimant allowed him to envision just distribution within the current economic and industrial structure. It also encouraged him to imagine a noncombative relationship between employers and employees: workers were not being robbed of their rightful wages by employers; workers' wages were the result of their efforts in concert with those of employers, investors, and innovators. Finally, his theory suggested that workers could have at least some degree of control over their wages.[30] Walker divorced wage payments from preliminary investment by capitalists and linked them instead to production. Provided that wage rates remained constant, if workers increased their productivity without any additional investment from capital, they would logically increase their wages: distribution, he suggested, was in part a matter of choice.

Pointing out that workers could theoretically control their wages offered Walker a partial solution to the labor question. As he explained at the 1888 AEA annual meeting in Philadelphia, the Manchester School of Adam Smith and Ricardo had "held doctrine, in politics" as well as in economics, "of the

guardianship of the lower by the upper classes." This "aristocratic economics" strongly implied that "it was not important, or indeed, desirable, that
the laboring class should take an active part in the distribution of wealth."[31]
Belief in the wages fund, Walker had explained in 1875, had not negated the
real purpose of wages, which was "to purchase labor," "not that he may keep
it employed, but as a means to the production of wealth." This theory had
ensured that the unintended consequence of the employer's belief that he
"advanced" wages was a detrimental, paternalistic relationship. Large-scale
industrial production and the labor movement made this belief unsustainable
by the latter half of the nineteenth century. Now, "under impulses new to this
age," the laboring classes, previously designated the "wards" of capital, had
"come forward to allege the competency to manage their own affairs."[32] While
reaffirming Walker's strong faith in self-reliance, individual responsibility,
and "the power of individual effort," his theory of wages argued that wage
earners *as* wage earners were independent rather than dependent actors in
the economy of industrial capitalism.

But for many economists, Walker's determined belief in the power of the
individual to change or affect his life no longer applied to a modern society
dominated by corporations and classes. Stuart Wood in particular took aim
at Walker in an article on wage theory that, though generally forgotten to-
day, was remarkably significant for postbellum economists. Wood was not,
at first glance, a likely candidate to be one of the "independent discovers
of the marginal productivity theory." A Philadelphia businessman, he had
earned a doctorate in politics at Harvard, where he worked under Dunbar.
Although economist George Stigler acerbically described Wood's thesis as
"undistinguished" by much except a "flowery" style and an unfortunately
"low" "standard of craftsmanship," he produced several enormously influential essays between 1888 and 1891, including his attack on Walker, before he
turned most of his attention again to business.[33] In "The Theory of Wages,"
Wood laid out a new theory that posited consumption rather than production as the driving force behind wage rates. Although, he acquiesced in the
direction of Ricardo that a natural price of labor might exist, it was strictly
theoretical. For Wood as a historical economist, this theoretic natural price
did little to describe the actual social circumstances that determined wages.
He instead turned to the role of market price in setting wages. Unlike natural price, market price reflected the historically specific circumstances that
determined wages; but, argued Wood, market price was set not by employers
or employees but by consumers. With Walker's argument about the residual
claimant in mind, Wood argued that labor's wage was not determined by the

effort (or, as he called it, "pain") of the work itself. Anticipating Clark's arguments about marginal productivity, Wood argued that the price of labor was regulated by the final utility, by "how much . . . men pay for the least useful or least productive portion of labor," and that final utility had to be determined by "taste." "The relative demand for labor and for the use of capital," he argued, "will not depend solely upon the existing rates of wages and of interest, but will depend in part also on taste."[34] Although the prices of some items (he mentioned green vegetables) reflected wage rates fairly accurately and others (for example, textiles) had prices more closely determined by interest (that is, investment), in the end, cost had to be determined by a combination of capital investment, labor costs, and consumer preference.

Wood's emphasis on the role of taste in driving consumption represented a departure from popular early-nineteenth-century explanations of economic behavior. Instead of positing individual rational behavior (and asking whether a person maximized income or pleasure), Wood assumed that individual consumers made choices unconsciously dictated by social taste, which was not natural, rational, or predictable but above all else reflected social norms, predilections, and whims. If taste was an integral part in setting final utility, then the self-interested individual, whose economic choices were always rational and comprehensible, was thrown right out of the picture. In his place, Wood put a much less tidy and much more diffuse "society," ill defined but clearly present, that was neither entirely predictable nor consistently rational. Wood's idea of the irrational consumer certainly seems to prefigure the arguments of Thorstein Veblen in *The Theory of the Leisure Class,* but unlike Veblen, Wood remained neutral on the moral effects of consumption, seeing himself as merely describing how wages and profits were now constituted.[35]

Wood's significant rethinking of the nature of profits—specifically, his argument that both wages and profits were largely determined by consumer taste and preference—had two significant implications for economists trying to answer the labor question. First, Wood showed that "the problem of wages and of interest [or profits] are one and the same, and that since it is not possible to ascertain the amount of either one of them apart from the amount of the other, so therefore neither of them can properly be treated as a mere residuum which is left after defraying the other out of the total product of industry."[36] In other words, Walker's argument that labor was the "residual claimant" on industry was misleading. Profits were not the sale price minus labor and cost of production, nor were wages the main drag on profits. Rather, both profits and wages depended on the rate of sales over time in conjunction with cost per unit of production. The most important determining factor for both profits and wages was not production costs (raw materials, plant, and wages) or final price but amount sold. The labor question, then, was less a problem of modulating production and more a matter of understanding and managing rates of consumption, an argument that the trade union movement would reiterate.

Second, Wood emphasized the role of the consumer more than that of the capitalist or employer in determining wages. His reformulation of Walker's theory of wages argued that the consumer was an equally integral part of determining wages as well as commodity value. Any law of wages, argued Wood, had to take into account that wage rates are partially set by commodity price and that price is partly determined by supply and demand. But, he cautioned, supply and demand reflect both quantifiable conditions (such as price) and subjective factors (such as taste): "In order to be useful [or productive], labor and capital must be efficient in producing objects; but this is not enough, unless the objects produced are also the objects of human desire. Their relative utilities are in proportion to the sum of objects produced, and in proportion likewise to the power of those objects to satisfy the cravings of appetite." As an illustration of the role of consumer demand or desire, Wood noted, "I know of regions which have a marvelous facility for producing Canada thistles, but I have yet to hear of a single farmer who has regularly adopted this branch of agriculture." Price, profit, and wages—the "direction of industry" more generally—"will always in the last resort be dictated by human appetites or desires." Relative price might guide desires (the "choice of [desire]'s objects is modified by the consideration of their relative cost"), but desire sets demand.[37] Wood's theory of wages turned away from investment and production and toward consumption as the central determinant of wages. Workers' "economical virtues," as Walker had called them, could no longer be seen as determining their wages. The result, if Wood was correct, was double-edged for labor: low wages did not reflect moral turpitude on the part of workers, but as producers, they also had limited influence on wage rates. At the same time, Wood suggested that capitalists and manufacturers had similarly limited influence on wages and profits; society as a whole and the consumer (whether seen as an individual or an aggregate) in particular were as important, if not more important, in determining the rewards to all three.

During the 1880s and 1890s, most economists, like Wood, began to turn to consumption rather than production as the central factor in setting wages. Even Taussig, who continued to hold onto the general idea of a wages fund (though in a highly modified form), agreed with Wood's basic assessments. Although Taussig, like Walker, believed firmly in the virtues of self-reliance and individual independence (he consistently opposed minimum-wage laws, even for women), his investigations of postbellum economic and social conditions told him that sobriety and diligence could not automatically raise labor's wage. Taussig's version of the wages-fund theory was broader than that of most employers, who were, according to Taussig at least, wedded to too narrow an understanding of it. The wages-fund theory, he argued, was "right in looking at the advance of funds from capitalists to laborers as the first step in the process by which wages were determined." The idea that "the real ultimate source from which wages were paid lay in the income of the consumers who brought the products made by laborers," which was also espoused by the popular labor economist George Gunton and was strongly suggested by Wood, was too circular to make sense to Taussig. If the "consumer's income was said to be the source of wages," then how could economists account for the fact that the "wages themselves were a very important part, probably the most important part, of [the] consumer's income?" Taussig's answer to this conundrum continued to emphasize the supply side of the equation: the real source of wages was to be found in the "recurring supply of finished and consumable commodities which was being constantly produced and consumed." But even as he focused on production as the dominant factor determining profits and wages, he also argued, much as Wood had, that consumer spending was "*the* important factor . . . in determining . . . whether the demand for labor shall be in one direction or another, and whether particular groups of laborers shall get high or low wages."[38] Even for Taussig, wages now seemed to depend on rates of consumption rather than cost of production.

Theories of Value

"It is," pointed out John Bates Clark, "one thing to determine from what sum the amount of wealth represented by wages is deducted, and quite a different thing to ascertain how that abstract quantity comes to embody itself in bread, meat, clothing, implements, etc."[39] Refuting the wages-fund theory went a long way toward substantiating workers' demands for high wages, but this refutation did not determine just how much "bread, meat, clothing, implements, etc." any one social group deserved. And at the core of the labor problem lay the question, as Clark put it in 1899, "Does labor get all it deserves?" "The welfare of the laboring classes," he explained, "depends on whether they get much or little; but their attitude toward other classes—and, therefore, the stability of the social state—depends chiefly on the question, whether the amount that they get, be it large or small, is what they produce." If they feel that they "produce an ample amount and get only part of it, many would become revolutionists, and all would have the right to do so."[40] But what represented a just wage?

The popular version of the labor theory of value, which most Americans instinctively held to be true at some level, argued that commodity value reflected the quantity of labor power embodied within the commodity (assuming general compliance with contemporary production and efficiency standards).[41] This particular version of the labor theory of value had a great deal in common with the Manchester School's understanding of the economic role of labor. For Adam Smith, explained Adams to his Cornell undergraduates, it was self-evident that "labor is the real source of wealth." By *labor,* Smith meant "productive labor," which "effects an increased value in commodities." Consequently, Adams argued, Smith held that "labor is the measure of value."[42] Part and parcel of the popular version of the labor theory of value was a "sentimental glory" for workers. As Leon Fink has shown, this "sanctification of work" "in part . . . drew on nostalgia for a preindustrial past [and] on a defense of devalued craft skills, [and] in part also on a transcendent vision of a cooperative industrial future."[43] The Knights of Labor as well as middle-class reformers such as Henry Demarest Lloyd and Ely called for a "cooperative commonwealth" in which workers and capitalists would jointly own the means of production.[44] In this vision of an ideal society, the producing classes' "nobility of toil" would be rewarded, while parasitic nonproducers would suffer. Such reformers argued that as the producers of the world's wealth, workers should receive the fruits of their labor—that is, the surplus value of each commodity. If labor indeed created commodity value, then there was no doubt: labor was getting robbed by capital. Employers' rather extraordinary profits represented their parasitic siphoning of the surplus value (over and above the costs of plant, materials, and wages) created by workers' efforts. The only solution to this exploitation that would avoid violent class warfare and ultimately revolution had to be a radical reorganization of industrial relations, as Clark was prepared to admit.

But what if labor were not the measure of value, as economists increasingly argued? The solution gradually worked out by Adams and Clark became known marginalism, and the "marginal utility theory" they articulated between 1881 and 1886 held that labor did not produce all wealth. Rather, the consumer, in conjunction with society, did. Adams's first major work, the *Outline of Lectures upon Political Economy,* embraced British economist Stanley Jevons's formulation of commodity value, a description of value as changeable utility rather than as a quality inherent within the commodity itself. Both Adams and Jevons effectively jettisoned the labor theory of value: a commodity's value, they argued, did not reflect the amount of labor power necessary to create it. Instead, explained Jevons, "I hold labour to be *essentially variable, so that its value must be determined by the value of the product, not the value of the product by that of the labor.*"[45] Jevons, in other words, inverted the labor theory of value. The value of labor did not determine the value of the product; the value of the product, at the point of sale, determined the value of labor. Thus, labor's value was not natural or inherent in the act of work itself but reflected consumers' demands more than workers' efforts.[46] Adams did not follow this implication to its conclusion, however. Adams accepted Jevons's formulation but continued to believe that one man-hour of labor was the basic unit of the measurement of value and still focused on the productive capacity of each worker.[47] Adams explained that "while labor is no measure of value for the exchange of goods once thrown upon the market, the value of that procured by exchange, expressed in labor expended to secure the power of purchase, is that which determines the limit of production for exchange, of any commodity. This is something of a guarantee that goods will exchange in proportion to the labor expended in production."[48] It fell to Clark's marginal utility theory explicitly to reject the labor theory of value.

Beginning in the 1870s, Clark began more systematically to refute the labor theory of value. Individual labor, he explained, was an inaccurate unit for the measurement of value. Too many individuals, groups, and factors went into creating commodity value; no individual's work was exactly comparable to that of another; and work itself "consists of different acts as heterogeneous as things."[49] Production, he suggested, contributed to commodity value but could not be understood as the labor of one or even several individuals. In an industrial society, dominated by manufacturing corporations and widespread distribution systems, production had been socialized. "The passing of goods from man to man enables all society to make all goods; and the two expressions, 'division of labor,' on the one hand, and 'exchange,' on the other, merely describe in different ways the organized process of creating wealth." In contrast to older forms of production, in which "a thing stays in one man's hands until it is finished and in use," now "society in its entirety is an all-around creator of goods."[50] This statement—a social theory of value—inverted the labor theory of value as Clark understood it but did so somewhat differently from Jevons's theory of value. While Jevons had held that the product determined the price of labor rather than the other way around, Clark suggested that the product's value was socially determined.[51] Jevons's theory of value remained fixed on the product as an object; Clark's turned to the product's social use. "A commodity," Clark insisted, was "actually measured for value on the basis of the social service that it renders." Consequently, he could abandon once and for all a man-hour of labor as the standard unit of value and replace it with "the social service that is before us in the using" of the particular commodity. Value, then, comes through "the product of labor," which Clark meant as "the social effect that the product will produce."[52]

If laborers could make any claim to the fruits of their labor, that claim could involve not concrete things or measurable profits but only the social effects of the products, or their utilities. Although Clark did not further pursue this line of reasoning, he was pushing the labor question away from producerist arguments based on the labor theory of value. The labor theory of value no longer described commodity value and no longer offered a platform from which to launch political or social demands. After all, Clark explained, one worker might make a "distinguishable commodity," but it always joined with other commodities to form an end product. Therefore, "the utility he creates is definite, but he can never get possession of it; and it would be useless to him if he did so. It has become an inseparable part of the shoe that represents the work of a little community of laborers." Indeed, workers made shoes (or parts of shoes) only "that they might part with them; what they claim as their own, to have and to hold, is the quantum of effective social utility that is embodied in them." The shoe represented merely "an aggregation of values," just as it represented an aggregation of labor. No one worker could claim the value of the final, finished shoe—too many other people had a hand in making it. "Once in the social cauldron a man's concrete product is lost beyond recovery; all that he can get is its essence,—the abstract quantum of abstract wealth it contains."[53] This abstract quantum—utility—lay at the center of Clark's theory of value, which he began working out in the essays published as the *Philosophy of Wealth* in 1886 and continued to revise through the 1899 *Distribution of Wealth*. At the most basic level, marginal utility theory held that a commodity's value came not from the cost of the labor time necessary to make it but rather from the utility it offered consumers.[54] But the multiple meanings incorporated in *utility* meant that marginal utility theory was more than an explanation of the source of commodity value; it was also a description of the dynamics of consumer society, in which social relations were increasingly understood through abstracted value.

Clark was not alone in thinking about the more abstract meanings of utility, though he was the American most closely and consistently associated with marginalism throughout the late nineteenth century. The British marginalists and their American readers had already begun thinking of subjective utility as a necessary factor in determining commodity value. Quoting Jevons directly, Adams had told his students, "Utility is conceived to be no intrinsic quality of things, but an attendant quality, which gives to commodities, at any time considered, the power to ward off pain or add to pleasure." Cairnes, fussed Adams, had confused "utility" and "usefulness," a basic error that had needlessly muddied the waters of economic theory. But as soon as economics accepted the distinction between the two terms, it "must adopt human wants as its starting point." Like Jevons, Adams believed that "the question of original cost in labor has no influence here. Labor once expended has no further influence upon the value of the commodities which it produced."[55] Labor might determine original cost, but it could not determine market value. Clark, however, insisted more fully on the abstract and subjective meanings of utility. In his work, *utility* did not mean "usefulness" in most quantifiable or objective senses. Rather, Clark held that utility was subjective, dependent on the particular judgment or desire of the consumer. Utility was that which had the perceived "power to modify our subjective condition, under actual circumstances, and is mentally measured by supposing something which we possess to be annihilated, or something which we lack to be attained."[56] This "effective" utility could be measured by tracking the rate of purchases over time: consumers were assumed to buy only what they needed or wanted so that their rate of purchase of a particular commodity would decrease over time. The marginal utility (or value) of the product is determined, however temporarily, by the price a consumer pays for the final purchase of the product before ceasing to purchase it.[57] For his fellow economists, Clark's emphasis on effective (or, as they also called it, "subjective") utility reflected the economic realities of industrial America: no longer driven by scarcity, consumption was replacing production as the crucial factor in economic growth. As Clark explained in *The Philosophy of Wealth,* Henry George had been right to argue that wages "come, not from capital, but from products." While George meant that wages come from the product of labor alone and ignored what Clark saw as the "productive action of capital," George's basic statement was "as conclusive as anything in mathematics." But George and others failed to note that although "wages are taken immediately from a reservoir of capital . . . the amount in that reservoir is undiminished, since the quantity which is drawn from it has already been added to it by the stream of products resulting from industry." Ultimately, felt Clark, "it is the volume of products which sets limits to the amount of wages."[58]

As sociologist and sometime Clark collaborator Frank Giddings explained in an effort to distinguish among utility, value, and cost, objective utility (that is, the meaning of *utility* used by Smith and Jean-Baptiste Say, the "inherent fitness or capability of certain things to satisfy the various wants of mankind") was an appropriate object of study in theories of production. But, argued Giddings, economists must turn to subjective utility (the ability of the object to satisfy wants) when discussing theories of exchange and distribution.[59] With the concept of subjective utility, economists turned their attention fully to the consumer's role in creating value. In the lively discussion following Clark's article "The Ultimate Standard of Value," which appeared in the January 1893 edition of the *Publications of the American Economic Association,* E. A. Ross concluded that "there must be something of the subjective experience of the consumer which is the ultimate standard. . . . Are we then not forced to measure value by the experiences of consumers?" Patten, perpetual prophet of abundance, concurred: "There are two ways of measuring [value], in terms of pain and in terms of pleasure. In primitive society pains are definite things, and therefore the ultimate standards are standards of pain." But by the late nineteenth century, pain and scarcity had been replaced by abundance; now, Patten explained, "I measure the dollar not in terms of what it costs but in terms of what I can get out of it. . . . We have moved from the point where the theory of cost was fundamental to a point where the theory of pleasure is fundamental."[60] That pleasure, though, was imagined more than experienced, for, as Giddings explained, "Men do not value goods directly in terms of a feeling now actual. They value them in terms of a judgment about an anticipated or foreseen feeling." In the end, any estimation of value was not only a question of figuring "a ration of pleasure to pain, or of an equilibrium of pleasures and pains; it is also a question of an equating of judgments about pleasures and pains." In other words, value reflected imagined, future utility.[61] It was quite literally abstract—an assessment of future pleasure, much as grain futures were an assessment (or, more accurately, a guess) of wheat's eventual sales price.

The general move toward studying utility and consumption completed mid-nineteenth-century economists' rebuffing of the popular forms of classical economics. Walker's rejection of the wages-fund theory had retained classical economics' emphasis on the role of production in creating both commodity value and workers' social status. Walker's belief that workers were the "residual claimants" in modern industry tied their individual and collective prosperity directly to their productivity and efficiency at the site of production. The new emphasis on consumption as both creator of value and stabilizer of the economy reversed Walker's claim. According to Hadley, "The labor is the residual claimant in modern industry," but, he hastened to add, "not solely nor chiefly on account of his profit in the increase of production, but on account of his profit in the increase of consumption."[62]

Residual Claimants and New "Economic Freedoms"

Hadley's version of a residual claimant theory took two divergent paths, both of which remained vigorous throughout the twentieth century: one pointed toward neoclassical economics, while the other pointed toward social economics and institutionalism. Clark's theoretical work in particular came to follow that first path. His theory of distribution ultimately relied on a static equilibrium framework that universalized economic laws across both time and space. Though he retained a strong sense that economists must approach the economy "from a social point of view," he also came to see an isolated individual at the center of his economic theory. In the process, Clark individualized society and made "it to be an entirely isolated being."[63] It is easy to see how critics of consumer society have cast a disapproving eye on Clark's work and on the work of late-nineteenth-century economists more generally. His reliance on an individual actor, his insistence on the justice within competition, and his static vision of the economy have enabled the argument that Clark and his colleagues privileged individual consumer choice at the expense of a larger social vision.[64] His static models also increasingly implied a separation of the market and society against which historical economics had always vigorously protested.

But for other economists, most notably Seligman, Clark's friend and Columbia colleague, acknowledging that labor was the residual claimant because of its role in consumption demanded a new and specifically social conception of value, an idea that had already been implied but not pursued in Wood's work. Seligman's conception of value made society, especially the particular social-historical context, more important than the individual consumer. After all, he countered in Clark's language, "value is not due to the labor of the individual who has made it, but to the social service it is going to render; that is, to the social sacrifice which it is going to save." Without that social service, it can have no value, "no matter how much time was spent on it."[65]

To illustrate his point, Seligman turned to the figure of Robinson Crusoe, whom Clark had used to argue that "the principles by which the economy of an isolated man are directed still guide the economy of a modern state."[66] Seligman readily acknowledged that for Crusoe, value was not socially constructed at all. He placed higher value on apples than on nuts, for example, solely based on their usefulness to him in relation to their quantity. But, countered Seligman, Crusoe considered only one of his wants in relation to another want to determine the relative value of each. His conception of value was "independent of exchange as between man and man. . . . [I]t is to be found in the desire on the part of the individual to satisfy his wants." In society, conversely, value "presupposed in addition [to two things] at least two men." Seligman believed that Clark was mistaken in grounding an economic theory on a model where the primary economic relationship exists between men (or an individualized society) and things and is governed by "fundamental truths" of the economy. Rather, Seligman used Crusoe to show how economic relationships must always be between historical men: "Value in society depends upon the fact not only that each individual measures the relative urgency of his own different wants, but that he compares them, consciously or unconsciously, with those of his neighbors." Herein lay the origin of a social marginal utility. For, value (or "real value," as Seligman called it) could only be the "estimate of what society thinks" any particular commodity is worth. "If an apple is worth twice as much as a nut, it is only because the community, after comparing and averaging individual preferences, finds that the desire unsatisfied by the lack of an apple is twice as keen as that unsatisfied by the lack of a nut." Because value was determined by social utility rather than individual utility, something that had "no direct utility to the individual may yet have value to him." Thus, a train locomotive may have no direct utility, "but, if I can dispose of it to a railroad company, it acquires a value, because in other hands it will serve a social purpose. The locomotive now has indirect utility for me, because through it I can secure things of direct utility. Its indirect individual marginal utility to me is the result of its direct marginal utility to the community as a whole. . . . Thus, while social utility is made up of a combination of individual utilities,—that is, while a thing cannot be useful to society unless it is useful to the individuals that compose society,—the indirect marginal utility of anything to an individual is the result of its social marginal utility." Here, Seligman clearly revealed his strong differences with Clark. While Clark thought about marginal productivity in an abstract state (as he readily admitted), Seligman posited value as the product of both historical factors and contemporary institutions, arguments that led to the creation of the field of institutional economics.[67]

Just as each value represents a socially constituted utility, it also represents a socially determined "disutility" (or what Jevons called "inutility")—that is, the amount of pain or sacrifice that each object was "worth." Like utility, this disutility or cost was a social conception of sacrifice. He explained, "We think no longer of the sacrifice imposed upon any one individual, but only of the social sacrifice, or cost, embodied in the commodity. Or, rather, the sacrifice, or cost, to the individual is the result and reflex of the sacrifice to the community. . . . If an individual desires to secure a commodity, he will normally give for it not what he chooses, but what society as a whole fixes as the proper figure."[68] In the end, then, commodity value was not determined by any one individual's labor but by society's assessment of its "service." Seligman's argument with Clark went beyond mere semantics, for their theories had vastly different political implications. Where Clark saw a world made up of self-regulating individuals, Seligman saw a broad network of complex interconnections, of socially determined and ever-changing norms. It was not only foolish but impossible, argued Seligman, to attempt to answer the labor question without considering the broader society: the labor question "cannot be solved by emphasizing the rights of the individual laborer."[69] Instead, any answer to the labor question had to consider labor's rights in a broader social context, beyond the interests or rights of any single, isolated individual.

For Patten, that broader context—a society marked by abundance—pointed to new standards of what he called "economic freedoms," including the right to a safe and comfortable home, the right to leisure, and the right to comfort. Recognized by his peers as one of the most—if not *the* most—original and nimble minds of his generation as well as one of the oddest, Patten had pursued the study of contemporary social questions in a way that differed from the approach of his fellow economists. He freely mixed psychology and economics, borrowed from sociology (though he strenuously resisted sociologists' efforts to incorporate economics), and combined Lamarckian eugenics with theories of monopoly growth.[70] His originality and catholic approach to economics was already visible when he, like his friend James, traveled to Germany to study in Halle with Johannes Conrad. After earning a doctorate in 1878, Patten returned to the United States, eager to transpose the lessons of the Verein to America. Overcome with an idiopathic and quite probably psychosomatic blindness, however, he retreated to his parents' Illinois farm for three years before regaining his sight. He had difficulty finding an academic appointment (Ely remembered that even Patten's "dearest friends . . . must admit he was something of a rough diamond"), but in 1888, he finally received an academic appointment at Wharton through the efforts of James,

82 · CHAPTER 3

then head of the newly formed school.[71] There, Patten amassed a group of de-
voted followers, who, as one enthusiastic former student remembered, "went
out from his classroom imbued not only with a love of knowledge, but with a
love of their fellowmen, and with a will to service."[72] His initial work was *The
Economic Basis of Protection,* an 1890 treatise in support of protective tariffs,
but he soon turned to the more general study of economic growth, prosperity,
and consumption. Like others of his generation, he worried about the paradox
of great poverty in the midst of growing prosperity. "Few men," he insisted,
"deny that the working people of industrial centres are ill paid, that employment is uncertain, housing is bad, sickness frequent, and that the abnormally
short working life ends in an old age of poverty and fear." At the same time,
however, "few . . . would deny the evidence of growing prosperity." Charting
a safe course through this new civilization, he argued, would necessitate a
wholesale abandonment of the "ancient outlook" of classical economics and
an embrace of the social consequences of the new economics.[73] In his most
popular works, particularly *The Theory of Prosperity* (1902) and *The New Basis
of Civilization* (which went through eight editions between 1907 and 1923),
Patten attempted to lay out exactly what these social consequences might be.
Taking some of the economic theories of Clark and others, especially the idea
of utility and the rejection of the labor theory of value (though he did not find
all of marginalism useful), Patten presented a hypothetical new civilization
that would propel America farther down its exceptional road to progress.

While Wright, Adams, and others pointed to the end of scarcity following the depression of the 1870s, Patten identified the growing abundance
of industrial life as the wellspring of social change; the very problem of the
1870s—overproduction—suggested the solution to the social problems of
the early twentieth century. Patten cautioned, with some impatience, that
increased productive capacity was not sufficient: "Mental habits continue
long after the economic conditions which fashioned them have disappeared.
. . . The economic revolution is here, but the intellectual revolution that will
rouse men to its stupendous meaning has not done its work." The "social philosophy of deficit" that tainted the ideas of socialists and the "upper classes"
alike held too closely to Mill's insistence on "the niggardliness of nature."
Finally, though, Patten felt that "many of the obstacles that were insuperable
a century ago are falling before the young genius of the mechanical age":
for example, "famine no longer threatens a country where railroads carry
freight." Without the constraints and fears of scarcity, civilization's "bounds
are indefinitely widened because the unskilled laborer need no longer be
held to the plane of sheer animal terror by uncertainty of food and employ-

ment." Nonetheless, old habits, as Patten noted, died hard. "Men," he fretted, "are moulded into their classes by the pressure of social things accumulating generation after generation, which finally sum themselves into an acquired heredity binding men firmly to their place." For Patten, the results of such behavior were potential social degeneration. A firm believer in innate social traits, he saw southern African Americans as too long oppressed to have "established an agricultural civilization," and he feared that a general belief in scarcity rather than prosperity would make all Americans "cautious," with a "a keen sense of comradeship and the values of self-subordination." "Men," he argued, "are now squarely confronted with two issues. They may continue to cultivate ancestral qualities of strife and sacrifice in surroundings of peace and plenty, or they may consciously develop a new type of man fitted for the society without poverty toward which we aspire."[74]

Patten hoped that his "new type of man" represented a clean break both with the cautious property owner of the past, whose efforts were concentrated on securing and preserving his possessions, and with Malthusian man, downtrodden by scarcity and his own failings.[75] Freed from scarcity, this new man could be "fearless, independent and impulsive." In particular, the end of social organization premised on fear and scarcity heralded the arrival of a "workman with freedom of thought and mobility of movement [and of] the regulation and assurance of industry, with the worker squarely established in his environment, because he has become courageous enough to make use of what he already knows and to fit his acts to his situation."[76] Patten, though known as the great proponent of abundance, did not envision the rejection of scarcity to include a wholesale rejection of the Protestant virtues of self-control and abstinence. Indeed, in *The New Basis of Civilization,* he specifically lauded the individual's capacity to postpone pleasure today for greater pleasure tomorrow.[77] Nonetheless, in his *Theory of Prosperity* and *Product and Climax* (1909), Patten insisted that pleasure should not be deferred forever. As Daniel Horowitz has noted, Patten "recognized the difficulty of obtaining satisfaction from industrial work and turned instead to leisure to find rewards that were not connected with moral prohibitions." Leisure activities—specifically, working-class entertainments such as nickelodeons, sports, vaudeville, and ethnic social clubs—could, Patten argued in a probably unconscious echo of Florence Kelley, mediate between "conservative moralism, industrial work, and commercial consumption" by emphasizing a "spirit of communal celebration."[78] (Ironically, and somewhat sadly, Patten lived a quite Spartan existence. Giddings remembered that Patten, though "always happy in company," "moved among us as one detached, an obviously lonely man.")[79]

Patten, however, had more in mind than a new basis of civilization based on communal celebration and a restrained enjoyment of the abundance of industrial life. In *The Theory of Prosperity,* published five years before *The New Basis of Civilization,* Patten had argued that the end of scarcity and the rise of prosperity necessitated the recognition of new social rights. In the earlier work, Patten plumbed the implications of economics' move away from the labor theory of value in search of "a modern equivalent for the rights that in earlier times went with the land." For Patten, that modern equivalent was a new set of "economic rights" or "freedoms" (he used both terms). If, he suggested, consumers were the fulcrum on which the economy of large-scale production rested, then as consumers, they should have certain rights in industrial society. "The rights upon which political freedom depends have already been worked out," he explained, referring to earlier times when landownership formed the basis of social relations. Now, though, he went on, rights had to include what he called "public or market rights" (such as the right to participate in an open market and the right to have a modicum of security in every transaction). The most important new rights, however, were not market rights or industrial rights but what we might call social rights: the right to a sanitary and safe home, the right to education, the right to "comfort," and the right to leisure. Without these rights, according to Patten, political rights were meaningless.[80]

The most important economic right for Patten was the "right to comfort" and its "corollary," the right to leisure. "No matter what income a person receives," he said, "he cannot be comfortable without some time for enjoyment." For Patten, leisure included much more than time away from work; at heart, leisure provided the chance for "a full revival of mental and physical powers." In part, Patten held that comfort, leisure, and recreation were rights precisely because they were pleasurable.[81] Patten consistently argued that the right to comfort was, at heart, "the right to share in the social surplus," a demand "that the workman get on each increment of his production some surplus above its cost."[82] For Ely, this idea of a social surplus remained the most significant—and most unappreciated—aspect of Patten's economic thought. According to Ely, Patten saw social surplus as "rapidly increasing with the progress of economic society and [as] bringing about the passing from the deficit or pain economy, such as Ricardo and his friends had in mind, to a surplus or pleasure economy of the future." Patten believed that "through wise consumption . . . this surplus fund could be increased and through wise consumption it could be widely distributed."[83]

Patten's emphasis on the right to share in the social surplus effectively suggested a shift in the labor question itself. The social surplus and work-ers' right to it, including the specific right to comfort or leisure, were found outside of work and were divorced from control of the means of production. Workers' insistence that they enjoy the fruits of their labor thus moved away from producerite demands for the end of the wage system and a return to workers' ownership of the means of production. Now, Patten implied, work-ers should and legitimately could demand to enjoy the fruits of their labor outside of work, in the realm of leisure, and their ownership of the means of production was a moot point.

While as David Montgomery and others have shown, many skilled work-ers fought their dismemberment into so many hands, Patten imagined that workers could reacquire wholeness outside of the workplace. Some histori-ans have pointed out that Patten, though theoretically committed to ending poverty and improving the lives of Americans generally, did little if anything to challenge the rigid divisions of industrial labor.[84] In the end, Patten was better at making sweeping pronouncements than at enacting specific poli-cies, and he was often quite squeamish when confronted with the vicissitudes of daily life. But to see his ideas and those of his fellow social economists as promoting a "self-expression" or personality over a more politically rigor-ous "self-employment" or character misses Patten's central point: control or ownership of production, productive work, and indeed the act of labor itself was no longer the sole site or basis of social authority.[85] Work might be the fate of postlapsarian man, but it was not the only fate. By arguing that "to be free is to be comfortable, to have a home and the decencies that go with it," he moved the locus of the labor question from the shop floor to the parlor.[86] The AFL faced the task of making that shift a political demand.

4

"Labor Wants More!"

The AFL and the Idea
of Economic Liberty

Simon Nelson Patten never fully worked out his insistence that the "right to share in the social surplus" was the "new basis of civilization." Given more to broad pronouncements and rhetorical flourishes than proscriptive tracts, he left the details hazy and vague. By the 1890s, however, the American Federation of Labor (AFL) had already begun to work out those details through a relentlessly practical politics of more. "More" became the AFL's official answer to the general social crises of the late nineteenth century and to the labor question in particular. The fledgling AFL's president, Samuel Gompers, griped that labor was tired of "Sympathy without relief, Mustard without beef."[1] America's workers, he insisted, wanted "more"—"more leisure, more rest, more opportunity . . . for going to the parks, of having better homes, of reading books, of creating more desires."[2]

The AFL and its leaders did not call for an end to wage labor. Instead, they demanded higher wages and shorter hours for workers, demands that were, in the AFL lexicon, self-consciously "practical."[3] The AFL has been criticized since its inception for its program of "pure and simple" unionism, with its emphasis on the bread-and-butter issues of wages and hours to the exclusion of any sustained interest in sweeping political or social change. The issues of daily life, these critics have implied, were less revolutionary and less radical than were political action or social protest. Gompers and other members of the AFL leadership, however, held the inverse to be true.[4] If in the antebellum period, democracy had been linked to political participation, now it was linked just as firmly to economic participation. Without the ability to enjoy the abundance of industrial production, wage workers would remain economically marginalized. And in a social order defined by mass production, mass consumption, publicly held companies, and wage work, such economic marginalization was equivalent to political disenfranchisement. As Gompers explained to the *North American Review*'s readers in 1892, "We tacitly declare that political liberty with[out] economic independence is illusory and deceptive, and that only in so far as we gain economic independence can our political liberty become tangible and important."[5] More, then, represented a new understanding of citizenship that included economic as well as political opportunities.[6] For the labor movement, economic citizenship provided a powerful base from which to make "pure and simple" demands for higher wages and shorter hours. For Americans more broadly, it suggested a new conception of democratic citizenship that stressed economic as much as political participation.

The Origins of the Politics of More

Although the AFL's politics of more came to forefront in the 1890s, it had its roots in the particular historical circumstances of depression, unemployment, and increasing proletarianization in the 1870s and 1880s as well as in the personal experiences of its founding members.[7] For men such as Gompers, president of the AFL for every year but one from its founding in 1886 until his death in 1924, the broad argument of more—that material and cultural life was as central to social power as political rights were—had been tacitly apparent since his early childhood.[8] Gompers was born in London in 1850, the son of Dutch Jews. His father, Solomon, and numerous uncles and cousins were cigar makers, active in the city's Cigarmakers' Society. The family placed considerable value on craft and guild solidarity but also emphasized the importance of education and the arts. As a child, Gompers attended a free Jewish school until the age of ten, when he began to work alongside his father. With his family's encouragement, he continued to take classes at night, and his education was supplemented by his grandfather, who took him to concerts and plays. By the time he was thirteen, Gompers could speak and read some French, Dutch, and Hebrew in addition to English and had a fairly wide-ranging knowledge of European literature and music. Later in life, he remembered his early years fondly and saw them as instrumental to shaping both his belief in trade unionism and his love of music and literature.[9]

As the Gompers family grew, its members had more and more difficulty making ends meet. "London," Gompers remembered later, "seemed to offer no response to our efforts toward betterment," and Solomon Gompers moved his family to New York in 1863.[10] The Gomperses arrived at Castle Island two weeks after the end of the draft riots, and New York was still smoldering. Despite the turmoil, the Gomperses were able to find more commodious lodging in the city than they had possessed in London, and Gompers and his father soon found work rolling cigars. Young Gompers continued his semiformal education in the city's theaters, concert halls, and music halls as well as at free lectures at the Cooper Union. There he met other young workers who shared his commitment to trade union politics and his passion for culture and philosophy, most notably P. J. McGuire, later president of the United Brotherhood of Carpenters, a fellow founder of the AFL, and the prime force behind the first Labor Day parade.

The theoretical connections between cultural life and labor politics slowly began to solidify in 1873 when Gompers started working in a cigar factory owned by David Hirsch, a German socialist. At Hirsch's factory, Gompers read the *Communist Manifesto,* translated by his friend and mentor, Karl Malcolm Ferdinand Laurrell. Inspired to read more, Gompers taught himself German and read as much German philosophy and economics as he could, including Carl Hillman's influential pamphlet, *Prakitsche Emanzipation-swinke.* Hillman, a member of Saxony's Socialist Democratic Workingmen's Party, produced what Gompers would remember as the perfect expression of "the fundamental possibilities of the trade union."[11] Hillman by no means dismissed the power of political organization, but he argued that a political organization that failed to address material concerns would be impotent. The "political life in today's state," he explained, had "firm economic and social underpinnings"; labor organizations had to acknowledge the latter if they wanted access to the former. Gompers completely absorbed Hillman's message. When Hillman claimed that "anyone who wants to attain practical results must deal with all actual conditions and circumstances," Gompers agreed. Theoretical abstractions, he felt, could offer little hope to workers, whose concerns lay more with rent and food than with revolution or what Hillman dismissed as "utopian dreams."[12]

Gompers's growing conviction that "practical emancipation" offered more hope to workers than purely political tactics did was confirmed by his experiences during the early years of the depression. Now married and supporting a quickly growing family, Gompers watched with alarm as the U.S. economy crashed in the winter of 1873–74. "The scenes downtown," he remembered, "were wild on that rainy day" when Cooke's investment house failed, but they were nothing compared to what followed. "Thousands in New York City were walking the streets in search of a job. As winter came on the misery grew to appalling proportions. Public officials made gestures which might have had a value for political purposes but did not give food to the hungry or solve the rent problem for those facing eviction." One fellow cigar maker's family was so hungry that they ate their beloved pet dog.[13] What workers needed most, Gompers felt, was economic security; without it they were powerless, politically and socially.

Though the depression certainly put basic economic concerns at the forefront of Gompers's thought, he did not abandon the lessons learned from his grandfather and from his visits to opera houses and theaters. "Mental hunger," he insisted, "is just as painful as physical hunger"; the labor movement had to address both. As a young man, he reveled in "a poem, a paper, a book" and was particularly known among his coworkers as an enthusiastic musician. In his autobiography, Gompers remembered that his grandfather "introduced me to a world that brought a lifetime of pleasure. Music appeals to my whole nature as does nothing else." Music provided him with solace: "The beauty of wonderful music would hold me speechless, motionless— only waking at the end to gasp to myself, 'God, how beautiful!'" When he was a young man rolling cigars, singing bolstered his and his comrades' spirits during work; soon after he married in 1867, he used money that his wife, Sophia, had saved for new clothing to buy a violin. She overcame her initial anger, and Gompers taught himself to read music and soon learned to play the violin with friends. Music—especially Italian operas such as *Tosca* and *Norma*—as well as lectures, literature (Gompers was particularly fond of Dickens), and theater were as important to Gompers as work. "The pure joy of living is good to know," he insisted, and no less important than high wages or political agitation.[14]

Increasingly in the 1870s, Gompers looked with disdain on those who did not see the importance of higher wages, shorter hours, and pleasant pastimes—that is, those who were not, as he put it, "practical." He was particularly dismissive of the "so-called Communists" agitating in January 1874 as exploitative opportunists: "Propaganda was for them the chief end of life," he complained. "They were perfectly willing to use human necessity as propaganda material. Practical results meant nothing in their program." Indeed, Gompers later blamed the communists and other "non-practical" organizers for the January 1874 debacle in Tompkins Square Park, where policemen freely battered protesters. Many participants and onlookers were seriously injured, among them Gompers's friend Laurrell, and Gompers only narrowly escaped being bludgeoned by jumping down into a cellarway. Soon thereafter, Gompers and other like-minded men formed the United Workers of America (UWA), specifically to repudiate what Gompers saw as the dilettante communists. Following Hillman's advice, the UWA held itself to practical goals, with organizers declaring, "The emancipation of the working class can be achieved through their own efforts and that emancipation will not bring about class rule and class privileges for them but equal rights and duties for all members of society. Economic betterment is the first step to that desired end." Gompers reserved particular ire for radicals he saw as "faddists, reformers, and sensation-loving spirits." He loathed "pseudo-Communists" and others who "did not realize that labor issues were tied up with the lives of men, women and children—issues not to be risked lightly."[15] The ideas behind the short-lived UWA became the foundation of subsequent organizations in which Gompers was involved, including the restructured International Cigar Makers' Union, headed by the equally "practical" Adolph Strasser, the Federation of Organized Trades and Labor Unions (founded by Gompers, Strasser, and McGuire in 1881), and finally the AFL. In each of these associations, organizers placed the "emancipation of the working class" within a broader context of "rights and duties"; specifically economic goals were at the forefront of their agendas but were always part of a larger program that sought to gain for workers better lives, greater social independence, and increased opportunities within American society.[16]

Gompers was equally dismissive of those who sought to return to an idealized past, marked by smaller shops and less mechanization. Following an 1869 strike by cigar makers protesting the introduction of molds that simplified the rolling process, he remembered that he "began to realize the futility of opposing progress." Cigar makers, he believed, "were powerless against the substitution of machines for human skills," but they could work together to prevent wage reductions and increases in work hours.[17] For Gompers, at least, these practical goals reached beyond "mere" economics. They were, he believed, also demands for "all" that was "essential to the exercise and enjoyment of liberty"—in short, demands for better lives.[18]

The Meanings of "More"

While the Knights of Labor continued to make the long-standing argument that wage work created dependent and weak men, antithetical to the American republican project, the AFL consistently suggested by the 1890s that the emergence of an economy of abundance, however unstable, offered new ways to imagine independence in general and independence for wage earners more specifically.[19] At the AFL's 1897 annual convention in Nashville, Gompers explained to the assembled delegates, "It is not the diminution of the productive power of labor which prompts our course, as it is to give greater leisure and larger opportunities to those who are employed, making of all a greater consumptive power, thus giving an impetus to and creating the opportunities for employment of those who now vainly seek it."[20] Knights of Labor grand secretary Robert Layton and others who saw overproduction as the problem believed that the solution was to limit each worker's productivity, thereby necessitating higher levels of employment to maintain productivity. But, the AFL argued, much as Bureau of Labor Statistics commissioner Carroll Davidson Wright had, that underconsumption was the root cause of the depressions. Instead of arguing for lower productivity per worker, Gompers insisted on shorter hours, higher wages, and steady (or even increasing) output. Shorter hours and higher wages were, he claimed, no oxymoron, and the specific circumstances in places such as Chicago backed him, as manufacturers watched their profits dwindle during the 1880s. The Great Uprising of 1877 had taught at least most of these businessmen that cutting wages was simply not a good option, but they had somehow to seek profit. They turned to increased mechanization in an effort to increase productivity without cutting wages. The result was, perhaps predictably, a glutted market, especially in Chicago's steel, brick, nail, box, and agricultural implement industries. Chicago's labor unrest intensified in mid-1880, even before the Great Upheaval, leading to a general sense that this state of affairs was now "a system-wide problem" that required "society-wide solutions."[21]

If the economic and social disasters plaguing the United States were caused by underconsumption, two things seemed immediately necessary: greater demand and higher levels of consumption. With more leisure, Gompers reasoned, workers would have more time to want more. More important, additional leisure would not just provide workers with the opportunity to want but would also encourage workers to want more than they had. Explained Gompers, "A man who goes to his work before the dawn of day requires no clean shirt; but a man who goes to work at 8 o'clock in the morning wants a clean shirt; he is afraid his friends will see him, so he does not want to be dirty. He also requires a newspaper; while a man who goes to work early . . . and stays at it late at night does not need a newspaper, for he has no time to read."[22] Time outside of work, in other words, would create new desires.

And these new desires, argued Gompers, would create "large opportunities for the use and consumption of things which labor can produce," "wants and desires" that would quickly "become demands."[23] Frank K. Foster, a former Boston printer and longtime advocate of the eight-hour day, explained in the *American Federationist* that the push of workers' consumer demands and the subsequent manufacturers' response would ensure "a gigantic commercial stimulus," creating markets for "products of many kinds which under a system of long hours there is no demand for." This "vital economic side of the shorter hours movement," in turn, would "cause such awakened aspirations and increased demands as to require additional employees."[24] Increased consumption by workers would both level out the economy by providing a consistent and perhaps even growing market and necessitate increased employment to meet the new production demands. This argument neatly inverted Say's Law—supply creates its own demand. Now, supply would follow demand.[25] With enlarged, consistent demand, labor activists hoped to avoid future repetitions of the economic depressions and accompanying unemployment. But as labor activists and economists knew all too well, consumer demand had to be backed by higher wages. For any such useful increase of consumption to occur, explained economist Richard Ely, a corresponding increase in purchasing power had to take place. "Wants are the motive power in industry," he explained, "but if for some reason or another wants are not accompanied with purchasing power, consumption falls off and production exceeds what is called effective demand, that is, demand which is able to receive an equivalent in exchange."[26] During the depression of the 1890s, which hit industrial workers with special ferocity, wants were accompanied by a decline in purchasing power, with disastrous results for workers and the general economy alike. As a glum Gompers explained to his longtime correspondent, French trade unionist Auguste Keufer, "the ability, or better the opportunity, of the wage-workers to keep pace in their consumptive power to their productive capacity has failed, and as a consequence, thousands, aye, hundreds of thousands have been thrown out of employment."[27]

Members of the labor movement, most notably Ira Steward, had insisted on the vital connection between workers' consumptive power and productive capacity since the 1860s. Steward had argued vigorously that increased desire for goods would raise wages, and higher consumer demand would ignite a consumption-driven economy at the site of production. At the same time, when the demand for goods was met, workers could realize a higher standard of living, further increasing their demand for consumer goods.[28] But while Steward had held that shorter hours and higher wages would eventually allow workers to accumulate sufficient capital to own their own cooperative enterprises, his follower George Gunton had come to believe by the 1880s that consumption by itself could radically change the material and social lives of working men and women.[29] The crisis of overproduction that characterized the late 1870s and 1880s signaled, Gunton argued, that the "problem of production" had been solved: industry was now capable of producing commodities consistently and with economies of scale: "It is only as capital produces more than it consumes that the laborer is enabled to consume more than he produces."[30] Or, as the Iron Molders' Union constitution declared, "The welfare of a community depends on the purchasing power of its members."[31] Large-scale industrial production, with ever-increasing output and tighter per-unit profit margins, meant that workers had new and vital roles as consumers: without their consistent and increasing consumption, the economy would grind to a halt. For eight-hour associations in places such as Chicago, shorter hours offered the promise not only of greater leisure time but also of higher wages, improved standards of living, and a stronger labor movement.[32]

More, however, was not only a potential solution to the economic problem of underconsumption in the 1890s; it also represented a broader range of goals for the labor movement beyond a solution to economic instability. The usefulness of more as a slogan lay precisely in its flexibility; it could be a demand for greater working-class consumption; it could be a demand for material goods; or it could be a wide-ranging demand for greater participation in society writ large. In the most immediate short term, more time and more money translated into more comforts for the family of any given wage worker. Gompers, who often dressed in fine overcoats and natty hats, enjoyed listing the various material benefits that higher wages and shorter hours could confer. In a May 1890 speech in Louisville, Kentucky, Gompers explained, "A man who works eight hours a day has sixteen hours a day left. He must do something with them. . . . When his friend visits him he wants to have, probably, a pretty picture on the wall, or perhaps a piano or organ in his parlor; and he wishes everything about him to be bright and attractive."[33] This vision of a cozy, comfortable worker's home rearticulated Ely's and Gunton's insistence that workers' consumption was necessary for the economy as a whole. It also offered a direct rebuttal to those Americans who blamed workers' troubles on their reckless spending and urged them to lead frugal, abstentious lives. Today's workers, such critics argued, expected material reward without working for it. New Jersey's *Patterson Labor Standard* quoted one unnamed detractor lambasting workers for extravagantly buying meat and indulgently eating wheat bread: "They even eat pie, which is no food for working people and does them no good."[34] Workers had troublingly rejected the older articulation of the work ethic that held that "life is a stern, hard service" in which any individual success is "the fruit of self-denial, patience, and toil."[35]

The AFL's call for more met with criticism from other quarters as well. Some contemporaries labeled the parlor pianos, pretty pictures, and clean shirts Gompers lauded as trivial items, clear attempts by the AFL to placate wage workers and turn them away from a more revolutionary course. One article in the New York socialist newspaper *People* sniped that "'pure and simple' imbecility" merely regurgitated "the old capitalistic sophism . . . that the American workman should be content to be less miserable than his foreign cousins."[36] For Gompers, however, the answer to such criticism was obvious: why should wage workers not have comfort in their lives? After all, their labor had produced the abundance of a consumer society. As both producers and consumers, they should enjoy the fruits of their labor in the here and now. Future revolutions could do little to improve today's dinner table. "The workingman," explained Gompers in an 1895 newspaper interview, "is tired of mere rhetoric and theory. . . . [T]he workingman . . . wants wages that will buy him lots of the things he needs."[37]

What this demand for "lots of the things he needs" did not mean was almost as important as what it did. More, for instance, emphatically did not refer to the kind of conspicuous consumption driven by a relentless quest for individual status that worried economist Thorstein Veblen and labor leaders such as Joseph McDonnell, in which the "relative success" of each man "becomes the end of action."[38] Underlying such concerns was the Protestant anxiety about excessive luxury and unearned pleasure. But also present was a fear that the lure of goods might detract men from serious work, whether it was struggles in the workplace (as McDonnell felt) or meaningful social relations (as Veblen argued).[39] In his insistence that workers deserved more comforts in their lives, Gompers had in mind something much broader than mere wages, a point missed by some commentators on the labor question. H. C. Daniels, a printer, held that workers merely had base material interests at heart, without any thought to higher aims of social change. In *Capital, Labor, Unionism,* his 1906 contribution to the debate over the labor question, Daniels claimed "that the majority, yes, eighty-five per cent. of the laboring class to-day would favor *more hours work* and *more money,* than *less hours work with no more money.*"[40] But Daniels missed the crucial element of Gompers's argument. Though higher wages were central to Gompers's demands for more, his broader understanding of more went beyond money or material goods without denying the real pleasures of newspapers or new chairs. "I am," he once explained, "in entire accord with" Heinrich Heine, a German romantic poet who insisted, "Freedom is bread. Bread is freedom." Heine, felt Gompers, "did not mean simply the pieces of bread . . . which one may eat, but all that the term implies," for "liberty can be neither exercised nor enjoyed by those who are in poverty."[41]

Indeed, more was, explained Gompers in an impromptu speech before the Boston Monday Evening Club in 1899, "a requirement for life." Labor demanded "more of the good things that go to make up life; better homes, better surroundings, higher education, higher aspirations, nobler thoughts, more human feelings, all the human instincts that go to make up a manhood that shall be free and independent and loving and noble and true and sympathetic. We want *more*."[42] Here, more necessarily moved beyond material goods and became a demand for intangibles, for social and cultural capital—"higher aspirations" and "nobler thoughts"—as well as for social opportunities such as education. In other speeches, Gompers called for better houses, nicer playgrounds, and "happier childhoods," all of which represented appeals for greater social welfare couched in the language of more. Gompers saw greater leisure time to read, to attend lectures, or otherwise to engage in mental improvement as just as integral to social welfare as cleaner streets, better homes, safer jobs, and pianos. Nor was Gompers alone in such demands. Individual unions including the Brotherhood of Clothing Cutters and Trimmers of Rochester, New York, included these ideas in their constitutions alongside demands for arbitration.[43] Leisure, self-improvement, and nice shirts all constituted part of full participation in American society, an outcome of economic liberty.[44]

Just what such economic independence implied was explored in a 1901 story that appeared in the *American Federationist*.[45] Fiction was not in the publication's usual purview, and this story certainly does not encapsulate all of either Gompers's or the AFL's philosophy. But "Economy That Proved Disastrous" reveals some of the intricacies of Gompers's understanding of more. Written by frequent contributor Lizzie Holmes, who more commonly reported on debates at union conventions, the story tells the tale of a "pleasant, busy little manufacturing town" brought to ruin by too much saving and too little consumption. The townspeople previously had been happy and well paid, living in comfortable houses with tidy gardens and ample furnishings. In their spare time, they had busied themselves with social activities— choirs, church groups, plays, and lectures. It was a model industrial town with a contented and well-remunerated population, represented in the story by a young engaged couple, both wage workers, portentously named Frank Towne and Ellen Worth. The town's idyllic existence was summarily ended not by exploitative employers but rather by the townspeople themselves. Under the influence of Mr. Blatchford, a major and benevolent employer, the townspeople begin to hoard their money. Blatchford had risen from rags to riches by accumulating money through shrewd business deals and by never "spend[ing] a cent that was unnecessary." The key to life, he preached, was "economy" and thrift. He bemoaned the townspeople's willingness to fritter away money on plays or a "pretty ribbon"; they must "learn to deny themselves the many useless expenditures in which they were wont to indulge. After all," he reasoned, "men needed very little to keep them healthy and in condition to work, so why spend money on other things?"

Blatchford's philosophy is essentially Ricardo's iron law of wages—the wage rate will always "naturally" veer toward the cost of subsistence—applied to personal expenditure. According to Blatchford, only items necessary for basic survival were worth purchasing; expenditures for such frivolous things as plays, ribbons, candy, and paper collars were merely a waste of money.[46] Frank Towne, whose name is synecdochic for the town, soon comes under Blatchford's influence. Although he and Ellen have been carefully buying furniture and other items for their new home with great pleasure (with "each new acquirement . . . the occasion of a small festival"), he now insists that "to spend money [is] a crime." When Ellen tries to convince him to buy "a delightful little center table," he balks, and the other townspeople soon follow suit, refusing to spend their money. Ellen, the only resident who resists Blatchford's economy, flees, and Frank rushes to the train station to follow her. When he reaches for money to pay for his ticket, however, he just "gaze[s] upon the little pile of gold and greenbacks and [thinks] how very small it would look when he had taken what he needed to go away." In the end, Frank cannot bear to part with his precious money, even for food, and he and the remaining townspeople leave for the hills, where they can live in caves and eat roots, no longer "obliged to spend any money whatsoever."[47]

The refusal to spend money literally destroys the town, both socially and economically. The townspeople's rejection of "useless frivolities" breaks the social bonds of the town as well as its ties with other places. Players and lecturers stop coming to the town, and the townspeople no longer gather together to sing or debate. Denying themselves "pretty ribbon[s]" and lace curtains, they become "starved of [their] love of the beautiful." Quite quickly, their parsimony devastates the town's economy. First, saloons, candy stores, and ice cream parlors close. Then, as a "spasm of economy" spreads over the entire country, orders for "artistic cabinet ware" decline and the town's furniture mills close. Like their mentor, Blatchford, the townspeople believe in utility, not pleasure. Since, as Blatchford had explained, "men need very little to keep them in a condition to work," the townspeople curb any interest in items superfluous to their ability to work. Only Ellen Worth resists this mentality, insisting that there is more to life than labor. Her pursuit of pleasure is always prudent—she does not spend beyond her means and earns all she spends—but she celebrates rather than shuns what Blatchford labors "useless expenditures." In the story, of course, Ellen's expenditures are not useless. Just as economists predicted when looking back at the depression of the 1870s, such spending ensured the town's economic stability and social harmony—its worth, as Ellen's name implies. In addition, Ellen's purchases bring her and initially Frank pleasure and happiness, both in the items they buy and the bright future home they imagine. Most important, Ellen has "economic liberty"—the ability to participate in what Gompers called "the promises of society" in both its material and intangible opportunities. Her discretionary income gives her the freedom to "aspire," practically and not theoretically, to a better life and to seek out great social and cultural capital.

But the promises of society that Ellen pursues differ radically from those sought by the producer-citizen, and those differences are marked most conspicuously by gender. Under the rubric of producerite ideology, wage work emasculated workers, making them dependent on others for their existence and even metaphorically destroying their physical selves by dividing each man up into so many hands. In contrast, the source of this emasculation—wage work—is exactly what creates the possibility of Ellen's independence from Blatchford, from Frank, and from the censure of the townspeople. She can spend her money as she chooses, on bonnet ribbons or tables, and she can leave the town when she chooses to do so, all because she has economic liberty. Her liberty depends on her ability to earn an income and to spend it. In contrast to Ellen stood workers trapped in the "peonage" of scrip payments and commissary (or, as Gompers called them, "Pluck You") stores. Scrip, Gompers argued, "practically bound [workers] to the soil." Without wages in legal tender, "they cannot move; can not quit."[48] Without payment in legal tender, these workers were unable to make choices about their expenditures or their movements; they had, for all practical purposes, no opportunities.

Ellen's central position suggests that economic liberty and autonomy are no longer exclusively masculine, as they had been under producerite ideology, and this story certainly was not alone in seeing wage work as liberating for women. Women's social inferiority, argued many advocates of women's rights, resulted directly from their exclusion from the workforce. "There is no logical reason," Gunton insisted, "why a woman should not be permitted to vote on the same conditions as man." But she could not be man's political or social equal "not because she does not vote" but "because of her industrial and social inferiority," which excluded her from the franchise. "In a word," continued Gunton, her disenfranchisement "is because she is poorer, and, consequently, less independent than man."[49] Reformer Florence Kelley posed a similar argument in a letter to Ely: "The economic dependence of the wife upon the husband passes away with the rest of the economic dependence of one person upon another."[50] Feminist economist Charlotte Perkins Gilman largely agreed. Earning freed women from seeking economic and social security through "the power of sex attraction." Indeed, claimed Gilman, the "increasing army of women wage-earners . . . are changing the face of the world by their steady advance to economic independence."[51]

But the use of a female hero in this story also points to some of the continuing anxieties about wage work in general and its potentially emasculating effects in particular. The same article in the *Social Economist* that enthusiastically lauded the growing trade union movement among women simultaneously chastised working women for depressing male wages and urging "single women alone" to seek employment.[52] Emasculation was thus linked to low wages—indeed, quite specifically to women's low wages—and not directly to wage work itself. But as the debates regarding Chinese immigration showed, the two concerns could not easily be separated. Economic instability, periodic or seasonal unemployment, and the omnipresent threat of lower wages reminded workingmen that they could easily become feminized, much like the Chinese. If white workingmen were unable to provide well for their families, if they were unable to serve as adequate breadwinners, then how could they lay claim to citizenship as American men? The AFL's rhetoric reinforced this anxiety: even as the *Federationist* portrayed Ellen Worth as a hero, the organization assiduously patrolled the gender line, emphasizing the ways in which male wage earning reinforced and reasserted men's status as breadwinners and family heads. Men's wages should be high enough, argued Gompers, that they could provide their families with pleasant homes, complete with framed pictures and pianos. They should be able to buy nice dresses for their wives or "best girls."[53] While the AFL equated wage earning with economic liberty for both men and women, it simultaneously privileged male wage earners' superior social and familial positions as family providers.[54] But linking men's social status to wage work and breadwinning also made any threat to high wages a threat to wage earners' claims to civilized manhood. Behind every acclamation of the male breadwinner norm lurked the image of John Chinaman in his "shuffling slippers," embodying the fragility of wage earners' social claims. Nevertheless, tenuous as it was, the divorce of independence from either property ownership or control of the means of production suggested that male workers' independence, like Ellen's, could be enacted outside of the workplace. Wages from work might be vital, but independence was not reducible to relations at the point of production.

"Pure and simple unionism" now confronted the problem of precisely how to make this economic independence a potent weapon for labor, how to reconcile formal, legal equality with practical equality.[55] The Fourteenth Amendment may have declared that all men, regardless of race or country of origin, were legally and politically equal, but glaring disparities in income obviously separated rich and poor, creating what economist Arthur Twining Hadley called "a contradiction between our political theories and the facts of industrial life."[56] As activist lawyer and labor advocate Clarence Darrow told those assembled at the AFL's 1898 convention, "Theoretically, every man stands equal before the law. The working man has plenty of theoretical rights. He has, in the language of the day, theoretical rights 'to burn.' . . . [B]ut when it comes to practical rights . . . the poor man has none."[57]

For the labor movement or at least the AFL to use more as a demand for social power, some basic tenets of classical economics had to be undermined. Gunton made such undermining a goal of his monthly publication, the *Social Economist* (later known as *Gunton's Magazine*). In the midst of the depression of the 1890s, Gunton's publication approvingly reported on the "sound economics" of Thomas Bracket Reed, a powerful Republican congressman from Maine, who argued "that wages are determined, not by supply and demand, but by the social standard of living in the community." The *Social Economist* understood Reed's statement as a frontal assault on classical economics, representing "the foundation of an essentially new school of economics and national policy; a school that is distinctly American," the contemporary equivalent of the *Wealth of Nations* in early-nineteenth-century England. That book was "the herald of middle class economics" and "represented the manufacturing and mercantile interests, as distinguished from those of the aristocracy." Workers' consumption did not yet represent a significant factor in production, and workers were regarded merely as part of production, a cost to be kept as low as possible. But in the United States, the situation was reversed, in part because of English trade policies. England, as preeminent manufacturer, sought to infiltrate foreign markets under the banner of free trade; the United States, concerned about its weaker domestic manufacturing, blocked English goods from entry and turned toward an internal market. Consequently, argued the *Social Economist,* "the consumption of our own people [became] the basis and limitation of our national production. . . . This really changed the market basis of society from the consumption and social standard of living of the middle class to that of the wage class," a turn away from "middle class economics to democratic economics." The basis of this "democratic" economics was the "idea that the standard of living and wages of the masses constitute the chief market for the products of modern industry," an idea that demanded "the discarding of the now-exploded idea that wages and prices are governed by supply and demand" in favor of the view "that wages ever tend to equal the cost of supplying the social necessities or established standard of living of the wage receivers; and that those wages constitute the great purchasing force in modern society." In other words, both industry and the nation relied on "the expansion of the social life and daily income of the wage class, and capital" can only expand with the "social life and consumption of the masses.[58]

Gunton repeated these ideas throughout the 1890s, seeking explicitly to create an American school of economics in opposition to Ricardian economics. Central to Gunton's argument was an embrace of mechanization as politically and socially liberating for working men and women. The "dismal science" of the Manchester School, argued Gunton, was predicated on the belief that profit depended either on cutting labor costs or on increasing productivity. This assumption had made a certain amount of sense in an economy determined by scarcity and productive uncertainty, in which "wages were regarded as a certain fixed quantity which was rightly due to labor" and which was set "by law." But circumstances had changed, and society was not, the *Social Economist* noted, "a fixed body of given and unchangeable conditions." By the late nineteenth century, despite the dire predictions of Henry George (for whom Gunton clearly had little but contempt), wages were not static factors to be overtaken by increasing rent. Rather, they rose steadily throughout the period.[59]

Economists more closely allied with the classical school, among them Edward Atkinson and Jacob Schoenhof, believed that high wages were possible only when free trade permitted expanding production for each individual worker. Adherents to producerite ideology thought that high worker incomes were possible only when the workers owned the means of production, thus bypassing the exploitation of wage labor. But, argued Gunton, these beliefs countered the historical evidence. American workers' wages had increased even as their hours had declined and their individual productivity had decreased. And workers had not regained control over the production process; indeed, they had been further deskilled by mechanization and increasing rationalization of the work process. Against both traditional economics and traditional labor politics, Gunton insisted that industrialization—that is, large-scale production performed by wage workers—had allowed manufacturers to increase production, lower prices, sell more, and consequently raise wages.[60] However counterintuitive this state of affairs might have seemed to believers in Ricardian economics, "it is true," explained Gunton, "that high wages are accompanied by low cost of production, but that cheapness does not come simultaneously with the high wages. It cannot come that way, because high wages make a dear man." Only with "production on a greater and cheaper scale" could "high wages mean large consumption." "The cheapening therefore comes as an indirect result of high wages, and not simultaneously with them."[61] This idea had staying power. Six years later, Wright argued in Gunton's magazine that machinery "has extended marvelously the power of production, and consequently of consumption. It has made the world cosmopolitan, upsetting old ideas and old customs," most notably the "pessimist's" belief that mechanization harmed workers. "Individual workmen" might well be displaced, concurred Wright, but "in the aggregate machinery secures employment to a larger relative proportion of the population."[62]

Such blithe words no doubt offered cold comfort to those individuals who were replaced by machines and saw their wages drop precipitously. Ironworkers, for example, fought vigorously throughout the late nineteenth century to control work processes and rhythms, while iron manufacturers sought to institute new, routinized, and more easily controlled work patterns. In light of these bitter struggles, historians have accused Gunton of being excessively optimistic about improving social conditions and of being a thoughtless apologist for capitalism.[63] Such charges may indeed ring true, and he certainly was not opposed to capitalism, industrialization, or permanent wage work. But his acceptance of these factors was predicated on a belief that social improvement was synonymous with a higher standard of living outside of the workplace. And in his quest for continuously improving standards of living, he had a quite expansive vision: he did not focus only on skilled workers or semiskilled workers or union members; he focused on everyone, from "the aristocracy of labor" to "dressmakers, milliners, barbers, machine sewers, bakers, miners and factory operatives and laborers in general."[64] When looking at all of these people, and not just at skilled and semiskilled labor, his paper could say confidently, "The working classes have increased in wealth far faster than any other class."[65] Moreover, Gunton's ideas did not differ from those of mainstream economists. Even Edward Atkinson, an entrepreneur and staunch defender of free trade, argued that only "in proportion as the workman raises his standard of comfort and welfare, he develops in the very mental conception of and in the desire for that higher standard, an increasing power to attain it; thus his increasing share of an increasing product becomes the basis for the attainment of a yet greater increase." Atkinson concurred with Gunton that such desires were the sign of "civilization," demarcated "not so much in the standard of living which is actually attained by common laborers, as in the standard set up by them as the mark of their attainment."[66] Gunton certainly would have placed more emphasis on workers' actual standard of living than Atkinson did but would not have disagreed with the textile manufacturer's larger point: civilization meant the ongoing expansion of workers' desires and demands.

This link between high wages and consumption on the one hand and "civilization" on the other was central to many of the *Social Economist*'s articles. These writings drew directly on the arguments of the historical economists, many of whom contributed to the publication, but the *Social Economist* consistently applied economic theory to the lives of working people.[67] In one very early unsigned article in the *Social Economist*, the author (almost certainly Gunton) declared that "wages are civilization because they represent the scale of living in every country, and the scale of living is only another name for development of every kind. Wages, therefore, are, as we said, civilization, which falls or rises as wages fall or rise."[68] While other turn-of-the-century invocations of "civilization" generally relied predominantly on "race, gender, and millennial assumptions about human evolutionary progress," they were less instrumental in shaping the connection between high wages and civilization advanced by Gunton. Though such assumptions were hardly absent from Gunton's thought, he and other labor advocates stressed economic equity (and occasionally even equality) instead of millennialism and more than assumptions of white male supremacy.[69]

In so doing, these authors borrowed not from Protestant theology but from Karl Marx. The idea of economic progression from feudalism to proprietary capitalism to industrial capitalism to corporate capitalism to the triumph of the proletariat lurked within much of their thought. Unlike more vigorous proponents of immediate regime change (socialists, communists, and anarchists), however, pure and simple unionists imagined a gradual change, prodded by workers' demands and actions as well as by changes within capitalist organizations. Thus, the process of proletarianization eliminated one form of worker independence (property ownership) but revealed another (high wages). Arguing for "wages as a criterion of civilization," W. E. Hart explained, "We want no species of abolition, or revolution, but only industrial evolution. We must take cities and the wages-system as they now are, and use them both to better advantage. In spite of the evils thus far connected with the wages-system, which have prevented its full development, it must be regarded as an advance on the part of the laboring classes towards a larger share in the results of civilization." And Hart viewed civilization as a process, not an end: "Civilization may be defined subjectively as an increasing percentage of gratified wants, objectively, as the distribution of an increasing amount of well-being among an increasing proportion of the human family." Such a definition, Hart acknowledged, repudiated older valorizations of self-denial and economic restraint. The "sour-grape theory of life," as he called it, or "pessimism in ecclesiastical garb," relied on the theory of supply and demand to determine wages. That is, wages reflected the truth of market relations, and no amount of workers' agitation could raise them. But, Hart argued, workers had long realized the power of demanding higher wages. These demands put workers' desires—not abstract and ahistorical theory—at the center of economics and, even more to the point, propelled change. "It was an increasing urgency of unsatisfied wants on the part of the laboring class, that brought about the transition from serfdom to wagedom. . . . The present demand for shorter hours and higher wages is likewise the result of another stride."[70]

Ellis Meriam was even more direct in his equation of a high standard of living with civilization. "We do not want less luxury but more," he insisted in the *Social Economist*. Rejecting "the false economic views" of those who feared the corrupting effects of material goods, Meriam defined civilization as precisely those frivolous goods that Protestant theology saw as corrupting: "flowers, music, fine fabrics, fine surroundings, which inspire to cleanliness, and manners, and morals; which bring better environment, and a higher standard of living for all classes."[71] Somewhat circuitously, the *Social Economist*'s arguments in favor of the "economics of luxury" insisted that high wages led to a high standard of living, which in turn resulted from shorter hours, higher wages, and workers' desire for better lives and better goods. With higher wages and ceaseless desires, workers could stimulate the economy through consumption, thereby ensuring their continued high wages as well as capitalists' high profits.[72] More important, the rejection of classical economics and the insistence on workers' vital economic roles underpinned labor's larger demand for economic liberty.

Not all factions of the labor movement agreed with Gompers's and Gunton's equation of high wages and economic competency with meaningful social power. For many people, more goods, expanded leisure time, and higher wages simply did not offer enough. Symmes M. Jelley, who edited the *Voice of Labor*, an 1885 volume of "plain talk . . . on labor's rights, wrongs, remedies, and prospects," insisted that "the wealth of the world would be no compensation to freemen for the degeneracy of their manhood and the debasement of the uplifting spirit that animates our glorious republican institutions."[73] Jelley understood the high wages and shorter hours that allowed Ellen Worth to claim economic liberty to be grossly insufficient to return workers to their former social positions. Wages could not reinstate producers' lost manhood, and wages could not confer republican independence on workers: only the reclamation of control of the means of production could do so. Demands for wages were short term, and they represented no concrete, measurable goals. Several decades later, the Reverend W. S. Harris held that the labor question could be easily (or at least succinctly) answered by curbing (indeed, essentially eliminating) monopolies in favor of small business. Large, necessary monopolies should be owned by the state and administered in the public interest. All other monopolies—the type that forced "small competitors to surrender . . . and die"—should be eliminated.[74]

Similarly, the leaders of the Knights of Labor maintained a strong belief in the power of the cooperative commonwealth through the 1880s. The 1887 revised Constitution of the General Assembly, for example, stressed the urgent need "to establish co-operative institutions, such as will tend to supersede the wage system."[75] The practical goals of the AFL, which had little use for cooperative commonwealths, were seen as insufficient, because they were for workers and unions whose primary concern remained control at the point of production. The United Hatters, for example, consistently protested the breakdown of the apprenticeship system because it prevented boys "from acquiring that thorough knowledge of the trade which is necessary, if we expect them to become competent journeymen and capable of superintending and managing hat factories." The Hatters wanted to reinforce traditional control of work and knowledge even as they saw it slipping away.[76] An audience member at an 1899 Gunton speech argued quite vigorously that workers had acquired higher wages and great consumer power only at the expense of their "individuality as a producer."[77] Despite their considerable differences, the Knights of Labor and AFL shared a great deal. On the local level in particular, neither organization was monolithic or necessarily rigorously consistent. And just as many local Knights assemblies pushed for higher wages with more enthusiasm than they professed for cooperative ventures, the AFL had a strong producerist wing not only in local organizations but also at the national level, as 1893's Plank 10 and John McBride's 1894 ouster of Gompers as AFL president showed. More important, the two organizations frequently shared members. Many workmen joined both organizations, and many others, including Chicagoan George Detwiler, moved from one to the other. Ed Nockles of the Chicago Federation of Labor stressed trade unionists' and Knights' mutual regard (though he would not have included Gompers and Terence Powderly among those who shared this regard). The AFL leadership had no use for the model of the cooperative commonwealth and considered the end of the wage system a hopeless fantasy, but the fight for the closed shop was just as much about "winning control of employment," albeit in a somewhat different sense. Nonetheless, at the level of national leadership, the two organizations understood themselves as having different goals, different methods, and different purposes, all of which were, in theory at least, irreconcilable.[78]

The Knights' strength and influence diminished markedly in the years following Haymarket, and by the 1890s and into the 1900s, the most salient and sustained critique of the AFL from within the labor movement came from the Socialist Party and in particular from its leader, Eugene Debs. Debs and Gompers often appeared more alike than not. They used strikingly similar rhetoric, relying on terms such as *personal liberty* and *manhood*. But they understood these terms to have quite different meanings that pointed toward two distinct understandings of American democratic life. Testifying before the Strike Commission following the Pullman Strike, Gompers declared, "I regard the strikes as the sign that the people are not yet willing to surrender every spark of their manhood and their honor and their independence."[79] Though a significant root cause of the initial strike at Pullman had been George Pullman's excessively paternalistic attitude toward the town's inhabitants, the proximate cause of the strike was the cut in wages necessitated by the Panic of 1893. And in the larger context of Gompers's thought, his invocation of independence and manhood can best be seen as an insistence that Americans (and he was not referring solely to workers but to "the people" more broadly) would make demands regarding wages and hours. High wages (often linked to manhood through the assumed male breadwinner norm) was both the sign and the right of American manhood; strikes merely constituted the expression of workers' recognition of that right.

But Debs would have perceived Gompers's appeal to manhood, honor, and independence as having completely different meaning. In the 1880s, Debs had not seen himself as opposed to the ideas of Gompers and other founders of Federation of Organized Trades and Labor Unions, but after 1886, Debs began to move toward what Nick Salvatore has called a "more radical critique" of contemporary America and toward a rejection of the ideas that formed the basis of the AFL's platform. In particular, Debs drew on both evangelical Protestantism's emphasis on individual free will and free labor ideology's equation of hard work with individual mobility to critique labor's contemporary economic and social circumstances. His particular "vernacular socialism" "stressed resistance to the obstacles placed in the individual's path by the machinations of a few powerful men." In particular, he saw the wage system, which the trade unions accepted as a given, as the potential source of America's decline into oligarchic tyranny. In Debs's understanding, the wage system represented the efforts of the few to control and dominate the independent, individual citizen, the core of American democracy. Not only workers were in danger of losing the "personal liberty" bequeathed to them by the American Revolution; small businessmen, too, risked emasculation at the hands of audacious millionaires who cared nothing for the "sacred fire, the very soul force of the Republic."[80] For Debs, the course was clear. The salvation of American manhood could be achieved only through the reassertion of the individual producer's position as the political center of the republic. Resistance to wage work, then, would have to take place through the action of a political party determined to end the control of the oligarchs and restore the republic. For the AFL and Gompers, however, the formation of a political party to represent labor's interest seemed neither feasible nor desirable.[81] Without the goal of reestablishing the producer-citizen, Gompers had little commitment to the kind of political action that Debs envisioned. But with the goal of economic liberty and a vision of economic citizenship, Gompers saw a clear path ahead through higher wages and shorter hours.

Historians by and large have sided with Debs against Gompers, criticizing the AFL's "pure and simple" unionism. Philip Foner, whose multivolume history of the American labor movement defined the parameters of labor history after World War II, has argued that while the early AFL was "practical and efficient," it "robbed [the unions] at the same time of the principles of labor solidarity and a sense of direction."[82] Subsequent historians have often replicated Foner's argument, suggesting that the AFL did little to challenge the capitalist system, unlike the "thunder on the left" of the Industrial Workers of the World (IWW) or the Congress of Industrial Organizations.[83] The AFL, these authors argue, was uninterested in "social reform per se" and "ideological" only in its support of capitalism.[84] When the Knights collapsed under the combined pressure of big business and the federal government, the AFL was uninterested in offering an alternative culture, like labor republicanism or producerism, to counter the avalanche of proletarianization. Indeed, the AFL has come to be characterized by its "business unionism," a far-from-complimentary term describing union policies of a centralized organization, paid organizers, exclusionary policies (particularly with regard to unskilled workers, women, and people of color), and a willingness to work with employers either on a case-by-case basis or through organizations such as the National Civic Federation.[85]

The historiographic readings of the AFL as conservative and even procapitalist focus on a very particular nineteenth-century American understanding of *radical* that was based on a particular understanding of citizenship and centered on the linked ideologies of labor republicanism and producerism.[86] In David Montgomery's influential formulation, labor republicanism gave the labor movement a "moral universality" that was lost when the "accomodationist" AFL collaborated with employers, business organizations, and the government.[87] This critique of the AFL, then, is based on its failure to uphold producerism and labor republicanism; in that failure, the AFL is seen as helping to destroy the democratic promise of the labor movement's alternative culture, whether exemplified by the Knights, the Socialist Party, or the IWW.[88]

If, however, we think of the AFL as existing within the broader spectrum of American socialisms, it ceases to seem quite as distinct as much of the historiography has made it seem. The emergence of the AFL as the dominant U.S. labor organization does not have to be understood as the moment that forestalled or curtailed meaningful social change but can instead be seen as part of a larger effort to answer the question of what constituted democratic life in an industrial society. Socialist thought (and socialism more formally) was, after all, not reducible to the thought of Powderly or Debs any more than it was reducible to the sensational pronouncements of William "Big Bill" Haywood, who denounced collective bargaining as collaborationist, demanded direct action, and advocated violence as a suitable tactic.[89] Equally prominent in socialist circles were "gradualists" such as John Spargo, Victor Berger, and Morris Hillquit, and in the context of their thought, the AFL seems to have a good deal in common with at least parts of the vast world of American socialism. Spargo, Berger, and Hillquit had as many differences as similarities, but they shared (among themselves and with Gompers) the belief that the only way "which the Socialist State could give to each Individual the full value of the product of his labor" was to go "back to the old hand-labor system of production." Such a return was quite frankly "unthinkable." At the same time, however, these men remained unconvinced that forward progress (and the immediate downfall of capitalism and the capitalist ruling class) was attainable through direct struggle by the working class. Instead, the gradualists espoused "boring from within" the system to gradually and relentlessly change it. For Spargo, this process recognized the futility of any "Utopian" desire to "take some abstract principle and make it the basis of plans and schemes for the arbitrary shaping of social institutions."[90] Rather, proponents of the strategy of working from within understood that socialism was inconceivable as anything "other than a development of the existing state. Its methods of production, distribution, and exchange must take their rise from the methods" already in existence. Berger's understanding of "boring from within" placed less emphasis on Spargo's strict reading of Marx and more on the processes of that boring. Berger, who imagined himself as the American Eduard Bernstein, shared the German socialist's view that the "movement" of socialist reform was more important than any end goal. In practical terms, this approach meant that Spargo, Berger, and Hillquit were comfortable forming alliances with middle-class reformers and Progressives, much to the dismay of Haywood and former Socialist Labor Party leader Daniel De Leon, who consistently "belittled reformers," demanding instead "a purely revolutionary stance."[91]

Boring from within also meant that such small, practical things as "clean water, better zoning, paved sidewalks," and "cleaner neighborhoods" were not only demands for better, healthier and more pleasant lives for workers and their families. As John Enyeart has shown in a study of socialist reforms in Butte, Montana, these practicalities also constituted demands "for greater power in industrial relations." Socialist efforts to ameliorate the daily lives of working people (and the rest of the city, too, since everyone would benefit from more rigorous enforcement of public health measures) sound a good deal like the AFL's demands. Gompers and the AFL leadership had an uneasy relationship with socialists, including Berger and Hillquit, but their processes—calling for improvements in daily life—were ultimately somewhat similar, as were some of their goals. Though the gradualists remained committed to political socialism, a commitment that the AFL did not formally share, they were also committed to other kinds of social democratic reform that were not necessarily explicitly tied to formal political change.[92] Like the AFL, these reformers sought to redistribute economic power toward noncapitalists and particularly toward the working classes along social lines.[93]

The practical nature of the AFL's demands, in contrast to what some AFL supporters saw as the Knights' inactivity, stressed "bread for the hungry, work for the unemployed" and insisted "that a recurrence of such a condition of affairs be made impossible."[94] Like the president of the International Cigar Makers' Union, Adolph Strasser, who proudly insisted before a congressional committee that "we are all practical men," Brotherhood of Carpenters' founder Gabriel Edmonston explained that trade unionists rejected "impractical theories" and instead "offered . . . a thoroughly practical foundation upon which would be built many vital and necessary reforms."[95] Or, as the *Patterson Labor Standard* scoffed, "What good is it to a man to know that he is the producer of all wealth, if he does not know how to obtain even the smallest share of it—sufficient to give his family the actual necessities of life?"[96] Nor did acceptance of wage work necessarily show a willingness to abandon any struggle for independence. Indeed, Gunton argued precisely the opposite: "I regard the doctrine of the economy of high wages as of no less importance than the Declaration of Independence."[97] Workers had not been reduced "to a dull conformity," he argued. Indeed, "never was the able man so influential and powerful, and never was the average man so independent and valuable." Gunton acknowledged that workingmen had lost much of their former "industrial importance," their control of the workplace and of work processes; but, he insisted, they had "gained in personal, social, and political importance."[98] Independence, Gunton admitted, might vanish at the point of production, but it would be replaced by greater social independence. With this understanding of independence in mind, James Duncan explained in the *American Federationist* that Labor Day and the Fourth of July were merely the political and economic halves of the same coin. Just as American independence from Britain had "foster[ed] a republican government as against dependence on a foreign monarchy" so too would economic independence "introduce for all time industrial democracy based upon justice." Though politics could not assure that justice, practical unionism could: "It aims to raise the standard of a living wage from a mere pittance to a guarantee of sufficiency. It does not strike at the condition of the well to do, but insists that all shall be well to do."[99] This was not a claim for workers' rights to the fruits of their labor but a demand for all to share in the fruits of industry.

As Stuart Kaufman has noted, this emphasis on practical rather than political action reflected Gompers's belief that "political success was economically determined," an idea he learned from his readings of Marx. In the pages of the *American Federationist,* British labor leader John Turner explained that the "economic emancipation" of the working class had to precede any political action. "Marx himself," argued Turner, "based his philosophy on the teaching that 'all social and political institutions were the outcome and result of economic conditions.'"[100] Furthermore, Gompers held that the practical demand of more was useful precisely because it both represented immediate concessions to workers' needs and was purposefully vague; it did not point to any specific, identifiable long-term objectives. Gompers illustrated these advantages in a parable about a donkey, the very embodiment of the equine working class. After a long day's work, the donkey was tethered on a short rope in his master's yard. Having eaten all the grass he could reach from his tether, the donkey asked his master for a slightly longer rope so that he could reach more and nicer grass. His owner obliged him, and the donkey grazed happily. The next day, the donkey asked for an even longer length of rope to reach even more grass. The owner was deeply annoyed: "You ungrateful donkey, do you not know that your father was contented with a space half as large as that which you demand?" Continued Gompers, "This allusion to his father caused the donkey to hang his head in shame for a moment, but brightening up he said: 'Well, sir, but do you not know that my father was an ass?'"[101]

Demands for more rope and more grass not only get the donkey more grazing room but more crucially establish a particular relationship between the animal and his master in which the master can expect further demands to be forthcoming. Indeed, the demands become the ordering principle of their relationship. There is no obvious limit to the amount of grass the donkey will want or the length of rope he will need. The master, rather reluctantly, seems to accept the existence of this desire, even if he may not acquiesce to the donkey's demands. At the same time, the donkey accepts his relationship to his owner. He could, in theory, chew through his rope and escape. But where to? Donkeys have no home in the wild; indeed, the particular term *donkey* refers to a domesticated ass. Instead, the donkey stays with his master but continues, we imagine, to request a longer and longer rope.

Like the donkey, suggested Gompers, the working classes had few if any viable options outside of wage work. And, like the donkey, workers faced the problem of how to wrest concessions from employers without establishing a point at which concessions would stop. Just as the donkey wanted more room than his father had had and more grass than he had had a day earlier, Gompers explained that the working classes would always "insist that we are entitled to more, and we shall never cease to demand it until we get it." Indeed, the act of repeating the demand was as important as any single measurement of material gain. The working classes, explained Gompers to anyone who would listen, could never be satisfied: their rallying cry had to remain "More! More today and more tomorrow; and then . . . more and more" if they were to claim economic emancipation and social enfranchisement as consumers rather than as producers.[102] *More,* a word whose meaning shifted continuously over time, represented no fixed amount, no quantifiable end point, much to the dismay of employers who hoped to placate labor once and for all and have done with strikes and unions. Nor did more represent, strictly speaking, a political revolution or a bid for control of the means of production. At the same time, asking for "more of the good things that go to make up life" was not a passive acquiescence to capital's control over labor. As Gompers's parable of the discontented donkey suggests, the demand for more assumed an employer-employee relationship of continuous, dialectical interaction rather than of domination and subordination. Indeed, more's flexible and ongoing nature, its persistence and vagueness, put the demands of workers front and center in public debates about distribution and consumption of wealth into the twentieth century.[103]

More's flexibility did not go unnoticed by corporate leaders, eager to stem the tide of labor activism and violence. The welfare programs with which various corporations experimented in the early twentieth century, for example, sought to give workers more—more leisure activities, more breaks, nice gardens, good washrooms, personal lockers, hot coffee, and so on—but did so explicitly to control unionization and worker unrest. As New York's *Syracuse Standard* noted, "In every factory, no matter how well regulated, there are improvements that might be made at no great expense which would make the working hours far pleasanter for the men and women employed." The article went on to suggest the employment of "a 'social agent' whose sole duty" would be "to look out for unpleasantness and to remedy it so far as possible." Such a change, the *Standard* concluded, would surely "make conditions pleasanter" in the workplace while doing "much toward maintaining pleasant relations between employer and employed," all without the pesky interference of a union.[104] Many companies apparently were persuaded by this line of reasoning. An American Institute of Social Service report found that union activity had ceased at Brooklyn's J. H. Williams Company in 1893, when the company had established baths and begun to keep the locker rooms heated and cleaned, to supply cuspidors, and to clean the floors.[105] One International Harvester administrator was blunter still: providing insurance for workers' families, he argued to the managers of all of the company's plants, "would greatly strengthen the loyalty of employes to the company, as not only the man's interest but the interests of his family would all bend in the direction. . . . I believe at first sight that a weapon of this kind would be much stronger than any profit sharing proposition toward breaking up unionism."[106] International Harvester was so convinced that welfare programs would halt union activity that the company established a welfare department, with noted reformer Gertrude Beeks at its head. Quipped the *Chicago Post* in a story on Beeks's push to provide mirrors in women's changing rooms, "Could any woman have the heart to strike in a factory which gives her plenty of looking-glasses?"[107]

Although more offered one avenue of action for corporations hoping to decrease or completely suppress union activity, it held far greater power for labor. The AFL leadership's language of more helped to create the belief that workers were entitled to participate in the consumer marketplace not only because they had made America's abundance of goods and not only because their consumption ensured economic stability and growth. Workers' ability to participate constituted "an aspiration to a higher life" based on ongoing demands, changing desires, and the possibility that these goals would be fulfilled.[108] More offered the AFL a practical answer to the labor question, describing what labor should and could demand. But more also answered the labor question in broader terms. Beyond its delineation of workers' immediate goals for higher wages and shorter hours, more proposed that it was both right and reasonable for citizens to expect to partake in the economic abundance of industrial society. Inclusion in the polity, as Gompers often noted, had to encompass the ability to participate economically as well as politically. No longer producers or proprietors, workers—and indeed, most other Americans—had little claim to citizenship. As economic actors, however, they could make such a claim by insisting that the definition of American democracy include economic participation as well as political involvement.

By the middle of the twentieth century, a much narrower understanding of economic citizenship had emerged, linked directly to whether an individual earned and, more crucially, to whether he earned through the right kind of work. As Alice Kessler-Harris has shown, New Deal labor legislation and welfare policies (especially unemployment insurance, overtime pay, and social security) repeated and codified long-held assumptions about who should work (men rather than women), who made the best worker (white men), and what kind of work was most valuable (industrial and consistent employment rather than rural, seasonal, or domestic labor).[109] While this narrow understanding of economic citizenship provided the basis for expanding the rights of American citizens, it best served those who worked at full-time jobs in support of families—in other words, male breadwinners. Women and nonwhite men were largely excluded from claiming the benefits of both economic citizenship and the new federal policies. Furthermore, it was difficult and frequently almost impossible for those excluded from economic citizenship to make demands on society and the state in any language other than that of individual economic rights—precisely the language that had excluded such people.[110] The idea of economic citizenship that Kessler-Harris describes as shaping and motivating policy and legislation, then, proved extremely limiting for many Americans, and the ease with which federal policies solidified these limitations made the twentieth-century welfare state exceptionally restrictive both to individuals and to broader social reform.[111]

The AFL's vision of economic citizenship echoed many of the limitations that Kessler-Harris details for twentieth-century federal policy. In general, the AFL assumed that the right to work was a significant part of economic citizenship. The AFL also generally supported the male breadwinner norm and assumed that women should not work full time. But the AFL's vision of economic citizenship was much more expansive than that of twentieth-century liberals, even as it shared some of the same assumptions. In part, the difference between the two versions of economic citizenship is one of location. As Kessler-Harris tells us, economic citizenship was enacted most forcefully in public policy.[112] For the AFL, economic citizenship was enacted in private life and included more than protection for labor organizations, hours legislation, overtime pay, and unemployment insurance; it also encompassed sofas, vacations, and dime novels.

More important, the AFL's idea of economic citizenship was relentlessly historical and far from naturalized. As political scientist Roberto Alejandro has argued, categories such as "citizen" or "we, the people" are "universals that we are able to locate in time, but whose historicity" is lost in the undifferentiated, ontological nature of the rights claim.[113] But more's continuing nature depended on its specific, current, and ever-shifting historical context, unlike static, universal categories that mask more directly recognized social and economic inequalities. Gompers firmly believed that wage work was a condition of industrial capitalism and that workers could change their position within industrial society only by boring from within, by demanding the practical and material benefits of industrial production. Thus would each worker be "furnished with the weapons which shall secure for him industrial emancipation."[114]

In the politics of more and in the vision of economic citizenship that more contained, the AFL's programs reached beyond the labor movement. As Meg Jacobs's work on "pocketbook politics" in the twentieth century shows, economic citizenship formed the basis for "state-building from the bottom up," as ordinary Americans formed cross-class coalitions to protect and expand their ability to participate in economic life.[115] But the ability to make such demands was predicated on the new vision of democracy embedded in the AFL's politics of more, a vision of an economic democracy that Walter Weyl would christen the "new democracy."

5

The End of the Labor Question

In *Twenty Years at Hull House,* Jane Addams wryly recounts her disastrous meeting with Leo Tolstoy. Addams had long revered the Russian's writings on social reform and made a visit to his farm a central part of her 1896 trip to Europe. But the encounter did not quite unfold as she had imagined. She had hoped "to find a clew to the tangled affairs of city poverty," new ways to revive the democratic promise of America. Instead, she got a thorough scolding from the great man himself, first for the "monstrous" size of her fashionable dress sleeves and then for her apparent unwillingness to "till [her] own soil." Addams cringed. Could Tolstoy be right? Could "the wrongs of life be reduced to the terms of unrequited labor and all be made right if each person performed the amount necessary to satisfy his own wants?" she wondered. And "what about the historic view, the inevitable shadings and modifications which life itself brings to its own interpretation?" Chased back to America by this "horde of perplexing questions," Addams resolved at least to bake bread each morning and thus to rely less on the labor of others to support and feed her. Her conscience was momentarily assuaged, though the question of how her baking would square with the work of "the German union baker who presided over the Hull-House bakery" continued to nag at her. But when Addams returned to Chicago, she changed her mind. "Suddenly the whole scheme seemed to me as utterly preposterous as it doubtless was. The half-dozen people invariably waiting to see me after breakfast, the piles of letters to be opened and answered, the demand of actual and pressing wants—were these all to be pushed aside and asked to wait while I saved my soul by two hours' work at baking bread?"[1]

Addams means this episode as more than an amusing anecdote. She follows her chapter on "Tolstoyism" with a lengthy discussion of "public activities and investigations," beginning with an account of the difficulties—and smells—posed by urban garbage. The considerable garbage problems on Halsted Street were social problems that reached past the street and the ward and lay beyond the power of any single individual to solve. In the end, the garbage troubles were somewhat ameliorated—it would be difficult to argue that they were truly ended—by the many small, combined efforts of many individuals that extended across both geographical and class lines.[2] Addams's juxtaposition of Tolstoyism and garbage reform is not accidental. She is contrasting not only two divergent attempts to tackle "tangled affairs of city poverty" but two different historical moments. Addams, unlike Tolstoy, lived in 1890s Chicago, a world marked not by self-sufficiency but by large-scale industry, wage work, and consumption—that is, by interdependence.

Addams's Tolstoyian tale lays out in one amusing incident the transition that defined the 1890s. The decade was, as Henry Steele Commager has argued, not only "the end of an era" but "the beginning of one." In every sense, "economically and politically" as well as "intellectually and psychologically," the 1890s pushed the United States into the twentieth century. The continuing efforts to answer the labor question, to rethink the parameters of American democracy, helped propel this transformation. By the early twentieth century, the labor question had produced two new models of democracy—a "democracy in social terms" and a "democracy of choice." These answers in many ways dissolved the labor question of the nineteenth century and changed it into questions for the twentieth, questions that would set the "pattern to which Americans of the next two generations were to conform, set the problems which they were required to solve."[3]

"Democracy in social terms" is Addams's phrase, though she was hardly the only American to espouse it.[4] She came to the idea through an examination of precisely the juxtaposition she describes between herself and Tolstoy. As she struggled with the problem of democratic life in an industrial world, she turned away from the producerism that Tolstoy offered and the vision of society it implied. His producerism valorized an individual's labor as the source of his social and political value and reflected nineteenth-century American producerism's stress on an individual's right to the fruits of his labor and the priority of self-employment over the wage system. For her part, Addams rejected that "republican liberal" understanding of democratic society in favor of her understanding of "democracy in social terms."[5] That phrase had two meanings for her. First, it meant that democratic life had to reach into the economic and cultural realms as well as the political realm. Second, democracy in social terms was historically specific, a product of the interconnected, interpenetrated world of industrial corporate America. The figure at the center of this economic democracy, then, was no Tolstoyian laborer but a social individual, constituted by an interdependence constantly predicated on and reaffirmed by the organizational and technological structures of industrial life.

These same circumstances of modern life also produced another answer to the labor question that continued to celebrate individual independence and autonomy, for, despite Addams's insistence, the producer did not vanish in the twentieth century. He reappeared as an autonomous individual, defined by and through his freedom of choice. He shared many characteristics—most notably independence and self-rule—with the nineteenth-century producer but neither controlled nor sought to control the means of production. If he was a renovation of the producer, he was a producer stripped of production, a shadow of his former self. This autonomous individual was as much a product of modern life as Addams's socialized democracy. He also inhabited a world of consumers and wage workers; his qualities were equally products of incorporation, mass production, and mass consumption. Like them as well, he was defined by his actions within American economic life. In his case, though, his economic actions, his free choices, made him autonomous and self-reliant. In Addams's vision, participation in economic life constituted both the emblem of citizenship and the action that continuously confirmed that membership in the polity. The ideals of a democracy of free choice and a democracy in social terms were thus diametrically opposed, as one stressed the autonomous individual and the other stressed the social whole. But they were also intrinsically related, twentieth-century answers to the labor question that turned away from production and property and toward economic life as the site of democratic striving.

These two answers profoundly changed the labor question, so that by the early years of the twentieth century, the nineteenth-century labor question had ceased to exist. It had moved away from the problem of wage work, away from the demands to control the means of production, and away from calls for workers to receive the full fruits of their labor. Instead, it turned to the question of participation in social life and calls for the ability to enjoy the full fruits of industrial abundance, whether through Addams's socialized democracy or through the autonomous individual's capacity for free choice. In another sense, however, the labor question was reborn. Its expansion into all aspects of daily life helped structure future debates about citizenship and democracy, shaping legislation, legal rulings, labor movements, cultural politics, and social movements.

The Crisis of the 1890s

To say that the Pullman Strike marked the end of the labor question is of course an exaggeration. Americans continued to debate the relationship between wage work and democratic life into the twentieth century. But in another sense, Pullman indeed represents a moment in which the labor question changed profoundly. At first glance, the events leading up to the strike and boycott seem similar to events in the 1880s and even 1870s. The crisis was precipitated by economic disaster—in this case, the May 1893 collapse of the New York Stock Market, which led to yet another wave of devastating business failures, high unemployment, and violence. In the immediate aftermath of the financial meltdown, runs decimated the holdings of local banks, and demands for specie depleted the U.S. Treasury's reserves. By the following December, 500 banks and 16,000 businesses had failed. Within six months, 156 railroads with approximately $2.5 billion in capitalization were in receivership.[6] Unemployment soared above 12 percent and remained above 10 percent until 1898.[7] When capitalists tried to stanch the flow of money from their coffers by cutting wages, workers struck. In the spring of 1894 alone, at least 750,000 laborers, including coal miners, iron miners, brick makers, shoemakers, silk workers, and railroad workers protested the drastic lowering of wages.[8] The strikers included the members of the newly formed American Railway Union (ARU), the industrial union headed by Eugene Debs, which struck against the Great Northern Railroad in April 1894. The Great Northern ground to a halt, and in short order the ARU won a reversal of almost all of the wage cuts. Coming not two years after labor's disastrous defeat at Homestead, this victory must have seemed especially heartening. Workers and capitalists across the country paid close attention.[9]

That summer, all eyes turned to Chicago and to the actions of workers at the Pullman Palace Car Company. By 1894, George Pullman had found himself in the same predicament as many other manufacturers. Demand for his sleeping cars was diminishing, but demands from his stockholders were not. Faced with the prospect of serious loss, he repeatedly cut his workers' wages, with the cuts averaging 33 percent total between August 1893 and the spring of 1894. Despite the pay cuts, however, Pullman did not lower the substantial rents in the model town in which his workers lived, and by May 11, frustrated and furious, 90 percent of Pullman's workers struck. Pullman had the rest fired, closed his plant, and headed for his New Jersey summer house. The strike against Pullman began as a local affair but assumed national proportions when Debs and the ARU, buoyed by their swift success against the Great Northern Railroad, stepped in on the side of the Pullman workers. ARU members refused to work with Pullman cars and threatened to strike if any member was disciplined for doing so. By 1894, however, Chicago's railroads were also organized under the auspices of a General Managers' Association, and they did not allow the ARU to replicate its spring success. On July 2, the U.S. Circuit Court issued an injunction against Debs, the ARU, and anyone else interfering in railroad traffic. To enforce the injunction, troops were ordered to Chicago from Fort Sheridan, Illinois, marching into the city just after midnight on July 4. The irony of their arrival on Independence Day was not lost on Debs. The Pullman Strike and the boycott ended in defeat for labor, and Debs found himself imprisoned for violating the injunction.

This broad outline of events only hints at the differences between the Pullman Strike and earlier major labor unrest. A closer examination of the events of 1894, however, shows that they not only represented a disastrous defeat for labor at the hands of the railroads, the army, and the courts. These events also marked the end of an era in which the linked languages of producerism and proprietary competitive capitalism had widespread salience. Debs had rallied popular support for the ARU and the Pullman workers in the language of producerism, describing the strike as "a contest between the producing classes and the money power of the country."[10] Producerism had long been a crucial element in discussions of the labor question, playing a central role in popular responses to the depression of 1873 and shaping discussions and redefinitions of wage labor in the 1880s. Producerism likewise formed the backbone the Knights of Labor's vision of a cooperative commonwealth in the 1880s, which many in the American Federation of Labor (AFL) used as a foil against which to describe the practical politics of more.[11] But after 1894, as Shelton Stromquist has argued, no single organization or movement "enjoyed the mass following that nineteenth century producerism had attracted."[12] At the AFL's 1894 annual convention, the defeat of the socialist political platform, which was replete with producerite ideas and language, merely confirmed its demise as a central language in the mainstream discussion of the labor question.

The labor movement was not alone in finding producerism an increasingly problematic idiom. Pullman had, quite self-consciously, set himself up as the paradigmatic business owner, and popular descriptions of the strike often pitted swarming hordes of workers against the isolated and beleaguered entrepreneur. But in the end, Pullman did not emerge from the ordeal as an ideal businessman. Fellow capitalists such as Marcus Hanna mocked Pullman's inflexibility and insensitivity to the demands of his workers, particularly on the issue of rent. The Strike Commission headed by Carroll Davidson Wright roundly condemned Pullman's actions as out of touch with the times. When Pullman died in 1897, his family followed his wishes and took the rather extreme precaution of burying him under concrete; Pullman apparently had expected that vengeful workers would attempt to dig up his body and take revenge on it.[13] No capitalist wanted to end up like Pullman, rich but reviled, under several feet of concrete. He had become an emblem of a past historical moment, the individual proprietor who despite his initial success failed in the new age.

Just what life in that new age would mean was not entirely clear in the immediate aftermath of the strike. One of the few things that did seem clear to many was that, in New York attorney Walter Logan's words, "the individual by himself doesn't amount to much. The only liberty he would have if he persisted in being left entirely alone, would be the liberty to starve and die."[14] Even Supreme Court justice David J. Brewer recognized as much in his decision in *In re Debs* invoking the need for the government to interfere in business (and strikes) for the protection of the "vast interests . . . of all the states." The Strike Commission, too, acknowledged this state of affairs, urging greater government regulation of "quasi-public corporations" such as railroads and lambasting both the courts and businessmen for holding tight to the "law of supply and demand" (and laissez-faire individualism in general) in a corporate age. As Carl Smith has written, "Far from restoring the ideal village community as a model for the future, the town of Pullman had proved that the entire nation was now an interconnected whole."[15] *Interdependence* was the new word for the new world.

For Addams, Pullman's greatest failing had been his inability to recognize the priority of this interdependence. He lived under old rules, and he could not see that industrial capitalism had changed the nature of democracy from individual political participation to "associative" governance of all aspects of life. An industrial organization, like Pullman's company, was always a "vast social operation," explained Addams. As it made employees ever more dependent on industrial work itself, it also made them ever more "highly socialized." If he had understood this fact, Addams implied, he might well have supported a form of industrial democracy in which workers had "representation in the administration of industry."[16]

Even more important, in Addams's view, Pullman would have realized that he as an individual could not force "progress" on the town or its inhabitants. Pullman could, it was true, legislate against certain behaviors such as drinking or gambling, but these efforts "imagined that virtue . . . meant the absence of vice." For Addams, both the town of Pullman and the man were profoundly undemocratic. They jointly provided many fine services but denied workers and their families the right or ability to participate in the decisions. He held, lamented Addams, a vision of progress as "perpendicular," guided only by his sense of absolute right, when he should have thought of progress as "lateral," reaching out to more people, including ever-greater numbers. Small but steady improvements—the "best possible" lateral steps—were truer expressions "of democratic faith and practice than those which underlie private venture."[17]

The New Interdependence

Addams was hardly alone in her belief that even a cursory glance at the organization of manufacturing, transportation, and finance showed the diminishing role of the stalwart individual, whether businessman or worker. Even a comparatively conservative economist such as Arthur Twining Hadley argued strongly that the autonomous individual—whether producer or proprietor—had lost his efficacy. Hadley did not share either the evangelical/abolitionist background or the youthful "moral enthusiasms" of many of his contemporaries, among them Richard Ely, John Bates Clark, and Henry Carter Adams. Hadley was very much a child of the midcentury bourgeoisie, the son of a successful businessman who had enjoyed a comfortable and privileged life and felt no need wholeheartedly to reject the status quo.[18] Nonetheless, like his more audacious colleagues, Hadley was convinced that classical economists as well as Americans who continued to venerate the figure of the self-interested "economic man" too frequently were "working on the assumption that individuals will act as individuals, when in point of fact the exigencies of modern industry compel them to act in masses."[19] That figure might have made sense in an earlier age, said Ely, when "economic individualism in theory corresponded to economic individualism in practice." Now, however, what Stanley Jevons had called "the exigencies of modern life"—proletarianization, incorporation, and mass consumption—had made such practices obsolete. According to Ely, "Our opportunities to work now depend on others as well as upon ourselves, for our whole economic life has become a great network in which each serves all and all serve each. We are bound to the other fellow by a multitude of ties."[20]

That "multitude of ties" was not merely theoretical; the ascendance of the corporation, both in industry and in daily life, increasingly compelled, as Wright put it, "the economic man of Ricardo" to develop "into the social man."[21] The changes in industry were sudden, explosive, and palpable. Before the depression of the 1890s, few firms had a capitalization of more than $10 million; after 1902, one hundred did. By 1899, 65 percent of all industrial wage workers labored for corporations, a figure that rose to 70 percent by 1905. Although the majority of manufacturers remained unincorporated, with small workforces, large manufacturing corporations represented 82.8 percent of all capital by 1905.[22] These new corporations, with their integration of production and distribution, made themselves felt at the most mundane levels of life and increasingly linked the country, literally and figuratively, as Americans nationwide ate midwestern grain and California produce and drank southwestern beer. Farmers in the heartland and New York cosmopolites could purchase the same goods from the same catalogs and could read the same newspapers.[23]

Corporations' arrival on the scene was no mere happenstance, as historians have long pointed out, but rather represented capital's efforts to resolve the social crisis of the late nineteenth century. For capital, the 1873–96 period was characterized by an exceptionally low rate of growth (particularly when measured by work hour), falling prices, rising cost of fixed capital, and high wage rates.[24] The relatively low rate of productivity and steadily rising real wages, in combination with the continued rising cost of plant or fixed capital, led to low rates of profit for capital, generally speaking, even as economies of scale, technological innovations in production, and manufacturers' willingness (or desperate need) to drop prices even below production costs meant that prices fell over the longer term.[25]

Two factors especially rankled capital: the low relative rate of productivity and the high wages paid to skilled workers. Such workers in particular had generally retained control of the productive processes, thereby ensuring that real wages continued to rise and resisting efforts to increase productivity through technological innovation, rationalization of the production process, or an increase in the number of hours worked.[26] Industrialists repeatedly tried to cut wages, and some did so, but in general, employers faced great difficulty in making significant and prolonged across-the-board wage cuts. Workers were more than willing to strike to protest wage cuts, and even when labor lost, the costs to capital often seemed excessive. If workers hoped to avoid the disaster of Pullman, capitalists were equally committed to steering clear of Pullman's fate. Faced with low productivity rates and immobile high wage costs, many capitalists felt serious pressure to produce more goods despite the lack of sufficient markets. The solution to this crisis was combination and incorporation, which enabled capitalists to control prices and production in such a way as to ensure reasonable levels of profits without having to cut wages. Equally significant, the corporate form—an entity owned by many dispersed individuals unknown to each other—separated ownership and control and severed the visceral connection between an individual and physical property.[27] Consequently, as James Livingston has argued, corporations, via managers, wrested control of production away from skilled labor, a development that permitted manufacturers to raise productivity through technological innovation and rationalization of the work process without resorting to lowering wages.[28]

Hadley understood that incorporation was more than a change in business organization; it was a social transformation. Consequently, it demanded a substantial rethinking of the figure of the individual, independent businessman, as Pullman had imagined himself and much as wage work had demanded a reassessment of the proprietary-producer. In contemporary America, Hadley explained, "The true basis for an estimate of a nation's wealth is to be found in the enjoyment of its members. The wealth of a community does not depend on the money value of its means for such enjoyment, nor even on their physical amount, but on their utilization." A business enterprise could no longer "strive to make money in the manner of an individual merchant" without acknowledging that "the prosperity of a nation depends far more on the use made of its wealth than upon the amount of such wealth in existence."[29] In 1893, therefore, Hadley roundly lambasted the recently deceased railroad speculator Jay Gould not because he was a speculator rather than a producer or because he made (and lost) fantastic amounts of money but because he saw business as a Spencerian "fight between buyer and seller" rather than "as a means of mutual service." Gould consequently was a mere "man of the street" committed to making money at others' expense, and Hadley surmised that for Gould, "great financial power was attended with a lack of normal moral development." Hadley contrasted the morally deficient Gould with Cornelius Vanderbilt, not because he was a paragon of "unselfish" altruism (Hadley made no claims about Vanderbilt's moral purity) but because he always "sought his gain in others' gain, not in their loss." "The interests of the investor," Hadley concluded, "are important; but the chief element of their importance lies in the fact that under good management they are identified with the far wider interests of the public."[30] By 1904, Adams felt confident enough about a national change in attitude to suggest hopefully to Edwin R.

A. Seligman, "We have almost come to the point where the individuality of business conduct is swallowed up in its collective character so that the individual point of view is now the exception rather than the rule."[31]

Economists were hardly the only ones to believe that the age of incorporation demanded a replacement for the individualistic "economic men" such as Gould. Some capitalists, too, urged a new conception of the individual. Prominent Chicago businessman and later secretary of the treasury, Franklin MacVeagh, for example, spent much of the 1900s urging his fellow businessmen to rethink the basis of American democratic life. To the capitalist intent on profit, MacVeagh warned, "You are in error if you think you could accumulate wealth without the very costly protection of society, or even without the active aid and cooperation of your fellows. . . . The fact is that no man's wealth would be worth a day's purchase . . . without the cooperation of society."[32] Like Hadley, MacVeagh saw no possibility of pretending that wealth was created through the efforts of one man alone and urged capitalists to accept that fact.

MacVeagh had come to his convictions slowly, amid the turbulence of late-nineteenth-century Chicago. A lawyer by training, he had moved to the city after the Civil War and joined Whitaker, Harmon, and Company, a wholesale grocer. After the Chicago fire, MacVeagh rebuilt the concern as Franklin MacVeagh and Company and quickly rose to prominence in the business community. In the 1870s, he served as president of the Citizens Association of Chicago, a mugwump organization dedicated to municipal reform under the guidance of the "best men." Following the Great Uprising of 1877, he and other city elites pushed for stricter control of city saloons. He was, in other words, a reformer from above. But by the end of the century, his attitudes had changed markedly. Like a number of other elite reformers, MacVeagh had made important contact with labor reformers in the late 1880s and 1890s, and his opinions and arguments changed significantly as a result.[33] MacVeagh did not, of course, represent all capitalists, but he did exemplify an important strain in American thought of the early twentieth century. As a prominent Chicago businessman and a significant figure in national business and politics through his work with the National Civic Federation and later in the Treasury Department, he helped shape the "new liberalism" of the early twentieth century, which, unlike the "old liberalism," emphasized conditional, historically contingent rather than innate or natural rights and sought corporatist or collective answers to social, business, and economic problems.[34]

"The time was sure to come—and has come," MacVeagh told a group of

South Bend, Indiana businessmen, "when the democratic spirit would lead the individual to see that he had played the first role to the limit; and that the complete conception of democracy is, not the individual leading a selfish life merely because he has his liberty and is therefore free to do so. The complete conception of democracy is the individual living freely, as an individual, the social life; and engaging himself in personal concerns [on] the one hand and in common concerns on the other."[35] MacVeagh saw the "complete conception of democracy" as a delicate balancing act. It had to accept and account for changes in the nature of American life. The "democratic evolution" of the turn of the century, he argued, had led to "great changes in the conception of personal and property rights," with greater changes to come. Businessmen no longer controlled their own businesses, either because of corporate governance or because "public opinion and not frequently public law" now "steps in and limits his exclusive control." In addition, unions, which MacVeagh supported as labor's version of the corporation, forced capital to consider the broader social picture. But MacVeagh was also gravely concerned about the threats of socialism, which he understood as statist and oppressive.[36] Contemporary "recognition of the claim of society, as contrasted with the liberties of the individual," he worried, "has . . . become so intense and insistent, as to be willing to practically abolish the individual altogether; and merge him into a social compound, which would take form as a socialistic state." At the same time, however, he understood such impulses as logical reactions to the excessive "abuse of individual liberty," and he fretted equally about the "anarchistic" drive to "pervert to extremes the liberties of the individual." Indeed, he feared that the "unabridged abstract rights of the individual and of his private property, can easily be pressed so far as to take out of our present institutions the essential features of their democratic character."[37]

To navigate a path between extreme socialism and extreme individualism, MacVeagh offered a variety of practical proposals, including greater state regulation of business and labor, incorporation, and unionization—all part of a "necessary limitation of personal and property rights." He also rethought the central figure in democratic life. In place of an autonomous individual, he proposed a "social-individual," "a man richly endowed with personal liberty" who also acknowledged himself as socially constituted. MacVeagh had no intention of throwing the individual overboard, but he realized that individuals were not autonomous and unfettered.[38] They could be understood and understand themselves only in relation to others. Both Gould and Pullman had failed because they could not recognize the new imperatives of association.

Though MacVeagh's arguments for the social individual were most frequently directed at his fellow businessmen, this idea was restricted neither to businessmen nor to his writings. *Social individual* appears in a wide variety of places in the late nineteenth century. Marx uses the phrase in the *Grundrisse* to describe the individual in history, the product of social relations, as opposed to the Enlightenment's natural individual. George Herbert Mead, John Dewey, and Charles Cooley all used it, often interchangeably with the term *social self.* "A self is so evidently a social individual," wrote Mead, "that it can only exist in a group of individuals." Like MacVeagh, these men saw this figure emerging out of the social nature of modern industry (that is, the corporation) and emphasized the social individual's position in an interdependent world.[39] For Addams, the emergence of the social individual meant that Americans could finally uncover "a new impulse to [the] old gospel" of democracy. Though "we have refused" thus far "to move beyond the position of the eighteenth-century leaders, who believed that political equality alone would secure all good to all men," she explained, the Pullman strike and similar crises unquestionably showed that political equality alone had to be "given up as our ideal in social intercourse."[40] Instead, Addams insisted, "social intercourse"—that is, social relations—must "express the growing sense of the economic unit of society and . . . add the social function to democracy."[41]

Democratic Economics

How exactly to "add the social function to democracy" was the problem that worried George Gunton for the entire 1890s. Gunton had begun his study of the labor question as an immigrant textile worker in Fall River, Massachusetts, where he arrived in 1874, just as the depression was deepening. He soon became a labor organizer, and his agitation and fiery oratorical skills caught the attention of New England's most prominent labor leaders, Ira Steward and George McNeill. For the rest of the decade, Gunton worked tirelessly to obtain shorter work hours, and after Steward's death in 1883, Gunton compiled and edited Steward's voluminous and chaotic notes on the necessity of a shorter workday.[42] Though Gunton ultimately departed from Steward's ideas, those ideas provided the foundation for Gunton's democratic vision.

Steward had become an advocate for shorter hours through a combination of his own experiences as a machinist and the New England abolition movement.[43] Self-taught, he wrote voluminously but published rarely and usually only in pamphlet form. Probably drawing on the arguments of such

antislavery advocates as Cassius M. Clay, who held that slaves' lack of ability to consume stunted the South's economic growth, Steward advocated
what Lawrence Glickman has called "a kind of consumerist republicanism
in which the producers of the nation's wealth maintained their community
and extended their power through innovations in consumerist theory and
practice." Indeed, Steward saw that "'the anti-slavery crusade was not only a
battle for the right of the slave laborer' but for the right of the wage worker
'to [decide] how many necessities, luxuries, and entertainments will satisfy
his demands.'"[44]

Steward believed shorter hours to be necessary for maintaining—or, more
precisely, regaining—a virtuous and democratic American republic. Workingmen, now laboring for long hours, had been "debased by Excessive Toil"
and struggled on "almost without hope." The average worker, argued Steward
in his manifesto, *The Eight Hour Movement,* had become a real danger to
democratic life. Staggering to work at "half-past four in the morning, [he]
does not cease until half-past seven, P.M." Under such conditions, demanded
Steward, "how many newspapers can he read? What time has he to visit or
receive visits? to take baths? to write letters? to cultivate flowers? to walk with
his family?" Without time for debate or reflection, the workingman would as
likely vote against his political interest as for it. Disenfranchisement, Steward
argued, was not the result of being propertyless or of being a wage worker;
it was the result of the physical ignomiy of overwork, which made a man
too tired to care about the world around him. The solution to the problem of
the debased citizen was, therefore, obvious: "emancipate" him from poverty
and "excessive toil" through shorter hours and consumption.[45] Leisure time
to pursue educational and recreational activities in conjunction with the
disposable income to make such activities possible could ensure workingmen's political and social enfranchisement.

Steward's argument about the emancipatory effects of leisure time and
consumption both rejected and reinforced producerite conceptions of the
constitution of democratic life, broadly conceived. On the one hand, he recognized that work was no longer the basis of moral or social virtue. "I put
the question to any man who thinks," he sniped. "Is Henry Wilson respected
because he *did* make shoes or because he *does not*? Are Abraham Lincoln,
Andrew Johnson, and N. P. Banks honored because they once toiled with
their hands, or because they were fortunate enough to lift themselves into a
position where it was no longer necessary?" On the other hand, Steward saw
increased leisure and consumption on the part of the working class as a possible route to a producerite utopia. "In the reduction of hours," he believed

or hoped, "the Producer and the Consumer will come together . . . and in the good time coming, every man will be a Capitalist." Each man would work for himself, for "when *every* one has a fortune to let, no one will *hire*."[46] By the end of *The Eight-Hour Movement,* Steward had begun envisioning a cooperative commonwealth with no sharp divisions between workers and owners.

In many ways, Steward's emphasis on both production and consumption as routes toward some form of working-class emancipation, either from wage work or from exhaustion, exemplifies a transitional moment for the labor movement. As Eric Foner has pointed out, many labor leaders held onto the belief that labor and capital were at heart allies, and these leaders spoke with conviction about the possibility of "cooperation between capital and labor." At the same time, however, escalating class conflict and growing numbers of permanent wage workers led many other labor activists to see the relationship between capital and labor as inherently and permanently antagonistic.[47] Eight-hour-day supporters increasingly sounded outraged at the imposition of long hours on workers who could never expect to become employers themselves. William D. Kelley, a Republican congressman from Pennsylvania and father of social reformer Florence Kelley, bitterly remembered his years as a jewelry maker: "I never lighted my lamp for night-work," he wrote in 1872, "without feeling that humanity was outraged by the fact that the millions whose toil produced all the wealth were compelled at the cost of sight and health to labor thus, while those who only bought and sold their productions were free from such exactions."[48]

Gunton kept many of his mentor's ideas—most notably Steward's insistence on the benefits of leisure—but by the 1890s had long since moved away from Steward's consumerist republicanism. Gunton would have shared Kelley's outrage at long working hours but would not have shared the frustration at the prospect of never becoming an independent proprietor, one of those "who only bought and sold their production," rather than a wage worker. So when Gunton began promoting the AFL's 1890 eight-hour-day campaign, he showed no interest in Steward's cooperative commonwealth and did not advocate the elimination of wage work. Instead, Gunton closely echoed the AFL's and Samuel Gompers's politics of more. Like Gompers, Gunton argued that workers should no longer look to production or producerism as their source of social authority. The circumstances of modern industrial organization made doing so impossible, and as he emphasized workers' segmentation into so many "hands," he reiterated Gompers's insistence that new times called for new measures.[49] Wage work, he suggested, that source of dependence, might be the foundation of a new democracy. Gunton saw precisely the factors that were crushing producerism as offering a means to reimagine workers' social position. Gunton agreed with most critics of the wage system that "the division and concentration of industrial power" had "specialize[d] and limit[ed] the laborer's economic function," thereby "diminish[ing] his industrial individuality." But Gunton did not believe that this diminution constituted a tragedy. Wage work and the industrial labor process may have made each worker an "economic automaton" who lost "power to the employer," but they had simultaneously "generalize[d] and extend[ed] his social function" and "increase[d] his social and political individuality" not as a producer but as a consuming "social unit."[50]

In part, Gunton was repeating the argument for workers' vital economic role as consumers: without worker-consumers, manufacturers would find themselves even more deeply mired in excess product. But Gunton was not interested in merely replacing the figure of the producer with that of the consumer—that is, in substituting one kind of independent individual for another. Worker-consumers had no social impact as individuals, he argued, but could make themselves heard only as a part of a larger "social unit" of working-class consumers. Moreover, workers' importance as individual actors would continue to diminish as manufacturers further wrested control of production through technology and rationalization of the production process. By confirming their "increasing dependence on society" as part of a greater social union, however, workers would both confirm and legitimate their social claims. Thus, when Gunton argued that better-paid British workers had "more political influence and freedom . . . under a monarchy with higher wages, than they do in France under a republic of lower wages" and that "there is still more real democracy with higher wages under a republic in America than with lower wages under a monarchy in England," he was not merely saying that America was more democratic because workers could buy more goods. America was more democratic because workers were more important socially, an importance that was predicated on both their dependence on society and their ability to participate, economically as well as politically, in it. Gunton called this phenomenon "democratic economics."[51]

Reading Gunton's rather wholesale abandonment of producerist ideology, some historians have suggested that he was at best a "wayward disciple" of Steward who largely abandoned his vision of a "consumerist republic."[52] (At worst, he is seen as a traitor to the labor movement.) It is quite possible to interpret his idea of human social improvement as consumption at its most base level—that is, as the simple acquisition of goods—and his forecast of a new "democratic economics" as mere fantasy. He certainly spent a great deal of time and ink promoting workers as consumers. Following Steward, Gunton argued for shorter hours and higher wages as a means of increasing workers' consumption, thereby both ameliorating the lives of workers themselves and allowing for greater and more profitable industrial production. But his particular understanding of consumption in general and workers' consumption in particular was much broader than the mere purchase of goods. At a practical level, Gunton suggested that manufacturers' and marketers' recognition of workers as consumers would make workers' desires and needs, rather than just those of the middle class, the market standard. At a more theoretical level, Gunton suggested that the interdependence of wage workers—their status as social individuals, as MacVeagh might have put it—meant that their consumption was always more than just buying goods or services; it was also an act of participation in society, the very democratization of quotidian life.

For Addams, this approach meant, in the most practical of terms, that even the most mundane objects could contain the germs of democratic life. In *Democracy and Social Ethics,* Addams contrasts a middle-class charity visitor's belief, instilled from childhood, that it was "vulgar to spend much money on clothes, to care so much for 'appearances'" with working girls' desire "to bridge the difference" between themselves and women of financial means "by reproducing the street clothes which they have seen." Addams is, as usual, sympathetic to the charity visitor, whose dismay and disapproval at working girls' extravagant expenditures on clothing stem from her desire to see the women accumulating savings for a rainy day rather than sporting flamboyant hats. But Addams points out the clothes have a very different significance for working women. They are not, as the charity visitor may well believe, only about vanity. A working woman understands that "she is judged largely by her clothes" and that her clothes become "her background." Armed with the right clothes, explains Addams, "bright and ambitious [working] girls will come to . . . downtown [girls'] clubs to eat lunch and rest at noon, to study all sorts of subjects and listen to lectures," freed, however temporarily, from "being judged" by their neighborhoods and neighbors rather than "on their own merits and the unconscious social standing afforded by good clothes."[53]

Neither Addams nor the working women she describes had any illusions about the power of clothes. They did not believe that similar-looking clothes erased the differences in wealth, ethnicity, background, and education between a working woman and an upper-class socialite. Indeed, the working women would have recognized those differences better than anyone; after all, they made many of the clothes available in the early twentieth century. But they also understood the cultural—and, as Nan Enstad has shown, the cultural-political—importance of fancy sleeves and plumed hats.[54] Addams was not being snide when she asked, "Have we not worked out our democracy further in regard to clothes than anything else?" And when Walter Weyl argued for a "a real and not merely formal democracy [that] does not content itself with the mere right to vote," Addams would have understood him to mean, in part, the "democratic expression" of an "Italian peasant woman" exchanging "her picturesque kerchief" for "cheap street hat."[55]

Such arguments for a democratic economics pointed toward the need for an understanding of democracy and democratic life in cultural and economic as well as formal political terms. By the first decades of the twentieth century, cultural and economic participation (and *economic* was used broadly to include cultural and social life) came to occupy as important a position in democratic life as political participation. Indeed, the categories became almost inseparable, as Christopher Lasch points out. The new radicalism of intellectuals such as Addams, Randolph Bourne, Mabel Dodge Luhan, Lincoln Colcord, and Lincoln Steffens was marked, Lasch bemoans, by an unfortunate "tendency to see cultural issues as political ones."[56] Lasch might have also insisted that a number of turn-of-the-century intellectuals—including Addams, Gunton, Weyl, Simon Nelson Patten, Gompers, and Seligman—confused economics with politics as well. If Lasch saw these confusions as troubling (a sign of the new radicals' fondness for social control), turn-of-the-century intellectuals saw it as a historically necessary step. An economist and a founding editor of the *New Republic,* Weyl argued that "the democracy of to-morrow, being a real [social] and not merely a formal democracy, does not content itself with the mere right to vote, with political immunities, and generalizations about the rights of men." It would reject, Weyl claimed, "unalienable rights, negatively and individualistically interpreted," in favor of "those same rights, 'life, liberty, and the pursuit of happiness,' extended and given a social interpretation" in the everyday world.[57]

Disaccumulation and the New Democracy

Weyl's best-known work, *The New Democracy* (1912) maintained that democratic life, infused with "a new spirit, critical, concrete, insurgent," would henceforth be enacted in the economic, social, and cultural worlds of daily life. Weyl came to this vision of the new democracy from his work on the labor question. Born in 1873, Weyl found his life and education shaped by depression and the labor question. After completing a doctorate in economics at the University of Pennsylvania, where he studied with Patten, Weyl worked with United Mine Workers president John Mitchell on Mitchell's 1903 *Organized Labor: Its Problems, Purposes and Ideals.* Weyl subsequently turned to journalism, writing for popular magazines before joining Herbert Croly and Walter Lippmann at the *New Republic,* but remained concerned with labor issues. And to a much greater extent than was the case for Croly or Lippmann, with whom Weyl shared many ideas, his conception of a socialized democracy was shaped by the particular contours of the labor question.

Weyl's vision of economic democracy can be understood as the social corollary of the beginnings of what Martin J. Sklar and James Livingston have called capital disaccumulation, and the early stages of disaccumulation provided the starting point for Weyl's argument.[58] Disaccumulation was a twentieth-century phenomenon, following at least sixty years of capital accumulation from around 1840 until the early twentieth century, with an acceleration during and just after the Civil War. In this period, capitalists began investing heavily in the capital goods sector, pouring investments into creating more and more advanced means of production, and such investments drove economic growth. Changes in infrastructure (such as the completion of the Erie Canal), thought (the intellectual foment of the Second Great Awakening), and demographics (the rise of urban populations with cash to spend) encouraged capital accumulation.[59] The resultant growth— and the viability of investments in the capital goods sector—required and created, as Richard Schneirov reminds us, "a new social relationship, that of class-based or wage labor, which came to pervade society and culture."[60] Such investment and innovation in the capital goods sector and the resulting technological innovations in the means of production also increased the productivity of each worker in the consumer goods sector or at least of the productive output possible for each labor hour worked. In theory, this development meant that fewer laborers were required to produce the same number of goods. In practice, it meant that more workers toiled in the capital goods sector than in the consumer goods sector. And the expansion of the consumer goods sector depended on the expansion of the capital goods sector (the creation of more and better means of production).

The rate of investment in the capital goods sector rose steadily until 1873, when growth slowed as a consequence of manufacturers' difficulties in raising labor productivity to the levels made possible by technological innovation and as a consequence of the resistance encountered when wage cuts were attempted. Though economic growth continued and was still fueled by investment in the capital goods sector, the rate of growth was extremely low, leading economists to refer to this period as one of economic retardation. The corporate mergers of the 1890s helped overcome this retardation and restore profits to capital without reducing wages. Now capital was able to reap the benefits of its investment in the means of production and watch productivity per labor hour rise dramatically, for productivity per labor hour depended more on economies of scale, technological innovation, and rationalization of the work process than on the individual laborer's efforts, and the worker ceased to be as vital an element in production. (Marx suggests that workers become "watchmen" or "regulators.")[61]

In the early decades of the twentieth century, the process of accumulation was inverted.[62] Capitalists began to cease investing heavily in the capital goods sector because such investment was no longer necessary to increase consumer goods production. Consumer goods production—what we call mass production—could now increase via the economies of scale in place (thanks to previous investment in the means of production) and manufacturers' greater control over the workplace. To increase consumer goods production, it was no longer necessary to invest as heavily in the capital goods sector. As Sklar explains, functionally this development meant that fewer workers were required in the capital goods sector. The labor force was now increasingly concentrated in the consumer goods sector, and worker productivity, measured by labor hour, continued to increase. According to Sklar, "The process that appears under capitalism as disaccumulation means the on-going net release of labor-power, measured in aggregate social labor-time, from goods-production. In particular, it means that less and less labor-power is required for the production of the goods necessary for sustaining and reproducing physical and social life." Production, in other words, could lose the social significance it had enjoyed throughout most of the nineteenth century; the relations of production no longer stood as the necessary "determinant of social organization."[63]

Weyl recognized as much. The new democracy, he insisted, was being made possible by the emergence of "the social surplus," a socialized version of surplus capital that was equivalent to "our clear gain in wealth after the year's business is over," but not in a strictly or narrowly monetary sense. Rather, the social surplus represented "our excess of social product over social effort." Weyl understood it as a historically new occurrence, a result of the economic growth of the nineteenth century. Before the Industrial Revolution, Weyl explained, "production was limited by the narrow bounds of muscle power and simple tools." But as more investment went into factories and technologies of production, the direct link between productivity and "muscle power" broke down, and productivity increased exponentially. Machine production consequently had "multiplied almost *ad infinitum*" "the products of the social surplus"—most important among them "wealth, recreation, leisure, [and] culture." By the early twentieth century, with the beginnings of disaccumu-lation, Weyl argued that the wealth that had been accruing for more than a century had now "furnishe[d] the weapon with which democracy may be attained."[64] And that weapon was found in leisure, recreation, and culture.

Weyl contended that the existence and increase of the social surplus cre-ated the opportunity for socialized democracy for three reasons. First, he saw disaccumulation as both a sign and a source of a new economic and social importance of the people. The growth of the consumer goods sector meant that the majority of Americans now comprised the engine of eco-nomic growth and the central element in the creation of more social wealth. In other words, he pushed Gunton's argument about the social importance of workers as consumers to its logical conclusion. After all, Weyl explained, "everywhere it is the great mass which buys." In 1905, for example, Ameri-can industry had produced a rather staggering $390 million worth of boots and shoes, along with $692 million worth of clothing, $78 million in canned food, and $29 million in pickles. "How many" of these things, Weyl asked rhetorically, "did the rich consume?"[65]

Though Weyl saw this high level of mass consumption as important be-cause it indicated the central position of the masses, he also linked mass consumption to both an absolute rise in the general standard of living and a desire for an ever-improving standard of living—the second way in which he linked the social surplus to the new democracy. Much like Steward and Gunton, Weyl held that the possibility of mass consumption had led to "a complete revolution in popular standards of living." Even more important, it had pushed people to demand "a fuller life," wrote Weyl, echoing Gompers. With this new ethical demand came a concomitant new "theory of the dig-nity of human life" that demanded a "full life" as a condition of democracy, extending beyond the older condition of the preservation of life (in the most literal sense) and property.[66]

Finally, Weyl saw the social surplus as central to the new democracy be-cause it changed the nature of the questions that animated the push for a more democratic society. The current "progressive, though slow, diffusion of wealth," the idea that "bread and fishes" for all might no longer be a miracle, meant that demands for "a fairer distribution" of "food and material and moral goods for all" could become central to any meaningful conception of democracy. Now, said Weyl, the social surplus "makes us sensitive to misery, preventable death, sickness, hunger and deprivation." Thus, the equation of a full life with the new democracy, of material comfort with democratic life, made the "disequilibrium between social surplus and social misery" both a social and political problem. Such a change was a part of the "new economic, and therefore . . . new psychological world." Here, "the whole problem of the mutual relations of classes has moved from its old mooring" (relations to the means of production) toward a new series of social questions—about distribution, the quality of life, poverty, market regulation, wage and price stabilization—that were predicated on the hope for a "full life," for the full enjoyment of the social surplus.[67] For Weyl, disaccumulation changed the terms in which Americans could understand democracy from a political system to a social, economic, and political system. By politicizing the question of the accessibility of a full life for everyone, politics had become economic and cultural, and democratic life was inseparable from the details, however minor, of daily existence.[68]

Weyl might indeed seem overly naive (as some of his reviewers believed) in his equation of the material and the democratic, and many critics have continued to read *The New Democracy* as hopelessly optimistic.[69] But Weyl understood the demand for full life as simultaneously material and moral and mocked those who denied the importance of the material in a democratic life: "There are exalted and impatient souls who pay no heed to talks of mere material progress. They believe that the geniuses—the Shakespeares, Beethovens, Botticellis, Kants, Darwins—do not arise in pork-and-pig-iron-producing nations, that a full belly means an empty mind." But these naysayers overlooked or simply could not see the centrality of a satisfied stomach to early-twentieth-century American democracy. Without economic power, Weyl explained, political rights had little meaning. In the context of the times and "in the final analysis, however it may be clothed in legal rights and political immunities, democracy means material goods," accessible to all.[70]

Weyl's new democracy—or Addams's democracy in social terms or Gunton's democratic economics—can be seen as a variant of social democracy, advocated on both sides of the Atlantic by intellectuals such as Eduard Bernstein, Jean Jaurès, Croly, and Dewey. Like them, Weyl was committed to defining democracy economically and socially as well as politically. He similarly shared their beliefs that reform was more effective than harsh revolution and that no conflict need arise between individual and society. But his involvement in the labor question as the central social issue of the day meant that he, like Gunton, Addams, Gompers, and others, was more committed than other social democrats to the expansion of democracy into the economic and cultural realms; all of these men and women linked social democracy more directly to the practical matters surrounding the labor question. Weyl understood that socialized democracy was as much a process as an ideal, the result of small, endless efforts to improve seemingly trivial details such as sidewalks, libraries, and furnaces. "Our hope of this democracy," he explained, "does not depend upon the chance of a sudden, causeless turn of the wheel. The motor reactions of society, like those of individuals, proceed only from prior accumulations of nervous energy."[71]

The world of mass consumption was not the only place in late-nineteenth- and early-twentieth-century America where such an expansion of democracy—from formal and political to informal and social, economic, and cultural—was visible. We might look, for instance, at grassroots movements to prevent involuntary childhood vaccinations or establish better schools, voter registration drives and ballot initiatives. We might also look at the City Beautiful movement and efforts to establish playgrounds in urban neighborhoods such as the Bowery or at fights against urban corruption that turned to the extrapolitical city manager; legislation regulating medicines and food, corporations, and transportation; interest group lobbying and efforts to push forward women's suffrage or workplace safety legislation.[72] And of course we might look at the worlds of leisure and consumption. None of this argument implies that the workplace and the relations of work itself ceased to matter. Far from it. They remained and still remain central to the efforts of unions, reformers, and workers. Nor does this line of reasoning imply that formal politics have become unimportant. But as the "bright and ambitious" clubgoing working women knew, democratic politics expanded so that cultural and economic democracy—Weyl's "real" democracy—mattered as much as formal political democracy.

Latter-Day Crusoes

The same circumstances of modern life that generated the new democracy also produced another answer to the labor question. Instead of emphasizing interdependence and participation in social and economic life, this answer robustly reasserted the figure of the self-reliant, independent individual. Two versions of the self-reliant individual emerged, each seeking to reaffirm the most salient aspect of the proprietary producer—independence—in an era when fewer men, particularly workers, could hope to claim that status. The first variant appeared most frequently in popular literature. He was an isolated loner, always male, a marginal figure unfettered by the ties of either property or society. In literature, he often appeared in the recent past and was described with nostalgic tenderness. Or, as in Owen Wister's *The Virginian*, his independence was contingent and fragile, a fantasy that could not be sustained. The second variant of the self-reliant individual appeared forcefully in the legal rulings on labor issues. Here, the independent individual came to be defined through his (or possibly her) inherent freedom of choice rather than through property ownership or producerism. Freedom of choice, or what Illinois justice Benjamin Magruder called "the right to private judgment," equated independence with the capacity to choose and in particular to make economic choices. Claims to participate in economic or social life, then, could not be based on interdependence with one another—that is, on a larger social claim—but rather had to be predicated on the individual's abstract and theoretical ability to make choices. Freedom of choice offered a contemporary and definitely not nostalgic answer to the labor question, reaffirming an ideal of democratic life defined by an independent, autonomous citizenry even as it altered the premises of that life.

The valorization of the independent loner offered a vision of resistance to the demoralizing and enervating world of wage work, though this vision seemed rooted more in the past than in the present. Even when contemporary examples of such resilience to modern life were found, they were quite literally remote. For example, a tale of a modern frontiersman, "Dick Bassett, the hermit of Grand Traverse Bay," appeared in both the *Chicago Herald* and the *New York Times* in 1891. According to the article, Bassett, a frontiersman from birth, had been raised in the Rockies and had served in the Civil War, during which he was wounded in the lung. He subsequently found the mountain air too bracing and came "through some chance of providence" to northern Michigan in 1878. There, he "took possession" of a small island "about an acre large." His island was neither greedily large nor uselessly small. He built a cabin and, he explained, "started a garden, which has yielded much more than I can use myself. I have some nice fruit trees too." This "latter-day Crusoe" exemplifies an extreme version of the self-sufficient yeoman farmer. He relied on no one else for his livelihood. He did not even require the labor of a wife. When visitors came to see him—some out of curiosity, others to gather fruit—he cooked for them. His identity was so intrinsically tied to his land that he did not even need to own it legally. A few years earlier, he explained, "some one tried to gain possession of my little home by saying that it did not belong to me or to the United States." When he appealed to the Interior Department, "the reply came that no one could dispossess me of my claim; that [the island] was on their maps, and, inasmuch as I had made that my home for so many years, no one could take it from me." Bassett's position as a sort of ideal frontiersman and self-reliant farmer made him a celebrity. People came to his island just to see him and his house, and he regularly received fan mail.[73]

Bassett's popularity suggests that even as Americans read about Bassett in the mass media of the day and traveled to see him on efficient railways, they continued to idealize the independent proprietor. But this idolization only emphasized Bassett's rarity. No one would have thought to travel to the Old Northwest to gawk at frontiersmen at the beginning of the nineteenth century. By the 1890s, men such as Bassett were curiosities but hardly viable answers to the labor question. As Nelson Appleton Miles, the major general in charge of the federal troops ordered to Chicago to squash the Pullman "uprising," noted during the strike, overcrowding in cities, unemployment, and low wages had created huge "mobs" with excessive enthusiasm for "depredation and most fiendish atrocities."[74] While Miles despised these "mobs," he also saw that these men had few other options: "Up to within the last few decades, every community had to its westward a boundless territory of rich fields where the man who labored could at any time locate and establish in a few years an estate amply sufficient for his family or relations and of great and permanent value."[75] By the 1890s, however, "stout, able-bodied men" were trapped in "appalling" poverty; "thousands of men . . . are on the verge of starvation, laboring men . . . have been forced to poverty, not only by this rebellion, but by the depressed conditions of the times and impossibility of obtaining work."[76]

Under such conditions, efforts to reassert the self-sufficient individual could only dimly reflect the ideal of either the Jeffersonian yeoman or labor republicanism's proprietary producer.[77] The new self-sufficient individual appeared in many guises, though he was usually white and male. He could show up as a nostalgic figure from the past; as a loner in the present, existing uneasily on the fringes of industrial society; or as a resister of the enervating comforts of modern life. When popular literature, such as Irving Bacheller's *Eben Holden,* which spent two years as the fifth-best-selling novel in the United States, closely echoed producerite ideology's emphasis on both of those factors, the productive, proprietary individual was located firmly in the past. *Eben Holden* tells the story of Uncle Eb, a woodchopper who moves from Vermont to Upstate New York with his former employer's orphan in tow. Life in the Adirondacks is tough, but the adversity of farming there prepares the young boy for successful life in the city. Yet even as the novel praises Eb's self-sufficiency and resilience, both he and the novel are suffused with longing for a more rigorous, self-reliant past. At the novel's end, the narrator, now an old man, muses on today's "young folks," a "new kind of people." "It gives us comfort," he says, "to think they will never have to sing in choirs or 'pound the rock' for board money; but I know it is the worse luck for them. They are a fine lot of young men and women—comely and well-mannered—but they will not be the pathfinders of the future. What with balls and dinners and clubs and theatres, they find too great a solace in the rear rank." Bacheller's preface echoes these sentiments. The plot, he explains, is based on his experiences as a child, living with "hardy woodchoppers" in the "rigorous climate" of the wilderness, though he wrote the book "in the publicity of the Pullman car" and the "cheerless solitude of the hotel chamber." He realizes that he cannot return to his earlier life, and that realization invests Uncle Eb and his fellow Adirondack residents with both poignancy and moral authority, for the new young folks lack precisely the "old" values of "love of honour and of industry" that stem from honest work.[78]

Other works, especially those set in the West, reiterated *Eben Holden*'s gentle sense of nostalgic longing but moved their characters still further away from productive proprietorship. The illustrations of Frederic Remington, for example, frequently depict rugged men isolated from all but the rough tasks at hand. Rarely involved in productive labor, these illustrations are more likely to show cowboys or soldiers in remote locales, valiantly fighting nature, wild animals, or Native Americans. Remington's sculptures, which he began producing in the 1890s (his earliest well-known piece is *The Bronco Buster*, from 1895), only accentuate that isolation by literally removing the figures from any broader context, whether of land or social relations. Much like a literary embodiment of Remington's cowboys, the title character of Owen Wister's wildly popular novel, *The Virginian*, grabbed the popular imagination because he was the archetypal loner, dependent on no one but his horse, Monte. Though the Virginian works for a living, Wister makes that labor almost incidental to the Virginian's taciturn self-reliance. Yet the book's evocative power is self-consciously based on the impossibility of such independence in contemporary America. The cowboy, Wister states bluntly in the preface, "will never come again. He rides in his historic yesterday." Wister's cowboy stands as the antithesis of a modern corporate America. Because he is honest, "Wall Street would have found him behind the times." Because he is chivalrous toward women, Newport society would "have found him old-fashioned." But while that antimodern, chivalrous cowboy cannot exist in the modern world, the character of the Virginian can survive and even thrive as soon as he turns his back on his former independent cowboy life. By the end of the novel, the Virginian is married and a father. Monte ceases to be the symbol of the Virginian's independence but becomes the placid pony for his son. More important, the Virginian embraces the corporate world against which Wister had contrasted the character in the novel's introduction. Seeing the end of the cowboy life, the Virginian has wisely moved from cattle to coal. As he tells his new wife's great-aunt, "When I took up my land, I chose a place where there is coal," since, he predicts, "it will not be long before the new railroad needs that." The Virginian's existence as the paradigmatic independent loner, then, is tenuous at best, and in the end, he willingly succumbs to the demands of historical circumstance.[79]

Freedom of Choice

The variant of the autonomous individual defined through his freedom of choice faced no such conflict with the historical circumstances of the 1890s. He was instead grounded firmly in contemporary life and embodied no nostalgia for an era before mass production and consumption. His freedom of choice was almost always labeled a freedom of economic choice, whether it involved choice in work or choice in consumption. This autonomous individual contained vestiges of both producerism and free labor ideology, but with important distinctions. While he (or she—as the twentieth century wore on, this figure was not necessarily gendered male) shared the proprietor and producer's independence and self-reliance, the freely choosing individual was not as concerned with property ownership, control of the means of production, or securing the full fruits of his labor. And though labor contracts were often an important site where this individual could exercise freedom of choice, it was his ability to choose more than his formal equality with the other contractor that demonstrated his independence.

This figure was most conspicuous in the legal and popular discussions that upheld freedom of contract, particularly in opposition to legislation regulating wages and hours. The arguments against such legislation insisted that any effort to curtail workers' choices infringed on their natural independence.[80] In much the same way, organizations such as the National Association of Manufacturers, founded in 1902, the American Anti-Boycott Association (1902), and the Citizens' Industrial Alliance (1903) used the equation of liberty and choice to attack organized labor.[81] In these arguments, the collective action of workingmen through unions as well as the idea of the social individual appeared as the guarantor of servility, as A. J. F. Behrends's denouncement of the violent 1895 Brooklyn streetcar strike shows.[82] For Behrends, minister of Brooklyn's large Central Church and a prominent proponent of the social gospel, the strike and the strikers intended nothing less than the destruction of "individual liberty." Under the iron grip of unions, which forced each worker to accept the same terms of employment as every other man, a man could "not own himself" but was rather "bound hand and foot." Such an appalling denial of individual liberty moved Behrends to compare unions with chattel slavery: unionized workers, he insisted grandiosely, "are slaves as really as the humblest Negro whose back was bared to the lash in the South." As far as Behrends was concerned, unions sought to deny the "right of men of every color to receive the proceeds of [their] labor."[83]

Behrends's comparison of white workers to black slaves might well have seemed overblown by 1895, but he could not have made such a comparison lightly. Behrends was deeply involved in the American Missionary Association, serving as the group's vice president as well as on its executive committee. The association had begun as an abolitionist organization and after the Civil War worked throughout the South to establish schools and universities for former slaves. Behrends likely intended his comparison almost literally, as a perfect articulation of his fervent belief in the equation of freedom of contract with individual liberty. Behrends's commitment to freedom of contract continued midcentury abolitionists' insistence that slaves' inability to enter into contracts most defined them as slaves, a bald sign that slaves did not own property in themselves. Abolitionists consequently saw the right to make and enter contracts as a crucial aspect of freedom for ex-slaves, an outward sign of their self-ownership.[84] Such claims often were based on the premise of the equality of property owners in the marketplace, as in the case of *Godcharles v. Wigeman* (1886), in which the Pennsylvania Supreme Court struck down a law that required workers to be paid in legal tender rather than in company scrip. Writing for the majority, Justice Isaac R. Gordon explained that the law represented an "an insulting attempt to put the laborer under legislative tutelage, which is not only degrading to his manhood, but subversive of his rights as a citizen of the United States." Any man, Gordon argued, "may sell his labor for what he thinks best, whether money or goods, just as his employer may sell his iron or coal."[85]

In popular defenses of liberty of contract, however, the equality of property owners was often stressed less than the freedom of choice, as in *Ritchie v. People* (1895), which struck down a law limiting women's hours of labor. "As a 'person,'" claimed Justice Benjamin Magruder, a woman "has the right to claim the benefit of the constitutional provision that she shall not be deprived of life, liberty or property without due process of law. Involved in these rights thus guaranteed to her is the right to make and enforce contracts. The law accords to her, as to every other citizen, the right to gain a livelihood by intelligence, honesty and industry in the arts, the sciences, the professions or other vocations." Magruder and other judges linked autonomy through choice to property ownership, just as had been the case under a free labor ideology. All adult persons, explained Magruder, had the right to make contracts precisely because "the right to contract is the only way by which a person can rightfully acquire property by his own labor."[86] But Magruder augmented women's rights as property owners with what he called their "right to private judgment." Restrictive labor legislation, he argued, not only "assumes to dictate to what extent the capacity to labor may be exercised by the employe" but also "takes away the right of private judgment as to the amount and duration of the labor to be put forth in a specified period."[87] While he did not negate the rights associated with property ownership ("the fundamental rights of the citizen to control his or her own time and faculties"), he also emphasized the right of private judgment and allowed individual choice based on that private judgment to join property ownership as a justification for upholding freedom of contract.[88]

Justice Rufus W. Peckham's majority decision in an 1897 U.S. Supreme Court decision, *Allgeyer v. Louisiana,* amplified Magruder's right of private judgment. *Allgeyer* was not a labor case but an insurance case, but in it, Peckham made it clear that liberty "means not only the right of the citizen to be free from mere physical restraint of his person, as by incarceration." Liberty also included a citizen's right "to live and work where he will," to chose his occupation and his location independent of any legal constraint.[89] Peckham bolstered his argument by quoting Joseph Bradley's dissent in *Butchers' Union Co. v. Crescent City Co.* (1884): "If it does not abridge the privileges and immunities of a citizen of the United States to prohibit him from pursuing his chosen calling, and giving to others the exclusive right of pursuing it, it certainly does deprive him (to a certain extent) of his liberty; for it takes from him the freedom of adopting and following the pursuit which he prefers." Bradley was quick to point out that this pursuit "is a material part of the liberty of the citizen." Although, explained Peckham, "these remarks were made in regard to questions of monopoly . . . they well describe the rights which are covered by the word 'liberty,' as contained in the fourteenth amendment."[90]

Similarly, when Starr Hoyt Nichols attacked the union label campaign in an 1897 article in the *North American Review,* he did so by insisting that the union label nullified the right to contract and consequently abrogated workers', employers', and consumers' right to chose when to work, what to make, and what to buy. Since the union label campaign also backed the closed shop, Nichols held that the union label "threatened" workmen's "individual liberty" by denying their right "to make free contract with each other" and threatened to destroy small businesses by dictating who could and could not be hired. But he found the limitation of the rights of consumers to buy whatever they wanted equally alarming. By denying workers, manufacturers, and consumers the right to make free choices, the union label "abridge[d] the rights of others." Nichols's attack was especially pointed since he was a strong supporter of labor unions and had helped Gunton begin publishing the *Social Economist*. But Nichols was not willing to see unions acting like so many "self-made despots" and limiting consumers' or producers' opportunity to choose.[91] Others echoed Nichols's reasoning. Boston lawyer (and onetime partner of Louis Brandeis) Edward F. McClennen made similar arguments in relation to boycotts or other efforts to prevent a third party from entering into a contract with one of two parties in dispute. The gravest problem in that case, argued McClennen, was that the prohibiting party "destroys the freedom of the third party to choose"; thus, such prohibitions "should not be permitted."[92]

The link between individual independence and freedom of choice was more firmly cemented in efforts to define who could not be expected to exercise it. In *Lochner v. New York* (1905), the most famous or infamous of the freedom of contract cases, the question of who is capable of choice and thus independent and who is not rests at the heart of Peckham's majority decision. The ruling overturned a New York state law that limited the hours workers in a bakery could labor. Any such effort, Peckham argued, constituted "an illegal interference with the rights of individuals, both employers and employees, to make contracts regarding labor upon such terms as they may think best, or which they may agree upon." If the bakers in question had been incapable of "independence of judgment and of action," the New York law would have been constitutional. But since "there is no contention that bakers as a class are not equal in intelligence and capacity to men in other trades or manual occupations, or that they are not able to assert their rights and care for themselves without the protecting arm of the State, interfering with their independence of judgment and action," it was impossible to assume that they were in need of special protection.[93] Rather than protecting exploited workers, declared Peckham, the law declared that bakers were incapable of choosing for themselves how much they would work: "The employee may desire to earn the extra money which would arise from his working more than the prescribed time." But the New York law would forbid a worker from acquiring additional hours even if doing so "may seem to [the worker] appropriate or necessary for the support of himself and his family."[94]

Peckham's equation of the inability to chose with dependency echoed other rulings that upheld protective legislation precisely because the workers involved were seen as too weak and too dependent to chose wisely. In *Holden v. Hardy* (1898), the U.S. Supreme Court sustained a Utah law that prohibited miners from laboring for more than eight hours, precisely because mining's "morbid, noxious and often deadly effects on the mind" prevented miners from being able to make rational choices about their employment.[95] The opinion assumed that in most cases, workers could negotiate employment contracts independently, without interference or regulation from the state. The Utah law was upheld precisely because the miners were seen as too physically and perhaps mentally feeble to represent their own interests.[96]

Similar reasoning undergirded the majority decision in *Muller v. Oregon* (1908), in which the U.S. Supreme Court upheld an Oregon law that limited women's hours of labor and effectively overturned *Ritchie.* In this case, as in *Holden,* the justices suggested in part that women's right to contract was weaker than men's because of women's physical frailty. But unlike in *Holden,* the Court also insisted that women's political inequality with men also permitted and even necessitated protective legislation. Despite Magruder's earlier claims about women's equal property rights, the Court now suggested that women's lack of political rights demonstrated that they had less capacity to choose than did men. As Sybil Lipschultz argues, "The Court took advantage of women's inferior position in voting rights and contracts, and used this to uphold maximum hours in *Muller.*"[97]

Although *Holden* and *Muller* are generally seen as exemplifying the rise of a regulatory state (and thus standing in contrast to *Lochner*), the majority rulings in these two cases reinforced the central position of choice in distinguishing the self-reliant individual by declaring that miners and women, respectively, could be regulated precisely because they were not capable of making their own judgments and choices. Lawyer and historical novelist Frederic Jessup Stimson thus found it reasonable to argue that any effort to curtail the right of choice for an independent citizen ran counter to liberty and the "ethics of democracy." In an article for *Scribner's Magazine,* Stimson carefully surveyed all of what he called the "socialistic or communistic laws" passed by national and state legislatures in 1889 and 1890, finding an astonishing number (at least twelve hundred)—liquor laws; labor laws; "laws concerning soldiers, pensions, the [Grand Army of the Republic] and Sons of

Veterans"; libel laws; "laws concerning general morals"; and laws regulating manufactures. While Stimson conceded that some of these laws might fall under the heading of "allowable socialism," he worried that the trend pointed to an overall diminution of individual liberty. "Just how far our people are willing to subordinate the life of the individual to the ordering of the majority," he wrote, "is the greater question of the future—greater than the question whether the institution of property shall be maintained or not." Though he ended his article by asserting, "We are still free," he also included a warning against curtailments of liberty even in the best interests of society.[98] He made the right to choose, even foolishly, the most vibrant sign of an independent citizen. Pennsylvania industrialist A. B. Farquhar took an even more extreme stand, protesting to Congress in 1902 that labor legislation constituted nothing more than "pure undisguised paternalism": "It involves the assumption that business arrangements in which the contracting parties are alone concerned may not be made freely," an assumption that at worst might lead to "Oriental despotism."[99] But while one strain of popular thought linked "Oriental despotism" with workers' feared inability to sustain the "beef standard" deemed necessary for white workers, Farquhar equated Oriental despotism with what he saw as the subjugation of individual will to arbitrary, demeaning, and profoundly antidemocratic rules.

"The right of private judgment" never emerged as a specific substantive legal right, and it was never the central or defining argument in any of the liberty of contract cases. As James Gordley has argued, the "major premise" of cases such as *Lochner* "was that the United States Constitution protects contract rights." A more "minor premise" of these cases emphasized the right of property owners to choose. Nonetheless, this minor premise showed up consistently enough in court rulings about contract throughout the so-called *Lochner* era that legal scholar James Willard Hurst has identified the period between 1870 and 1900 as featuring a push for a "wider shoring of freedom of choice."[100]

Freedom of choice became an important part of individual liberty in the Progressive Era, offering an understanding of self-sufficiency that endured into the twentieth century when choice came to seem like a natural individual right; it became, in Wai-Chee Dimock's words, "solid, self-evident," like a piece of "moral furniture."[101] But freedom of choice constrained but could not evade the new democracy's vision of greater social participation in economic life. Proponents of this vision always couched their arguments in similar terms: democratic life, whether social or individualistic, was no longer tied to production; both answers to the labor question helped transform it from a question about wage work and democracy into a question about the extent and nature of participation in economic life, into the question of the new century.

* * *

In August 1879, E. Herbert Graham, Jeremiah E. Thomas, and Alexander Robb would not have imagined that the labor question would end with such answers. When these men spoke before Abram Hewitt's congressional committee in New York, they poignantly expressed their desire for "a chance to make [themselves] a home." They had invoked the American citizen's "sacred right to land." They had called for the "leveling" out of society, so that each man received the fruits of his labor, no more and no less. Their commitment to the world of the proprietary producer was absolute. At no moment could they have envisioned a society structured around something other than production or property. Thus, it is impossible to know what they would have made of the new democracy or the democracy of choice. After the turbulence of the 1880s and 1890s, would these witnesses, too, have turned away from producerism as the center of citizenship and democracy? Would they have embraced the new democracy or the politics of more? Would they have turned to freedom of choice? Or would they, like so many twentieth-century Americans, have accepted both, however contradictory they seemed?

By the early twentieth century, of course, they would have been old men, if indeed they were still alive. But their children and grandchildren inhabited in a world that had been shaped by the answers to the labor question. The questions that animated debates regarding democratic life in America were no longer about control of the means of production, the right to the fruits of one's labor, or the relationship between independence and property. The questions now concerned participation in economic and social life, leisure, entitlements, benefits, and security and were defined by words such as *access, opportunity,* and *inclusion* that set the terms of the new political, economic, and cultural debates, from the New Deal to the GI Bill, from civil rights to the women's movement, from the Great Society to the Reagan Revolution. In the end, all were questions of economic democracy.

Residues of the Labor Question

The Progressive Era's expansion of the labor question from a struggle over the means of production to a quest for economic democracy has been roundly criticized for at least fifty years. Selig Perlman, one of the originators of labor history, claimed that the American Federation of Labor (and by extension other proponents of economic democracy) substituted "a communism of opportunity" for a more rigorous and radical "communism of productive property," and the basic outline of this argument has not disappeared in the historiography or in popular culture.[1] Perlman understood the relations to the means of production as the most central, most crucial and most concrete relations in society. To abandon or expand the struggle over production, then, was to relinquish any notable quest for meaning or "real" change in social relations. Such an abandonment is one of the reasons—perhaps the main reason—why so many historians have been profoundly disappointed in the Progressive Era's answers to the labor question, answers that are seen as moving away from class analysis or class-based politics and toward a broader, most innocuous liberal politics that evades or elides the question of ownership of the means of production. Instead, elite and middle-class Progressive reformers allowed a politics of appeasement and reconciliation to overtake a producerist commitment to class-based reform.[2]

Such critiques assume that class was and remains determined by relations to the means of production. Reforms, whether political or social, that do not directly confront the question of ownership and control of the means of production cannot be seen as truly committed to radical systemic change and are equally uncommitted to the American democratic experiment. The substitution of economic democracy, which turns to daily life, including consumption, as the site of democratic engagement, for producerism must thus be read as the substitution of "trivial [acts] in the most basic sense" for actions of "larger social meaning."[3] In the Gilded Age and Progressive Era, this move away from class-based politics meant the cruel curtailment of any possibility for social revolution and hence historiography's emphasis on the defeats or declines of organizations and individuals such as the Industrial Workers of the World or the Knights of Labor that sought to wrest control of the means of production.[4] In contemporary America, the desertion of producerism has made any sustained engagement with or even recognition of the material bases of class difficult, even for those furthest removed from controlling the means of production. As a result, Thomas Frank claims in his study of conservative Kansas voters, Americans act and vote against their class interests, deluded into believing that they share ideological concerns with owners, capitalists, and other members of the economic elite.[5] The Progressive Era rejection of producerism seems to have had dire consequences for modern America: less democratic commitment, limited possibilities for social change, a more passive citizenry.

Such a tragic narrative makes for fairly depressing reading, especially in light of the grim economic news that has filled American newspapers since 2000. Real wages have fallen steadily even as productivity climbed, and wages are likely to continue their downward slide. The value of benefits, which had long offset the stagnating or falling real wage rate, began to decline as well, making the drop in wages more sharply felt.[6] Even the majority of Americans who do not fall below the poverty line have diminishing opportunities to participate in the American Dream of prosperity, the good life, and comfort. Ever more Americans work more than one job, and by 2001, Americans could claim the dubious honor of working more hours per week than citizens of any other industrialized nation.[7] Listening to Americans speak poignantly about their aspirations, their frustrations, and their hardships, the central components of the labor question—questions about the nature of citizenship and the meaning of democracy—seem to be ongoing concerns. Yet if so many early-twentieth-century Americans turned their backs on Perlman's "communism of productive property" in favor of a less rigorous "communism of opportunity," is there much point in continuing to hope for change? Are the debates regarding the labor question of any value today?

I think the proponents of economic democracy would say yes, largely by agreeing with Perlman's assessment of their ideas. Many Americans from a wide range of social and economic backgrounds indeed came to imagine that democratic life and social democratic reform might not be based on the productive world of work.[8] They did not understand social relations as reducible to relationship to the means of production, and their struggles for a better democratic life consequently did not center on efforts to recapture control or ownership of production. Instead, they tried to imagine a new kind of democracy that focused on economic participation in daily life. Such conceptions of democracy did not exclude the workplace as a site of democratic struggle.[9] As the struggles over industrial democracy during the Progressive Era and World War I showed, the workplace remained central to efforts to secure everything from higher wages to nationalization of factories to a vaguely defined "more democratic world."[10] But as workers celebrating Labor Day in the early twentieth century insisted, private recreation had its political aspects as well; picnics one day did not exclude strikes the next.[11] This phenomenon amounted to nothing less than a politicization of daily, private life. Economic citizenship and economic democracy, as both Samuel Gompers and Walter Weyl noted, were found as much in the home and on the street as in the workplace. When Gompers, for example, demanded "more of the good things that go to make up life" and that "go to make up a manhood that shall be free and independent," he included "better homes" and "better surrounding" with demands for higher wages and shorter hours. This idea formed no small part of Jane Addams's "democracy in social terms."[12]

Addams's socialized democracy, Weyl's new democracy, and Gompers's more were not denials of class but rather articulations of social distinction that were not reducible to relations to the means of production. These reformers were quite consciously attempting to negotiate the transition from one social order to another, from what we now routinely call proprietary competitive capitalism to corporate capitalism. And in so doing, they tried to make sense of seismic as well as miniscule shifts. Their arguments for economic democracy therefore recognized the social implications of the early stages the process of disaccumulation. If, as Martin J. Sklar argues, disaccumulation facilitated the "ongoing net release of labor-power, measured in aggregate social labor time, from goods production" so that it was no longer "the necessary focus and direct determinant of social organization for the mass of the people," then it made sense that relations to the means of production were no longer the only "direct determinant of social organization."[13] In the early years of the twentieth century, economic thinkers such as George Gunton and Weyl noted, too, the effects of rapidly rising real wages for unskilled industrial laborers, who could now claim a growing social role outside of work as consumers.[14] These thinkers saw as well the mundane but equally striking changes in daily life: the growing popularity of spectator sports such as baseball, the stunning successes of amusement parks and holiday resorts, the proliferation of nickelodeons, and the eager consumption of everything from hats to furniture. Like Henry Steele Commager forty years or so later, they understood that all of these phenomena, from changes in industrial organization to Coney Island's Cannon Coaster, signaled the end of one age and the beginning of another. Political scientist Michael Sandel is right to argue that the "shift from producer-based reform to consumer-based reform" was a move away from a republican tradition centered on productive labor. But where Progressive social theorists would understand this move as a response to historical change, Sandel sees it as an abandonment of a more rigorous democratic life. Work had mattered in the republican tradition because "the world of work was seen as the arena in which, for better or worse, the character of citizens was formed." Consumer politics such as Weyl's, Sandel argues, gave up on the idea of a virtuous citizenry in favor of individual satisfaction and "left the political economy of citizenship behind." Sandel specifically emphasizes the loss of republican virtue and the decline of an engaged citizenry, but his argument is closely related to those that link a decline in democratic life to the shift from character to personality or from the relations of production to those of consumption.[15]

Weyl would strenuously disagree with Sandel's assertions on specifically historical grounds. The arguments that stress material relations of production over the less concrete relations of consumption are, Weyl would say, part of the "old democracy" in which individual ownership of property formed the basis for legal and political rights. By the early twentieth century, Weyl argued, new factors—wage work, incorporation, mass distribution, urbanization—meant that conditions had changed: "To-day, the chief restrictions upon liberty are economic, not legal, and the chief prerogatives desired are economic, not political." If democracy were to continue in the United States, Americans would have to "revis[e] all [their] social conceptions" and turn from the "democracy of Jefferson and Jackson" to the "economic level of democratic striving." "The increasing social wealth," he insisted, "shifts the basis of social morality . . . to a new ethics which demands a full life of all members of society."[16] Historians of twentieth-century consumers and consumer culture have generally concurred with Weyl's identification of new sites of social and political struggle. As they have shown, consumers have often been extremely politically engaged and carefully attuned to distinctions in power, in no small part because of the transformation that Weyl described: social and political struggles in the twentieth century occurred outside as well as within the workplace.[17] Workers' demands for secure jobs and decent, safe workplaces also included demands for a higher standard of living for themselves and their families. During the 1930s, institutional economists and leaders of organized labor understood economic reforms as the primary avenue for creating meaningful social and political change, and the Social Security Act attempted to codify this belief. Franklin Roosevelt's Second Bill of Rights proclaimed that all citizens should have the right to jobs with sufficient incomes, reasonable profits, safe homes, medical care, economic security, and education. In the 1960s, Martin Luther King Jr.'s Poor People's Campaign linked economic and racial justice in a democratic vision.[18] All of these efforts have shared the belief that daily life—the small acts of buying, selling, enjoyment, work, recreation, amusement—is central to the quality of democratic life.

Yet a return to the labor question of the nineteenth century shows that economic citizenship and economic democracy emerged only in tension with producerism; consequently, it is hardly surprising that producerism, in a multitude of guises, retains considerable power in American culture. We might, for example, look at as seemingly trivial example as the 1990 movie *Pretty Woman,* a light romantic comedy in which a good-hearted prostitute saves the soul of an embittered, lonely expert in hostile takeovers. Except that Edward Lewis's soul is saved not precisely by love but by Vivian Ward's observation: "And you don't make anything and you don't build anything." She is absolutely right. Edward buys companies, takes them apart, and sells the parts for more than he paid for the whole. At the beginning of the movie, he is preparing to disembowel a shipbuilding company, still owned by the founding family, and he initially is completely unmoved when David Morse tells him, with some pride, "Men like my grandfather made this country." But Vivian's question gives him pause. What, he wonders, does he really *do?* In the end, he decides not to destroy the family shipyard but to go into business with David and his grandson, a move that finally makes Edward happy. He becomes a better man because he is now a producer, an honorable citizen. At the end, the grandfather-shipbuilder gives Lewis his paternal and patriarchal blessing: "I'm proud of you."

Nineteenth-century Americans would, I suspect, have a hard time accepting Edward Lewis, speculator, as the epitome of the virtuous producer. He is at best a spectral version of the older ideal. But the idea of "making something," of producing, of earning the fruits of one's labor, still matters in American social thought, as we can see in the word *earn.* On the one hand, *earn* means "to receive payment for labor rendered," and in this sense, the word is unrelated to individual moral qualities. On the other hand, it also means "to deserve or to merit," and it is a vestige of older producerist understandings of work. Arguments about welfare, health care, and other entitlements almost always contain a suspicion and a fear that someone undeserving will benefit. Ronald Reagan's fictitious "Welfare Queen" who fleeced the American government (and thus public) was shocking because she took without earning. When faced with a union drive for more comprehensive health insurance, people ask "'Why should those people in those unions get that good health care?' instead of saying, 'Why don't I get it?'" Or the Labor Department asks why coal miners deserve better health coverage than other Americans, especially the 35 million who lack health insurance, rather than demanding better coverage for everyone.[19]

At the same time, the terms of these debates have been and continue to be set by the premises of economic citizenship and economic democracy. The question is not "Is economic participation part of democratic life?" but "How much economic participation should there be in a democracy and under what circumstances?" In a sense—at least in Jane Addams's sense—the questions matter most in the end. They are the process by which Americans make their democracy. "We slowly learn," she wrote in *Democracy and Social Ethics,* "that life consists of processes as well as results. . . . We are thus brought to a conception of Democracy not merely as a sentiment which desires the well-being of all men, nor yet as a creed which believes in the essential dignity and equality of all men, but as that which affords a rule of living." She saw democracy not as an article of faith, a defined and solid belief, but as "that which affords a rule of living"—an undefined and unfixed idea, fluid, changeable, and flexible, that makes the ongoing quest for a better democracy a hope for the future.[20]

Notes

Introduction. The Labor Question in the Late Nineteenth Century

1. J. L. Spalding, "Are We in Danger of Revolution?" *Forum*, July 1886, 406.

2. John Swinton, *A Momentous Question: The Respective Attitudes of Labor and Capital* (Philadelphia: Keller, 1895), 36. Swinton's conspicuous failure to mention the enslavement of African Americans only heightened the rosiness of his nostalgia for a bucolic past, as did his willingness to overlook tensions within the northern working class.

3. T. H. Marshall, *Citizenship and Social Class, and Other Essays* (Cambridge: Cambridge University Press, 1950); William E. Forbath, "Caste, Class, and Equal Citizenship," in *Moral Problems in American Life: New Perspectives on Cultural History*, ed. Karen Halttunen and Lewis Perry (Ithaca: Cornell University Press, 1998), 167–200, esp. 169; William E. Forbath, "The New Deal Constitution in Exile," *Duke Law Journal* 51 (October 2001): 165–222; William J. Novak, "The Legal Transformation of Citizenship in Nineteenth-Century America," in *The Democratic Experiment*, ed. Meg Jacobs, William Novak, and Julian E. Zelizer (Princeton: Princeton University Press, 2003), 85–119. On more limited twentieth-century understandings of economic citizenship, see Alice Kessler-Harris, *In Pursuit of Equity: Women, Men, and the Quest for Economic Citizenship in Twentieth Century America* (New York: Oxford University Press, 2001).

4. Jane Addams, *Democracy and Social Ethics* (1902; New York: Macmillan, 1907), 269.

5. On the relevance of debates about the Progressive Era to contemporary U.S. society as well as on the desirability of "re-democratizing" the Progressive Era, see Robert D. Johnston's well-timed challenge to historians in "Re-Democratizing the Progressive Era: The Politics of Progressive Era Historiography," *Journal of the Gilded*

Age and Progressive Era 1 (January 2002): 68–92. In a more extensive review of the historiography than appears here, Johnston urges historians to turn away from the tragic narrative of democratic decline in the period and to recognize the "period's vigorous democratic potential" even as they acknowledge its "many kinds of oppressions" (69). For Johnston, that potential is most clearly found in the Populist tradition of a politically engaged middle class. Taking up Johnston's challenge, I, too, see democratic possibilities rather than suppression of democracy in the period, but I examine a quite different kind of democratic promise in the era—that is, a specifically social democratic vision emerging from the conditions of corporate industrial life.

6. Gabriel Kolko, *The Triumph of Conservatism: A Re-Interpretation of American History, 1900–1916* (Glencoe, Ill.: Free Press, 1963); James Weinstein, *The Corporate Ideal in the Liberal State, 1900–1918* (Boston: Beacon, 1968), xi. See also Richard Wiebe, *The Search for Order, 1877–1920* (New York: Hill and Wang, 1967). One could also trace this extreme skepticism of reformers back to the writings of Richard Hofstadter, who, particularly in *The Age of Reform* (New York: Knopf, 1955), was quite dubious of reformers' motivations. But unlike these historians, Hofstadter situated himself and his critique within precisely the reform tradition he was assessing. For a critique of this line of argument, see James Livingston, *Origins of the Federal Reserve System: Money, Class, and Corporate Capitalism* (Ithaca: Cornell University Press, 1986), 19–21.

7. Nancy Cohen, *The Reconstruction of American Liberalism, 1865–1914* (Chapel Hill: University of North Carolina Press, 2002). See also Jeffrey Sklansky, *The Soul's Economy: Market Society and Selfhood in American Thought, 1820–1920* (Chapel Hill: University of North Carolina Press, 2002); Shelton Stromquist, *Reinventing "The People": The Progressive Movement, the Class Problem, and the Origins of Modern Liberalism* (Urbana: University of Illinois Press, 2006).

8. Stephen Skowronek, *Building a New American State: The Expansion of National Administrative Capacities, 1877–1920* (Cambridge: Cambridge University Press, 1982); Robert Westbrook, "Politics as Consumption: Managing the Modern American Election," in *Culture of Consumption: Critical Essays in American History, 1880–1980*, ed. Richard Wrightman Fox and T. J. Jackson Lears (New York: Pantheon, 1983), 143–74; Michael McGerr, *The Decline of Popular Politics: The North, 1865–1928* (New York: Oxford University Press, 1986), vii, 214; Alexander Keyssar, *The Right to Vote: The Contested History of Democracy in the United States* (New York: Basic Books, 2000); Brian Balogh, "'Mirrors of Desires': Interest Groups, Elections, and the Targeted Style in Twentieth-Century America," in *The Democratic Experiment*, ed. Jacobs, Novak, and Zelizer, 222–49; Alexander Saxton, *Rise and Fall of the White Republic: Class, Politics, and Mass Culture in Nineteenth Century America* (New York: Verso, 1990); Mae M. Ngai, *Impossible Subjects: Illegal Aliens and the Making of Modern America* (Princeton: Princeton University Press, 2004); Gary Gerstle, *American Crucible: Race and Nation in the Twentieth Century* (Princeton: Princeton University Press,

2001); W. Fitzhugh Brundage, *Lynching in the South: Georgia and Virginia, 1880–1930* (Urbana: University of Illinois Press, 1993).

9. Christopher Lasch, *The True and Only Heaven: Progress and Its Critics* (New York: Norton, 1992), 334.

10. See, for example, Stuart Ewan, *Captains of Consciousness: The Emergence of Mass Advertising and Mass Consumption in the 1920s* (New York: McGraw-Hill, 1977); William Leach, *Land of Desire: Merchants, Power, and the Rise of a New American Culture* (New York: Vintage, 1993); Daniel Horowitz, *The Morality of Spending: Attitudes toward Consumer Society in America, 1875–1940* (Baltimore: Johns Hopkins University Press, 1985); Simon Bronner, ed., *Consuming Visions: Accumulation and Display of Goods in America, 1880–1920* (New York: Norton, 1989); T. J. Jackson Lears, *Fables of Abundance: A Cultural History of Advertising in America* (New York: Basic Books, 1991); Michael J. Sandel, *Democracy's Discontent: America in Search of a Public Philosophy* (Cambridge: Belknap Press of Harvard University Press, 1996); David Steigerwald, "All Hail the Republic of Choice: Consumer History as Contemporary Thought," *Journal of American History* 93 (September 2006): 385–403. A clear articulation of this connection can be found in Nancy Cohen, *Reconstruction of American Liberalism.* In the Gilded Age, Cohen argues, self-satisfaction "superseded self-rule in the purposes of life, and political participation was no longer a necessity or a good in and of itself. The promise of the fulfillment of all imaginable desires circumvented a debate about the nature of self-government in the new political economy" (225).

11. Lasch, *True and Only Heaven,* 224–25.

12. Sandel, *Democracy's Discontent,* 224–25.

13. See, for example, Nancy Cohen's argument that "new liberals assured [white working men] that the democratic promise would be fulfilled in the new marketplace of abundance" and "citizenship was reconceived as an attribute of the consuming individual, not the producer" (*Reconstruction of American Liberalism,* 225).

14. Scott Sandage, *Born Losers: A History of Failure in America* (Cambridge: Harvard University Press, 2005), 43, 45, 130; Warren Susman, *Culture as History: The Transformation of American Society in the Twentieth Century* (New York: Pantheon, 1984), 271–86. Susman's chapter on character and personality solidified this divide for cultural historians, but other U.S. historians have made use of a similar division. Gary Gerstle, for example, has argued that the New Deal abandoned an earlier vision of moral reform for purely economic reforms and that such a move severely limited the scope and promise of New Deal programs ("The Protean Character of American Liberalism," *American Historical Review* 99 [October 1994]: 1043–73).

15. Sklansky, *Soul's Economy,* 230; Robert E. Weir, *Beyond Labor's Veil: The Culture of the Knights of Labor* (University Park: Pennsylvania State University Press, 1996), 317–18.

16. Michael Kazin, *The Populist Persuasion: An American History,* rev. ed. (Ithaca: Cornell University Press, 1998), 35.

17. "The Social Economist," *Social Economist* 1 (March 1891): 1–2. Gunton's view that economic and social reform were inseparable was indeed widely shared, as the popularity of economic works shows. According to Henry George Jr., his father's *Progress and Poverty* (1879) sold more than two million copies in twenty-five years and was serialized heavily, giving only the Bible a greater readership in nineteenth-century America. The *Social Economist* (later renamed *Gunton's Magazine*) had a national subscription base of twenty thousand. (For comparison, *Harper's Weekly,* one of the most popular and influential newsweeklies, sold between one hundred thousand and three hundred thousand subscriptions annually between 1857 and 1912.) Simon Nelson Patten's publisher produced eight editions of *The New Basis of Civilization* (1912) in eleven years. See Henry George, *Progress and Poverty: An Inquiry in the Cause of Industrial Depressions and of Increase of Want with Increase of Wealth* (1897; New York: Schalkenbach, 1979), xxiv; Sklansky, *Soul's Economy,* 114; Jack Blicksilver, "George Gunton: Pioneer Spokesman for a Labor–Big Business Entente," *Business History Review* 31 (Spring 1957): 2–6; James Livingston, *Pragmatism and the Political Economy of Cultural Revolution, 1850–1940* (Chapel Hill: University of North Carolina Press, 1994), 68.

18. Jane Addams, "A New Impulse to an Old Gospel," *Forum,* November 1892, 346.

19. Theda Skocpol, *Protecting Soldiers and Mothers: The Political Origins of Social Policy in the United States* (Cambridge: Belknap Press of Harvard University Press, 1993); Elisabeth Clemens, *The People's Lobby: Organizational Innovation and the Rise of Interest Group Politics in the United States, 1870–1925* (Chicago: University of Chicago Press, 1997); Robert D. Johnston, *The Radical Middle Class: Populist Democracy and the Question of Capitalism in Progressive Era Portland, Oregon* (Princeton: Princeton University Press, 2003).

20. Richard Schneirov, *Labor and Urban Politics: Class Conflict and the Origins of Modern Liberalism in Chicago, 1864–1892* (Urbana: University of Illinois Press, 1998). For a very different argument that also highlights the ways Americans—in this case, farmers—used the existing political system to push for political, economic, and social reform, see also Elizabeth Sanders, *Roots of Reform: Farmers, Workers, and the American State, 1877–1917* (Chicago: University of Chicago Press, 1999).

21. Livingston, *Pragmatism and the Political Economy;* James Livingston, *Pragmatism, Feminism, and Democracy: Rethinking the Politics of American History* (New York: Routledge, 2001).

22. Lawrence B. Glickman, *A Living Wage: American Workers and the Making of Consumer Society* (Ithaca: Cornell University Press, 1997).

23. Andrew R. Heinze, *Adapting to Abundance: Jewish Immigrants, Mass Consumption, and the Search for American Identity* (New York: Columbia University Press, 1990); Charles McGovern, "Consumption and Citizenship in the United States, 1900–1940," in *Getting and Spending: European and American Consumer Societies in the Twentieth Century,* ed. Susan Strasser, Charles McGovern, and Matthias Judt

(Cambridge: Cambridge University Press, 1998), 37–58; Kathy Peiss, *Hope in a Jar: The Making of America's Beauty Culture* (New York: Metropolitan, 1998); Jennifer Scanlon, *Inarticulate Longings: The* Ladies' Home Journal, *Gender, and the Promises of Consumer Culture* (New York: Routledge, 1995); Nan Enstad, *Ladies of Leisure, Girls of Adventure: Working Women, Popular Culture, and Labor Politics at the Turn of the Twentieth Century* (New York: Columbia University Press, 1999); Elizabeth H. Pleck, *Celebrating the Family: Ethnicity, Consumer Culture, and Family Rituals* (Cambridge: Harvard University Press, 2000); Gary Cross, *An All-Consuming Century: Why Commercialism Won in Modern America* (New York: Columbia University Press, 2000); Leora Auslander, "Citizenship, Law, State Formation, and Everyday Aesthetics in Modern France and Germany, 1920–1940," in *The Politics of Consumption: Material Culture and Citizenship in Europe and America*, ed. Martin Daunton and Matthew Hilton (New York: Berg, 2001), 109–28.

24. Lizabeth Cohen, *A Consumer's Republic: The Politics of Mass Consumption in Postwar America* (New York: Knopf, 2003); Meg Jacobs, *Pocketbook Politics: Economic Citizenship in Twentieth-Century America* (Princeton: Princeton University Press, 2004). See also Kathleen Donohue, *Freedom from Want: American Liberalism and the Idea of the Consumer* (Baltimore: Johns Hopkins University Press, 2003). On the political implications of consumption, see Kathryn Kish Sklar, "The Consumers' White Label Campaign of the National Consumers' League, 1898–1918," in *Getting and Spending*, ed. Strasser, McGovern, and Judt, 17–36; Dana Frank, *Buy American: The Untold Story of Economic Nationalism* (Boston: Beacon, 1999); Ted Ownby, *American Dreams in Mississippi: Consumers, Poverty, and Culture, 1830–1998* (Chapel Hill: University of North Carolina Press, 1999); Lawrence B. Glickman, "The Strike in the Temple of Consumption: Consumer Activism and Twentieth-Century American Political Culture," *Journal of American History* 88 (June 2001): 99–128; Liette Gidlow, *The Big Vote: Gender, Consumer Culture, and the Politics of Exclusion, 1890s-1920s* (Baltimore: Johns Hopkins University Press, 2004).

25. Swinton, *Momentous Question;* George McNeill, ed., *The Labor Movement: The Problem of Today* (1887; New York: Kelley, 1971); S. M. Jelley, *The Voice of Labor: Plain Talk by Men of Intellect on Labor's Rights, Wrongs, Remedies, and Prospects* (New York: Franklin, 1888).

26. "Letters to the Editor," *New York Times,* September 23, 2008; posting to "The Caucus," "Congress Faces Major Issues in Final Week," *New York Times,* September 22, 2008.

One. The Cant of Economy

1. This transition, Richard Schneirov tells us, began in the early 1870s, and the depression itself was a sign of the changes in the dominant mode of production. The crash of 1873 ushered the Gilded Age, "a crisis period of capital accumulation characterized by 'overproduction,' a reconstruction of the party-electoral system directly attributable to that crisis, and the rise of class antagonisms which erupted

intermittently into broad social upheavals" ("Thoughts on Periodizing the Gilded Age: Capital Accumulation, Society, and Politics, 1873–1898," *Journal of Gilded Age and Progressive Era* 5 [July 2006], http://www.historycooperative.org.proxy.queensu .ca/journals/jga/5.3/schneirov.html [July 7, 2008]). Focusing on the "long Gilded Age," as Schneirov does, allows us to understand the period from 1873 to the early twentieth century as part of the extended transition from proprietary to corporate capitalism. We can thus read the depression itself, business failures, demands for greater government action (often through tariff bills but also through immigration control, industrial and railroad regulation, land grants, and military action in the West), and the labor movements of the late nineteenth century as both signs of the changing social order and efforts to define and negotiate those changes. This longer view of the transition emphasizes the continuity of the questions that animated debates regarding the labor question (as well as the women's movement, African American rights, populism, Progressive reform, democratic statism, and corporate liberalism). See also Rebecca Edwards, *New Spirits: Americans in the Gilded Age* (New York: Oxford University Press, 2006). Edwards also views the period as a whole but eschews the term *Gilded Age*.

2. U.S. Congress, House of Representatives, *Investigation by a Select Committee of the House of Representatives Relative to the Causes of the General Depression in Labor and Business, etc.*, 45th Cong., House of Representatives, Misc. Doc. 29 (Washington, D.C.: U.S. Government Printing Office, 1879), 8, 51, 71, 74, 108, 149.

3. By proprietary competitive capitalism, I follow Martin J. Sklar's definition: "capitalist property and market relations in which the dominant type of enterprise was headed by an owner-manager (or owner-managers), or a direct agent thereof, and in which such enterprise was a price-taker rather than a price-maker, price being determined by the conditions of supply and demand beyond the control of the enterprise short of anticompetitive inter-firm collusion" (*The Corporate Reconstruction of American Capitalism: The Market, the Law, and Politics* [Cambridge: Cambridge University Press, 1988], 4 n. 1).

4. Schneirov, "Periodizing the Gilded Age."

5. Ronald Schultz, "The Small-Producer Tradition and the Moral Origins of Artisan Radicalism in Philadelphia 1720–1810," *Past and Present* 127 (May 1990): 84–116.

6. Daniel Rodgers, *The Work Ethic in Industrial America, 1850–1920* (Chicago: University of Chicago Press, 1974), 11–14; Schultz, "Small-Producer Tradition," 87–89.

7. Ann Fabian, *Card Sharps and Bucket Shops: Gambling in Nineteenth-Century America*, 2nd ed. (New York: Routledge, 1999), 53, 66, 168.

8. David Montgomery, *Beyond Equality: Labor and the Radical Republicans, 1862–1872* (Urbana: University of Illinois Press, 1967), 143, 44, 233. As Eric Foner has shown, free labor itself had two main meanings (and many subtle permutations): it could refer to a wage worker entering voluntarily into labor arrangements or to an economically independent proprietary producer. Both originally emerged in "ideological tension" with unfree labor, whether slaves, indentured servants, impressed sailors, or

NOTES TO CHAPTER 1 · 159

apprentices, but by the nineteenth century, free labor was almost always contrasted with slave labor. Industrial producerism rejected the version of free labor that advanced a strict and narrow equation of freedom with the ability to sell one's labor in the marketplace, made socially and legally visible through a contract (Eric Foner, "Free Labor and Nineteenth-Century Political Ideology," in *The Market Revolution in America: Social, Political, and Religious Expressions, 1800–1880*, ed. Melvyn Stokes and Stephen Conway [Charlottesville: University of Virginia Press, 1996], 100).

9. Richard Schneirov, *Labor and Urban Politics: Class Conflict and the Origins of Modern Liberalism in Chicago, 1864–1897* (Urbana: University of Illinois Press, 1998), 40.

10. Quoted in Foner, "Free Labor," 111. "The aspirations of free labor were" as Foner earlier explains, "thus thoroughly middle class, for the successful laborer was one who achieved self-employment, and owned his own capital—a business, farm or shop" (*Free Soil, Free Labor, Free Men: The Ideology of the Republican Party before the Civil War*, 2nd ed. [New York: Oxford University Press, 1995], 15).

11. On vernacular socialism, see Rodgers, *Work Ethic*, 117–19. As Rodgers points out, Gronlund's insistent juxtaposition of virtuous and productive workers "fleeced" by lazy, nonproductive capitalists shared as much with the tale of *Ragged Dick,* which promised social mobility and individual virtue through hard work, as it did with the rhetoric of proletarian revolution.

12. William E. Forbath, "The Ambiguities of Free Labor: Labor and the Law in the Gilded Age," *Wisconsin Law Review* 4 (July–August 1985): 812. As Kim Voss explains, the Knights saw cooperatives "as a way to 'republicanize' industry" and give workers the power to decide "what to produce and how to produce it" without necessarily returning to the "old days of independent proprietorship" (*Making of American Exceptionalism: The Knights of Labor and Class Formation in the Nineteenth Century* [Ithaca: Cornell University Press, 1993], 84, 82).

13. Forbath, "Ambiguities," 816.

14. Sean Dennis Cashman, *America in the Gilded Age: From the Death of Lincoln to the Rise of Theodore Roosevelt*, 3rd ed. (New York: New York University Press, 1993), 8, 11, 29; Richard Franklin Bensel, *The Political Economy of American Industrialization, 1877–1900* (New York: Cambridge University Press, 2000), 20.

15. James Livingston, "The Social Analysis of Economic History and Theory: Conjectures on Late Nineteenth-Century American Development," *American Historical Review* 92 (February 1987): 69–95; Alfred Chandler, *The Visible Hand: The Managerial Revolution in American Business* (Cambridge: Harvard University Press, 1977), 282.

16. For example, the rate of growth per year per worker grew at a rate of 1.00 percent for the overlapping decade of 1878/82–1888/92, .58 percent for 1883/87–1893/97, 1.50 percent for 1888/92–1898/1902, 2.36 percent for 1893/97–1903/7, and 1.01 percent for 1903/7–1913/17 (Livingston, "Social Analysis," table 2, 74; Simon Kuznets, *Economic Growth and Structure: Selected Essays* [New York: Norton, 1965], 315; National Bureau

of Economic Research, "Business Cycle Expansion and Contraction," http://www
.nber.org/cycles.html [May 1, 2010]).

17. Allan Nevins, *The Emergence of Modern America, 1865–1878* (New York: Macmillan, 1927), 291–92.

18. Rendigs Fels, "American Business Cycles, 1865–79," *American Economic Review*
41 (June 1951): 338–40. The clearinghouse was an association of New York banks
that adjudicated interbank disputes and prevented banks from ruining each other
by summarily demanding repayment of loans (Harry E. Miller, "Earlier Theories of
Crises and Cycles in the United States," *Quarterly Journal of Economics* 38 [February
1924]: 326–28; Richard H. Timberlake, "The Central Baking Role of Clearinghouse
Associations," *Journal of Money, Credit, and Banking* 16 [February 1984]: 3–5).

19. "Another Panic," *New York Times*, September 19, 1873. See also "Effect of Jay
Cooke & Co.'s Failure in Chicago," *New York Times*, September 19, 1873. For equally
optimistic views of the brevity of the downturn, see, for example, "A Hopeful Feature
. . . ," *Amherst (New Hampshire) Farmers' Cabinet*, November 11, 1873, which saw "signs
of the silver lining" "already." See also "Fall Trade," *Philadelphia Inquirer*, September
7, 1874; "The Commercial Outlook in New England," *Keene New Hampshire Sentinel*,
October 20, 1873.

20. "The News in Other Cities," *New York Times*, September 19, 1873.

21. Fels, "American Business Cycles," 344.

22. "Winter and the Working Classes," *New York Times*, November 11, 1873.

23. Samuel Rezneck, "Distress, Relief, and Discontent in the United States during the Depression of 1873–1877," *Journal of Political Economy* 58 (December 1950):
495–96; Fels, "American Business Cycles," 326; Samuel Rezneck "Unemployment,
Unrest, and Relief in the United States during the Depression of 1893–1897," *Journal
of Political Economy* 61 (August 1953): 324–45.

24. European investors turned instead to U.S. government bonds, which were seen
as a more secure investment (Fels, "American Business Cycles," 337). For contemporary assessments, see "The Sorrow of Capitalists," *Nation*, March 25, 1875, 201–2;
"The Law of Panics," *Nation*, October 25, 1877, 251–52.

25. Rezneck, "Distress, Relief, and Discontent," 496–97.

26. See, for example, "Strikes," *Boise Idaho Tri-Weekly Statesman*, January 8, 1874.

27. Rezneck, "Distress, Relief, and Discontent," 498; "Destitution in Rhode Island,"
Middletown (Connecticut) Daily Constitution, January 15, 1874; Alexander Keyssar,
Out of Work: The First Century of Unemployment in Massachusetts (New York: Cam-
bridge University Press, 1986), 1–5, 50–52.

28. U.S. Congress, Senate, Committee on Finance, *Wholesale Prices, Wages, and
Transportation*, Report 1349, "The Aldrich Report," 52nd Cong., 2nd sess., March 3,
1893; Nevins, *Emergence*, 302; "Prices," *Philadelphia Inquirer*, March 18, 1874.

29. Drew R. McCoy, *The Elusive Republic: Political Economy in Jeffersonian America*
(Chapel Hill: University of North Carolina Press, 1980), 237. See also James L. Huston, "The American Revolutionaries, the Political Economy of Aristocracy, and the

American Concept of the Distribution of Wealth, 1765–1900," *American Historical Review* 98 (October 1993): 1079–1105.

30. "The Week," *Nation*, September 25, 1873, 201; "The Wall-Street Crash," *Nation*, September 25, 1873, 204.

31. *Congressional Record,* 45th Cong., 1st sess., November 1, 1877, 216. On the sudden "revulsion from excess" in 1873–77, see Charles P. Kindleberger, *Manias, Panics, and Crashes: A History of Financial Crises,* 4th ed. (New York: Wiley, 2004), 2, 17.

32. *Congressional Record,* January 17, 1873, 43rd Cong., 1st sess. (Washington, D.C.: U.S. Government Printing Office, 1874), 2:735.

33. Testimony of William Graham Sumner, August 22, 1878, in U.S. Congress, House of Representatives, "Investigation," 193–94.

34. "Financial Problems; Address of Prof. Bonamy Price," *New York Times,* October 2, 1874.

35. See, for example, "The Labor Committee," *Cincinnati Daily Gazette,* August 7, 1878, which reported on a Danbury man insisting that government loans on real estate would end the depression; "Little Locals," *Wilkes-Barre (Pennsylvania) Leader,* August 15, 1878, which reported on the testimony of men from the Wyoming Valley.

36. "New York Reformers," *Philadelphia Inquirer,* August 6, 1878; "Our New York Letter," *Philadelphia Inquirer,* August 7, 1878; "Where Wise Men Pause: The Great Problem of the Time Solved Instantly," *New York Times,* August 7, 1878; "The Great Social Problem; False Views and Unsound Doctrines," *New York Times,* August 6, 1878; "Three Wise Boston Men; A Printer, an Editor, and a Stonecutter," *New York Times,* August 22, 1878. The *Times* coverage continued in a similar vein until Sumner took the stand on August 23, 1878.

37. Testimony of William Wagner, August 6, 1878, testimony of William Hanson, August 6, 1878, testimony of A. Mervin, August 6, 1878, all in U.S. Congress, House of Representatives, "Investigation," 143, 137–38, 146.

38. Testimony of Alexander Robb, August 5, 1878, in ibid., 86.

39. "Where Wise Men Fear to Tread," *New York Times,* August 7, 1878.

40. Testimony of E. Herbert Graham, August 5, 1878, in U.S. Congress, House of Representatives, "Investigation," 89–93.

41. Testimony of George McNeill, August 6, 1878, testimony of William Wittick, August 6, 1878, testimony of Valentine Becker, August 5, 1878, all in ibid., 115–24, 108–10, 143.

42. Not all producers' cooperatives did so, of course, but for one particularly striking example, see Steve Leikin's discussion of the coopers' cooperative in Minneapolis (*Practical Utopians: American Workers and the Cooperative Movement in the Gilded Age* [Detroit: Wayne State University Press, 2005]).

43. "Topics of the Times," *Scribner's Monthly,* October 1877, 854–55; "Erroneous Social Economy," *Manufacturer and Builder* 5 (December 1873): 282; "Study of a New England Factory Town," *Atlantic Monthly,* June 1879, 701–2.

44. "Letters to the Editor; The Cant of Economy," *New York Times,* May 20, 1876.

45. When Rothschild testified before the congressional committee that the unemployed and homeless had brought their fate on themselves, Hewitt was apparently so startled that he interrupted to ask, "Their own improvidence?" "Yes, sir," Rothschild replied. He went on to explain that "when wages were large, they were careless; they followed all sorts of luxuries" (testimony of Henry Rothschild, August 6, 1878, in U.S. Congress, House of Representatives, "Investigation," 133–34).

46. "Letters to the Editor; Economy Yet a Virtue," *New York Times,* May 27, 1876.

47. "Displacements of Labor," *New York Times,* September 25, 1881.

48. Karen Halttunen, *Confidence Men and Painted Women: A Study of Middle-Class Culture in America, 1830–1870* (New Haven: Yale University Press, 1982), 206–7.

49. George Basil Dixwell, "Review of Bastiat's Sophism of Protection," *Bulletin of the National Association of Wool Manufacturers* 9 (1881): 303–4, in Joseph Dorfman, *The Economic Mind in American Civilization,* vol. 3, *1865–1918* (New York: Viking, 1949), 133–34; David A. Wells, "How Shall the Nation Regain Prosperity?" *North American Review* 125 (July 1877): 129.

50. "Topics of the Times," 854.

51. Carroll Davidson Wright, "Industrial Necessities," *Forum* 2 (March 1886): 310, 311. See also "The Problems of Labor; First Report of Commissioner Wright," *New York Times,* March 22, 1886. For more on the emergence of modern labor theory in the 1880s, see Clarence Wunderlin Jr., *Visions of a New Industrial Order: Social Science and Labor Theory in America's Progressive Era* (New York: Columbia University Press, 1992), 1–26.

52. The ad continued, "If mills don't produce how can the hands get pay? . . . Better sell at prices that will enable mills to employ hands and machinery and so prevent stagnation. . . . When WE'RE overstocked we CUT prices and soon are in the market to buy again" (advertisement for Hearn's, *New York Times,* December 7, 1884).

53. "Not Agreeing with George; Socialists Who Think He Don't Go Far Enough," *New York Times,* July 26, 1887.

54. F. Spencer Baldwin, "Some Aspects of Luxury," *North American Review* 168 (February 1899): 157–61.

55. Wells, "How Shall the Nation Regain Prosperity?" 128–30.

56. *The Nation*'s adherence to steadfastly classical economics and antebellum liberalism was much remarked on by decidedly anticlassical economists in the postbellum period. As late as 1894, Henry Carter Adams was fuming to E. R. A. Seligman, "The New York *Nation* is a decided Bourbon. Its editors have learned nothing during the last twenty-five years and I doubt if they are capable of learning anything. Perhaps in the general shifting of social forces, it is necessary to have classical expression of incompetent ideas, but I must say I weary of the reiteration of major premises which are found in the columns of this paper" (Henry Carter Adams to E. R. A. Seligman, August 28, 1894, in Joseph Dorfman, "The Seligman Correspondence II," *Political Science Quarterly* 56 [June 1941]: 273).

57. "'The Poor Man' in Politics," *Nation,* September 19, 1878, 173–74.

58. David W. Blight, *Race and Reunion: The Civil War in American Memory* (Cambridge: Harvard University Press, 2002), 211–54.

59. Lyman Abbott, "Danger Ahead," *Century* 21 (November 1885): 57. For an extended discussion of this article, which emphasized the dangers of immigration and radicalism more than the loss of the republic, see Carl Smith, *Urban Disorder and the Shape of Belief: The Great Chicago Fire, the Haymarket Bomb, and the Model Town of Pullman* (Chicago: University of Chicago Press, 1995), 118–19.

60. *Congressional Record,* May 8, 1879, 46th Cong., 1st sess., 1156.

61. "The Late Riots," *Nation,* August 2, 1877, 68–69. The solution, according to the *Nation,* was permanently to station federal troops in major industrial centers ("The Rioters and the Regular Army," *Nation,* August 9, 1877, 85–86; "Why the Regular Army Should Be Increased," *Nation,* August 30, 1877, 130–31).

62. "Among the Ruins," *Pittsburgh Daily Post,* July 25, 1877; "Reign of the Mob," *Pittsburgh Daily Post,* July 23, 1877.

63. E. H. Heywood, *The Great Strike: Its Relations to Labor, Property, and Government* (Princeton, Mass.: Co-Operative, 1878), 16. By 1877, Americans had tired of the project of Reconstruction, but the labor unrest of the 1870s permanently turned attention away from the South. Industrial class warfare in northern and midwestern cities seemed more threatening—and more ideologically disturbing—than the increasing abrogation of African American rights in the South. Many if not most white Americans had no trouble accepting racial hierarchies but were uncomfortable confronting the possibility of permanent class divisions. Federal attention shifted from the South to industrial centers as well, symbolized most poignantly by the redeployment of federal troops from the South to Pittsburgh during the Great Uprising of 1877 (Eric Foner, *Reconstruction: America's Unfinished Revolution* [New York: Harper and Row, 1988], 584–85).

64. An early comparison of the United States with France appeared in Samuel Eliot, "The Relief of Labor," *Journal of Social Science* 4 (1871): 133. He cautioned, "The same ideas are floating far and wide . . . and if blood is shed one day at Paris, it is shed another in Scranton."

65. "The Socialistic Spectre of Europe," *New York Times,* April 2, 1877.

66. Dacus quoted in Nell Irvin Painter, *Standing at Armageddon: The United States, 1877–1919* (New York: Norton, 1987), 18.

67. "The Late Riots," 68–69.

68. Eric J. Hobsbawm, *The Age of Capital, 1848–1875* (New York: Scribner's, 1975), 4.

69. Vernon Parrington, *Main Currents in American Thought: The Beginnings of Critical Realism in America* (New York: Harcourt and Brace, 1930), 3:173. Parrington's assessment has dominated most subsequent interpretations. On interpretations of Hay's novel in historical writings, see, for example, Rezneck, "Distress, Relief, and Discontent," 511; William Appleman Williams, *Contours of American History* (Cleveland: World, 1961), 317; Kenneth McCartney and John G. Turnbull, "The Novel in the

Study of the American Labor Movement," *Journal of Higher Education* 24 (January 1953): 8; Larry Isaac, "Counter 'The Very Devil' and More: The Making of Independent Capitalist Militia in the Gilded Age," *American Journal of Sociology* 108 (September 2002): 386.

70. John Hay, *The Bread-Winners: A Social Study* (New York: Harper, 1884), 246, 99, 307. Brook Thomas's reading of the novel argues that Hay "combats self-interestedness," which he associates with both Andrew Jackson and his namesake, Offitt, "by retaining the hierarchical assumptions of classical republicanism." But though Farnham's social class and caste assure him his home and a pretty wife by the end of the novel, they are no guarantee that another working-class revolt will not take both away from him in the future. See Brook Thomas, *American Literary Realism and the Failed Promise of Contract* (Berkeley: University of California Press, 1997), 103.

71. Rodgers, *Work Ethic,* 216.

72. Henry George, *Progress and Poverty: An Inquiry into the Cause of Industrial Depressions and of Increase of Want with Increase of Wealth* (1879; New York: Schalkenbach, 1979), 433–74; John L. Thomas, *Alternative America: Henry George, Edward Bellamy, Henry Demarest Lloyd, and the Adversary Tradition* (Cambridge: Harvard University Press, 1983), 118–23. Jeffrey Sklansky has argued that George had a much more "romantic" and socially contingent view of rights, land, and value; for Sklansky, George is almost a proto-marginalist. Contemporary assessments of George by economists such as Scligman, however, hewed more closely (and more critically) to Thomas's analysis.

Two. Meat versus Rice

1. Testimony of Isaac Cohen, December 11, 1878, in *Investigation by a Select Committee of the House of Representatives Relative to the Causes of the General Depression in Labor and Business, etc.,* 45th Cong., House of Representatives, Misc. Doc. 29 (Washington, D.C.: U.S. Government Printing Office, 1879), 418.

2. On the long history of Orientalism and anti-Chinese sentiment in America, see John Kuo Wei Tchen, *New York before Chinatown: Orientalism and the Shaping of American Culture, 1776–1882* (Baltimore: Johns Hopkins University Press, 1999); Erika Lee, "Orientalisms in the Americas: A Hemispheric Approach to Asian American History," *Journal of Asian American Studies* 83 (October 2005): 235–56.

3. "Domestic Chinese Question," *Salem (Massachusetts) Friend,* December 12, 1879; "Current Topics," *Duluth (Minnesota) Lake Superior News,* May 20, 1880; "Second District Farmers Men Who Made the Kingdom of Laws Aiming to Down Him," *Omaha (Nebraska) Daily World-Herald,* July 29, 1890; "Can It Be Enforced? Some Doubt Concerning the Chinese Exclusion Act," *Omaha (Nebraska) Daily World-Herald,* August 24, 1892; "Have Chinese Enough: A Bill to Exclude Almond-Eyed Immigrants before California's Legislature: It Is Believed," *Chicago Daily Inter-Ocean,* February 20, 1891; "Worshiping Idols: Rev. Curtis Lee Laws Says This Is Practiced in Baltimore," *Baltimore Sun,* September 4, 1899.

4. George McNeill, W. W. Stone, and William W. Morrow, "The Chinese and the Labor Question," in *The Labor Movement: The Problem of Today,* ed. George McNeill (1887; New York: Kelley, 1971), 429–53.

5. Alexander Saxton, *The Indispensable Enemy: Labor and the Anti-Chinese Movement in California* (Berkeley: University of California Press, 1971).

6. Helen H. Jun has argued that the Chinese provided a similar foil for African Americans, who strove to define themselves as responsible and desirable citizens in contrast to the problematic and undesirable Chinese ("Black Orientalism: Nineteenth-Century Narratives of Race and U.S. Citizenship," *American Quarterly* 58 [December 2006]: 1047–66).

7. Bruce Laurie, *Artisans into Workers: Labor in Nineteenth Century America* (New York: Hill and Wang, 1989), 116; Eric Foner, "Free Labor and Nineteenth-Century Political Ideology," in *The Market Revolution in America: Social, Political, and Religious Expressions, 1800–1880,* ed. Melvyn Stokes and Stephen Conway (Charlottesville: University Press of Virginia, 1996), 103; Daniel Rodgers, *The Work Ethic in Industrial America, 1850–1920* (Chicago: University of Chicago Press, 1974), 19; John R. Commons, "American Shoemakers, 1648–1895: A Sketch of Industrial Evolution," *Quarterly Journal of Economics* 24 (November 1909): 39–84.

8. John Swinton, *A Momentous Question: The Respective Attitudes of Labor and Capital* (Philadelphia: Keller, 1895), 176.

9. Ronald Schultz, "The Small-Producer Tradition and the Moral Origins of Artisan Radicalism in Philadelphia, 1720–1810," *Past and Present* 127 (May 1990): 87–88. The producers' republic was part of the larger Jeffersonian vision of a republic defined by small-scale production and proprietary capitalism and occupied by yeomen farmers and urban artisans. Labor was the precondition of property ownership and the source of all wealth.

10. The term *heroic artisan* is Michael Kimmel's (*Manhood in America: A Cultural History* [New York: Free Press, 1996], 16–18, 27–25). See also Melissa Dabakis, *Visualizing Labor in American Sculpture: Monuments, Manliness, and the Work Ethic, 1880–1935* (Cambridge: Cambridge University Press, 1999).

11. Webster quoted in Eric Foner, *Free Soil, Free Labor, Free Men* (New York: Oxford University Press, 1970), 15.

12. *An Address from the Friends of the Workingman to the Pulpit, the Platform, and the Press, in the United States of America* (Boston: Conference of Labor Reformers, 1872), 3–4.

13. Stanley Lebergott, "The Pattern of Employment since 1800," in *American Economic History,* ed. Seymour E. Harris (New York: McGraw-Hill, 1961), 290.

14. Margo Anderson, "The Language of Class in Twentieth-Century America," *Social Science History* 12 (Winter 1988): 352.

15. Before the 1870s, few firms employed large numbers of workers; between 1867 and 1868, only 57 firms employed 500 or more workers, and only 31 employed 1,000 or more. The largest, a cotton-spinning firm in Worcester, Massachusetts, employed

3,158 people (James L. Huston, *Securing the Fruits of Labor: The American Concept of Wealth Distribution, 1765–1900* [Baton Rouge: Louisiana State University Press, 1998], 112–15).

16. In comparison, agriculture generated 33 percent of the total national income, a direct inversion from 1869, when agriculture had generated 53 percent of the income and manufacturing 33 percent (Gary Walton and Hugh Rockoff, *History of the American Economy,* 6th ed. [New York: Harcourt Brace Jovanovich, 1990], 344–45; Alfred Chandler Jr., *The Visible Hand: The Managerial Revolution in American Business* [Cambridge: Belknap Press of Harvard University Press, 1977], 207–83).

17. Unskilled workers emerged as a major class in industrial production between 1880 and 1900; before 1880, most industrial workers were skilled or semiskilled. Huston has argued that the "wretched conditions of labor in the Gilded Age, the sudden intrusion of large-scale shops and impersonal management, and the cycles of boom and bust were bad enough, but the loss of skill was the loss of self-identification and was unbearable" (*Securing the Fruits of Labor,* 147). See also David Brody, "The American Worker in the Progressive Era: A Comprehensive Analysis," in *Workers in Industrial America: Essays on the Twentieth Century Struggle* (New York: Oxford University Press, 1980), 3–47.

18. Alexander Keyssar, *Out of Work: The First Century of Unemployment in Massachusetts* (New York: Cambridge University Press, 1986), 300–302, 340–41.

19. Drew R. McCoy, *The Elusive Republic: Political Economy in Jeffersonian America* (Chapel Hill: University of North Carolina Press, 1980), 237. See also Huston, *Securing the Fruits of Labor,* 3–28.

20. D. O. Kellog, "Thoughts on the Labor Question," in *Labor Politics,* ed. Leon Stein and Philip Taft (New York: Arno, 1971), 2:8.

21. C. M. Morse, "The Church and the Working Man," *Forum* 6 (February 1888): 655.

22. On white workers' use of the term *wage slavery,* see David Roediger, *The Wages of Whiteness: Race and the Making of the American Working Class* (New York: Verso, 1991), 65–94.

23. Alice Wellington Rollins, "The New Uncle Tom's Cabin," *Forum* 4 (October 1887): 221. Though her analogy of wage work to chattel slavery must have been impossible for African Americans or abolitionists to accept, it would have resonated with many whites sympathetic to the plight of the heroic artisan.

24. Moon-Ho Jung, "Outlawing 'Coolies': Race, Nation, and Empire in the Age of Emancipation," *American Quarterly* 57 (September 2005): 677–78.

25. Lisa Lowe, "The Power of Culture," *Journal of Asian American Studies* 1 (February 1998): 7; Najia Aarim-Heriot, *Chinese Immigrants, African Americans, and Racial Anxiety in the United States, 1848–1882* (Urbana: University of Illinois Press, 2003), 84–102.

26. On the history of the Chinese in the United States, see Roger Daniels, *Asian America: Chinese and Japanese in the United States since 1850* (Seattle: University of

Washington Press, 1988); Ronald Takaki, *Strangers from a Different Shore: A History of Asian Americans* (Boston: Little, Brown, 1989); Gary Y. Okihiro, *Margins and Mainstreams: Asians in American History and Culture* (Seattle: University of Washington Press, 1994). On the anti-Chinese movement and the Exclusion Acts, see Elmer Clarence Sandmeyer, *The Anti-Chinese Movement in California* (Urbana: University of Illinois Press, 1939); John Higham, *Strangers in the Land: Patterns of American Nativism, 1860–1925,* 2nd ed. (New York: Athenaeum, 1966), 165–75; Stuart Creighton Miller, *The Unwelcome Immigrant: The American Image of the Chinese, 1785–1882* (Berkeley: University of California Press, 1969); Saxton, *Indispensable Enemy;* Alexander Saxton, *The Rise and Fall of the White Republic: Class Politics and Mass Culture in Nineteenth-Century America* (New York: Verso, 1990); Andrew Gyory, *Closing the Gate: Race, Politics, and the Chinese Exclusion Act* (Chapel Hill: University of North Carolina Press, 1998); Mae M. Ngai, *Impossible Subjects: Illegal Aliens and the Making of Modern America* (Princeton: Princeton University Press, 2004); Roger Daniels, *Guarding the Golden Door: American Immigration Policy and Immigrants since 1882* (New York: Hill and Wang, 2004), 3–26.

27. As Saxton has pointed out, while newspapers and politicians frequently inflated their statistics, they at least "warrant a conclusion that large numbers of Chinese did follow these lines of work" (*Indispensable Enemy,* 5, 7). All in all, Chinese made up about a quarter of San Francisco's total population (Takaki, *Strangers from a Different Shore,* 79).

28. Saxton, *Indispensable Enemy,* 6. Though Chinese labor was soon excluded from locally based trades such as construction, the Chinese came to dominate in industries such as cigar making that competed with eastern goods. Employers in these industries favored Chinese workers in part because they accepted lower wages but also because they were more willing to accept rationalization of the work process. By 1885, the Chinese made up almost 87 percent of the labor force in the cigar industry. White workers responded by urging smokers to boycott Chinese-made cigars and by labeling non-Chinese products "white only."

29. Earlier restriction laws had made little distinction between the Chinese, Native Americans, and African Americans. By the 1870s, however, white Californians felt sufficiently threatened to pass a series of laws aimed specifically against the Chinese. In 1870, San Francisco passed a Cubic Air Act to minimize crowded housing in Chinatown as well as a Queue Act, designed symbolically to emasculate Chinese men. By 1878, the state denied Chinese immigrants the possibility of naturalization, and in 1879 they were banned from working on public construction projects (Saxton, *Indispensable Enemy,* 113–37).

30. James A. Whitney, *The Chinese and the Chinese Question,* 2nd ed. (New York: Tibbals, 1888), 122; "The Mongols in Brooklyn," *Sacramento Bee,* January 1, 1881.

31. Despite the fact that the Chinese population of the United States decreased as a result of these measures, the United States passed thirteen more racially specific laws aimed at restricting Chinese opportunities within the United States. For an

extended discussion of the political debates at the congressional level, see Gyory, *Closing the Gate.*

32. Nayan Shah, *Contagious Divides: Epidemics and Race in San Francisco's Chinatown* (Berkeley: University of California Press, 2001), 1–104.

33. *Chinatown Declared a Nuisance!* (San Francisco: Workingmen's Committee of California, 1880), 4.

34. Albert Sydney Willis, *Chinese Immigration: A Report in the House of Representatives of the United States, February 25, 1878* (Washington, D.C.: Polkinhorn, 1878), 6.

35. G. B. Densmore, *The Chinese in California: Descriptions of Chinese Life in San Francisco* (San Francisco: Pettit and Russ, 1880), 29–30.

36. Edwin R. Meade, *The Chinese Question: A Paper Read at the Annual Meeting of the Social Science Association of America, Saratoga Springs, N.Y., September 7, 1877* (New York: Arthur and Bonnell, 1877), 13–14.

37. Testimony of C. C. O'Donnell in *Causes of General Depression in Labor and Business: Chinese Immigration: Investigation by a Select Committee of the House of Representatives Relative to the Causes of the General Depression in Labor and Business; and as to Chinese Immigration,* 46th Cong., 2nd sess., House of Representatives, Misc. Doc. 5 (Washington, D.C.: U.S. Government Printing Office, 1879), 267. O'Donnell recovered sufficiently to describe these horrors at some length.

38. L. T. Townsend, *The Chinese Problem* (Boston: Lee and Shepard, 1876), 24.

39. Willis, *Chinese Immigration,* 4.

40. Whitney, *Chinese and the Chinese Question,* 35.

41. Charles N. Felton, *The Evils of Mongolian Immigration: The Chinese Question* (Washington, D.C.: n.p., 1892), 4–5.

42. Thomas Magee, "China's Menace to the World," *Forum* 10 (October 1890): 197–200.

43. Ibid., 200.

44. Testimony of Adolph Strasser in *Investigation,* 103.

45. McNeill, Stone, and Morrow, "Chinese and the Labor Question," 433.

46. Whitney, *Chinese and the Chinese Question,* 35–36.

47. McNeill, Stone, and Morrow, "Chinese and the Labor Question," 432.

48. Meade, *Chinese Question,* 8.

49. McNeill, Stone, and Morrow, "Chinese and the Labor Question," 430. Detractors believed that the lack of family had two effects on Chinese workers. First, it showed that they were in some way perverted. As Shah has shown, public health officials frequently noted the "variety of households and domestic arrangements" in Chinatown, including large numbers of men living together, as "definitive evidence that typical Chinatown domesticity contradicted the nuclear family ideal" (*Contagious Divides,* 83). Instead of supporting wives and children, Chinese men frequented prostitutes, mocking the American family. Second, because Chinese men had no families (at least in the United States, the only area with which American

commentators concerned themselves), they could work for less money and live in meaner surroundings.

50. For descriptions of the Chinese as bees, see, for example, Meade, *Chinese Question,* 5.

51. William W. Corlett, *The Labor Question as Affected by Chinese Immigration: Speech in the House of Representatives, January 28, 1879* (Washington, D.C.: n.p., 1879), 19.

52. Henry Grimm, *The Chinese Must Go! A Farce in Four Acts* (San Francisco: Bancroft, 1879).

53. J. N. Larned, *Talks about Labor, and Concerning the Evolution of Justice between Laborers and Capitalists* (New York: Appleton, 1876), 13.

54. James Ayers, *Chinese Exclusion: Speech Delivered in Committee on the Whole of the Constitutional Convention, Monday, December 8, 1878* (Los Angeles: Evening Express Newspaper and Printing, 1878), 11.

55. Iota, *The Raid of the Red Dragons into Eagle-Land: A Plague(y) Pamphlet* (San Francisco: Mission Mirror Job Printing, 1876), 9.

56. Ibid., 19.

57. *An Address from the Workingmen of San Francisco to Their Brothers throughout the Pacific Coast* (San Francisco: Workingman's Party of California, 1888), 2, 23. This document was generated after an August 16, 1888, mass meeting at Metropolitan Hall in San Francisco.

58. Carlos A. Schwantes, "Protest in a Promised Land: Unemployment, Disinheritance, and the Origin of Labor Militancy in the Pacific Northwest, 1885–1886," *Western Historical Quarterly* 13 (October 1982): 380.

59. *Portland Oregonian,* May 5, 1886 quoted in ibid., 388.

60. Saxton, *Indispensable Enemy,* 214–15.

61. Few anti-Chinese tracts stressed one of the central tenets of free labor ideology: the right of each individual worker to make a contract freely. Though the Civil Rights Act of 1866 enshrined the right to contract as a primary signifier of individual freedom, anti-Chinese rhetoric stressed economic comfort and security far more than the ability to enter into contracts. For a succinct discussion of the two strands of free labor ideology—that is, producerism and right to contract freely—often in tension if not outright conflict with each other, see Foner, "Free Labor," 99–127.

62. Willis, *Chinese Immigration,* 5.

63. "How the Hun Lives," *Swinton's Paper,* May 4, 1884.

64. Corlett, *Labor Question,* 19.

65. Testimony of T. B. Shannon, August 15, 1879, in *Causes,* 242. Others also compared the Chinese to grasshoppers; see, for example, testimony of William Haley in *Causes,* 79.

66. McNeill, Stone, and Morrow, "Chinese and the Labor Question," 435.

67. William W. Morrow, *Chinese Immigration: Speech of Hon. William W. Morrow,*

of California, in the House of Representatives, June 28, 1886 (Washington, D.C.: n.p., 1886), 14–15.

68. George Perkins, *Chinese Exclusion: Remarks on the Nature and Effect of the Competition of Chinese with American Labor, and the Necessity of a Stringent Exclusion Law: In the Senate of the United States, April 8, 1902* (Washington, D.C.: U.S. Government Printing Office, 1902), 16, 6.

69. Whitney, *Chinese and the Chinese Question*, 120.

70. Perkins, *Chinese Exclusion*, 20. Perkins was not alone in noting this phenomenon. See also Thomas H. Brent, *Chinese Immigration: Speech in the House of Representatives, March 18, 1882* (Washington, D.C.: n.p., [1882?]), 2. Earlier commentators had also mentioned the Chinese practice of returning bones to China and refusing to patronize American cemeteries, but by the end of the century, such practices were almost always couched in terms of Chinese underconsumption and were frequently noted.

71. Perkins, *Chinese Exclusion*, 5.

72. Gail Bederman, *Manliness and Civilization: A Cultural History of Gender and Race in the United States, 1880–1917* (Chicago: University of Chicago Press, 1995), 25. According to Bederman, white Americans were especially concerned about men and women who dressed in a manner inappropriate to their gender. So, at the 1893 Columbian Exposition in Chicago, "respectable" audiences fixated on their inability to distinguish Dahomey men and women from each other. Both, the *New York Times* noted, "may be seen at almost any hour . . . clad mainly in a brief grass skirt" (35–36).

73. Testimony of Charles Litchman in *Chinese Exclusion*, U.S. Senate, Committee on Immigration, 57th Cong., 2nd sess. (Washington, D.C.: U.S. Government Printing Office, 1902), 282.

74. Testimony of Edward Livernash in ibid., 143.

75. Whitney, *Chinese and the Chinese Question*, 135–36.

76. Elias Merriman, "The Economics of Luxury," *Social Economist* 1 (June 1891): 235.

77. Steward quoted in Timothy Messer-Kruse, "Eight Hours, Greenbacks, and 'Chinamen': Wendell Phillips, Ira Steward, and the Fate of Labor Reform in Massachusetts," *Labor History* 42 (May 2001): 151–52. Messer-Kruse argues that by the end of his life, "Steward's fear of the coming of the Chinese was intrinsically linked with his understanding of the economics of wages, hours, and even of history and human progress itself" (151). Steward was hardly alone in making this connection.

78. Testimony of Samuel Gompers in *Chinese Exclusion*, 265; Lawrence Glickman, *A Living Wage: American Workers and the Making of Consumer Society* (Ithaca: Cornell University Press, 1997), 78–92.

79. Testimony of Samuel Gompers in *Chinese Exclusion*, 270.

80. In 1907, the United States and Japan entered into a "gentleman's agreement" barring further Japanese immigration to the United States. In 1913, California passed

the Alien Land Law, which effectively prohibited Asians from owning land. In 1924, the Johnson-Reed Act ended Asian immigration.

81. Samuel Gompers and Herman Guttstadt, *Some Reasons for Chinese Exclusion: Meat vs. Rice: American Manhood against Asiatic Coolieism: Which Shall Survive?* U.S. Senate Document 137 (Washington, D.C.: American Federation of Labor, 1902), 6, 10, 15, 13, 22.

82. In other words, contrary to what early scholars of whiteness have argued, white workers' racism was not the one source of a working-class consciousness, nor was it only a bold ploy to claim the "psychological wage" of whiteness that mitigated the humiliation of permanent wage work. See, for example, Roediger, *Wages of Whiteness,* 12, 115–32. For a pointed critique of whiteness studies, see Eric Arneson, "Whiteness and the Historians' Imagination," *International Labor and Working-Class History* 60 (October 2001): 3–42.

83. Samuel Gompers to the Charles H. Eliot Company, January 16, 1901, in *The Samuel Gompers Papers,* vol. 5, *An Expanding Movement at the Turn of the Century, 1989–1902,* ed. Stuart B. Kaufman, Peter J. Albert, and Grace Palladino (Urbana: University of Illinois Press, 1996), 319.

84. As Glickman has shown, anti-Chinese rhetoric helped shaped the "American standard of living" based on high levels of consumption (*Living Wage,* 84–89). See also Shah, *Contagious Divides,* 158–78.

85. Testimony of Samuel Gompers in *Chinese Exclusion,* 264, 263.

86. "For Eight Hours," *Seattle Post-Intelligencer,* March 23, 1891, in *The Samuel Gompers Papers,* vol. 3, *Unrest and Depression, 1891–94,* ed. Stuart B. Kaufman and Peter J. Albert (Urbana: University of Illinois Press, 1989), 54.

Three. The Value of Wages

1. Henry Carter Adams to Elizabeth Adams, [1886?], Henry Carter Adams Papers, Box 2, Correspondence 1883–90, Bentley Historical Library, University of Michigan, Ann Arbor.

2. Edwin R. A. Seligman, review of *Nouveau Dictionnaire d'Économie Politique, Political Science Quarterly* 5 (June 1890): 336. Also quoted in Dorothy Ross, *The Origins of American Social Science* (New York: Cambridge University Press, 1991), 187.

3. Henry Carter Adams to Elizabeth Adams, [1886?], Adams Papers, Box 2, Correspondence 1883–90.

4. Richard Theodore Ely, *The Labor Movement in America* (New York: Crowell, 1886), 113.

5. The most significant and sophisticated proponents of this argument have followed Samuel P. Hays's *The Response to Industrialism, 1885–1914* (Chicago: University of Chicago Press, 1954). See, for example, Gabriel Kolko, *The Triumph of Conservatism: A Re-Interpretation of American History, 1900–1916* (Glencoe, Ill.: Free Press, 1963); James Weinstein, *The Corporate Ideal in the Liberal State, 1900–1918* (Boston: Beacon, 1968); Christopher Lasch, *The True and Only Heaven: Progress and*

Its Critics (New York: Norton, 1991). A recent, compelling version of this narrative is Nancy Cohen's *The Reconstruction of American Liberalism, 1865–1914* (Chapel Hill: University of North Carolina Press, 2002). Casting historical economics as antidemocratic relies on a very precise definition of democracy as popular political engagement in public life, social governance, and policy formation. These works implicitly argue that such a vigorous democracy existed prior to its execution at the hands of a liberal administrative state. Recent works on antebellum and midcentury political life, though, question that assumption. See, for example, Stuart Blumin and Glen Altschuler, *Rude Republic: Americans and Their Politics in the Nineteenth Century* (Princeton: Princeton University Press, 2000). These works assume a relatively straightforward correlation between a middle-class identity and enthusiastic support for corporate capitalism, managerial government, and the suppression of labor. But other historians have argued that the American middle class was hardly ideologically monolithic. See, for example, Burton J. Bledstein and Robert D. Johnston, ed., *The Middling Sorts: Explorations in the History of the American Middle Class* (New York: Routledge, 2001).

6. As Ellen Fitzpatrick has rightly pointed out, "Their enduring respect for the demands of social democracy determined their approach to political change" ("Rethinking the Intellectual Origins of American Labor History," *American Historical Review* 96 [April 1991]: 425).

7. Bradley W. Bateman and Ethan B. Kapstein, "Retrospective: Between God and the Market: The Religious Roots of the American Economic Association," *Journal of Economic Perspectives* 13 (Autumn 1999): 249–57; Bradley W. Bateman, "Make a Righteous Number: Social Surveys, the Men and Religion Forward Movement, and Quantification in American Economics," *History of Political Economy* 33 (Annual Supplement 2001): 57–85.

8. John F. Henry, *John Bates Clark: The Making of a Neoclassical Economist* (London: Macmillan, 1995), 1–2. Clark applied to Yale Divinity School before Amherst's president, Julius Seelye, urged Clark to consider political economy as a field of study instead.

9. Edwin R. A. Seligman, "Dinner in Honor of John Bates Clark," *American Economic Review* 17 (June 1927): 16. The dinner was held on Clark's eightieth birthday.

10. Henry C. Taylor and George S. Wehrwein, "Richard T. Ely," *Journal of Land and Public Utility Economics* 19 (August 1943): 387; Sidney Fine, "Richard T. Ely, Forerunner of Progressivism, 1880–1901," *Mississippi Valley Historical Review* 37 (March 1951): 601–3.

11. Steven A. Sass, *The Pragmatic Imagination: A History of the Wharton School, 1881–1891* (Philadelphia: University of Pennsylvania Press, 1982), 59, 92.

12. J. A. Schumpeter, A. H. Cole, and E. S. Mason, "Frank William Taussig," *Quarterly Journal of Economics* 65 (May 1941): 337–63; "Dr. Helen Taussig Dies," *New York Times*, May 22, 1986; "Arthur Twining Hadley," *American Economic Review* 20 (June 1930): 364–68.

13. Arthur T. Hadley, "The Relation between Economics and Politics," *Yale Law Review* 8 (January 1899): 206. On the similarities as well as differences between the economists, see Mary O. Furner, "The Republican Tradition and the New Liberalism: Social Investigation, State Building, and Social Learning in the Gilded Age," in *The State and Social Investigation in Britain and the United States,* ed. Michael J. Lacey and Mary O. Furner (Washington, D.C.: Woodrow Wilson Center Press and Cambridge University Press, 1993), 183–84.

14. Erik Grimmer-Solem, *The Rise of Historical Economic and Social Reform in Germany, 1864–1894* (Oxford: Clarendon, 2003), 25, 130–31.

15. Clarence E. Wunderlin Jr., *Visions of a New Industrial Order: Social Science and Labor Theory in America's Progressive Era* (New York: Columbia University Press, 1992), 1–10.

16. On the influence of the Verein, see Daniel Rodgers, *Atlantic Crossings: Social Politics in a Progressive Age* (Cambridge: Belknap Press of Harvard University Press, 1998), 90–106.

17. Schumpeter, Cole, and Mason, "Frank William Taussig," 339. On July 4, 1886, Taussig insisted to Adams, "We must look to Germany for suggestions, but must work out our own salvation in our own way" (Adams Papers, Box 2, Correspondence 1883–90).

18. Simon N. Patten to Richard T. Ely, October 22, 1909, quoted in "Memorial to Former President Simon N. Patten," *American Economic Review* 13 (March 1923): 260.

19. For a retrospective assessment of the AEA's heady early days, see Richard T. Ely, "The Founding and Early History of the American Economic Association," *American Economic Review* 26 (March 1936): 144, 145. On the founding of the AEA, see Thomas L. Haskell, *The Emergence of the Professional Social Science: The American Social Science Association and the Nineteenth-Century Crisis of Authority* (Urbana: University of Illinois Press, 1977), 168–89.

20. The aftermath of Haymarket did mark a change in the work of these economists. After Cornell pushed Adams out and Wisconsin's Board of Regents attacked Ely, most of these men were much more cautious in their statements But they continued to press their agenda, albeit in more specialized and remote venues. On the impact of Haymarket, see Mary O. Furner, *Advocacy and Objectivity: A Crisis in the Professionalization of American Social Science* (Lexington: University Press of Kentucky for the Organization of American Historians, 1975), 142–228. On Clark's continued interest in social justice, see Henry, *John Bates Clark,* 44–45. On Clark's static theories of economics, see the scathing article by Thorstein Veblen, "The Limitations of Marginal Utility," *Journal of Political Economy* 17 (November 1901): 620–21. Veblen had been Clark's favorite student at Carleton, and Clark remained an avid supporter of his former pupil's work, even when it directly attacked that of Clark. For a recent and thorough reassessment of Clark that sees him as neither a Progressive nor an apologist for capital, see Thomas C. Leonard, "'A Certain Rude Honesty': John

Bates Clark as a Pioneering Neoclassical Economist," *History of Political Economy* 35 (Fall 2003): 521–58.

21. Francis A. Walker, "The Wage-Fund Theory," *North American Review* 120 (January 1875): 85.

22. Ibid., 88.

23. Furner, *Advocacy*, 18–19.

24. Charles F. Dunbar, "The Career of Francis Amasa Walker," *Quarterly Journal of Economics* 11 (July 1897): 438.

25. Francis A. Walker, "Recent Progress of Political Economy in the United States," *Publications of the American Economic Association* 4 (July 1889): 29.

26. Joseph Dorfman, *The Economic Mind in American Civilization*, vol. 3, *1865–1918* (New York: Viking, 1949), 102.

27. Carroll Davidson Wright, "Francis Amasa Walker," *Publications of the American Statistical Association* 5 (June 1897): 254–55.

28. Walker, "Wage-Fund Theory," 114, 115–16, 117.

29. Francis A. Walker, "The Labor Problem of To-Day: An Address Delivered before the Alumni Association of Lehigh University, June 22, 1887," in *Wages, Hours, and Strikes: Labor Panaceas in the Twentieth Century*, ed. Leon Stein and Philip Taft (New York: Arno, 1969), 5–8.

30. On the lingering effects of Walker's idea of the residual claimant on theories of distribution based on the idea of marginal return, see Furner, "Republican Tradition," 178–79.

31. Walker, "Recent Progress," 33.

32. Walker, "Wage-Fund Theory," 102; Walker, "Recent Progress," 35.

33. George J. Stigler, "Stuart Wood and the Marginal Productivity Theory," *Quarterly Journal of Economics* 61 (August 1947): 640. Wood is often misidentified as the first American to earn a doctorate in economics, but Harvard had no department of political economy when he graduated in 1875 at the age of twenty-two (Edward S. Mason and Thomas S. Lamont, "The Harvard Department of Economics from the Beginning to World War II," *Quarterly Journal of Economics* 97 [August 1982]: 389).

34. Stuart Wood, "The Theory of Wages," *Publications of the American Economic Association* 4 (March 1889): 6, 9, 12–13.

35. On Veblen's vexed relationship with consumption and consumers, see Kathleen G. Donohue, *Freedom from Want: American Liberalism and the Idea of the Consumer* (Baltimore: Johns Hopkins University Press, 2003), 8–40.

36. Wood, "Theory of Wages," 16.

37. Ibid., 20, 23–24, 27. Indeed, noted Wood wryly, "In utter disregard of the rights of private property, the State of Pennsylvania has even made it a misdemeanor to have a single specimen of this enterprising vegetable grown on one's estate."

38. F. W. Taussig, "The Wages-Fund at the Hands of the German Economists," *Publications of the American Economic Association* 9 (January 1894): 68–69.

39. John Bates Clark, *The Philosophy of Wealth: Economic Principles Newly Formulated* (Boston: Ginn, 1887), 127.

40. John Bates Clark, *The Distribution of Wealth: A Theory of Wages, Interests, and Profits* (New York: Macmillan, 1899), 4.

41. Joseph R. Schumpeter, *Capitalism, Socialism, and Democracy* (New York: Harper and Row, 1942), 23.

42. Henry Carter Adams, *Outlines of Lectures upon Political Economy* (Baltimore: n.p., 1881), 9.

43. Leon Fink, *Workingman's Democracy: The Knights of Labor and American Politics* (Urbana: University of Illinois Press, 1985), 9. For a comparison of the Knights' vision with that of employers, see Sarah Lyon Watts, *Order against Chaos: Business Culture and Labor Ideology in America, 1880–1915* (Westport, Conn.: Greenwood, 1991), 9.

44. Chester MacArthur Destler, *Henry Demarest Lloyd and the Empire of Reform* (Philadelphia: University of Pennsylvania Press, 1963), 380–99.

45. W. Stanley Jevons, *The Theory of Political Economy,* 4th ed. (London: Macmillan, 1911), 187.

46. Louis Dumont, *From Mandeville to Marx: The Genesis and Triumph of Economic Ideology* (Chicago: University of Chicago Press, 1977), 86.

47. Dorfman, *Economic Mind,* 165. See also Adams, *Outline,* 16–18, 23–27, 37.

48. Adams, *Outline,* 37.

49. Clark's theory that capital and labor were equally important factors in creating value was fully explored in *The Philosophy of Wealth* and reiterated numerous times. See J. B. Clark, "The Ultimate Standard of Value," *Publications of the American Economic Association* 8 (January 1893): 83. Clark was by no means the first to point out the role of nonworkers in the process of production. In 1881, Adams had pointed to the roles of landlords, capitalists, and "undertakers" (by which he meant "managers of industry," or entrepreneurs) in production (*Outline,* 20).

50. Clark, *Distribution,* 11–12. Clark qualified this statement in a footnote: "An article is not finished, in the economic sense, till the retail merchant has found the customer whose needs it satisfies. The sale of completed articles is thus the terminal act of social production" (11). See also John Bates Clark to Richard Theodore Ely, December 18, 1889, Richard Theodore Ely Papers, Correspondence, Mss MK, Box 2, Folder 10, Wisconsin Historical Society.

51. Although a great deal of cross-pollination clearly took place between European marginalists and Americans (Adams quotes Jevons liberally, for example), Clark maintained that he read Jevons only after beginning to elaborate his ideas while at Smith (John Bates Clark to Henry Carter Adams, December 10, 1886, Adams Papers, Box 2, Correspondence, 1883–90).

52. Clark, *Distribution,* 397.

53. John Bates Clark, "Capital and Its Earnings," *Publications of the American Economic Association* 3 (May 1888): 58–60. Clark's ideas soon appeared in less academic

venues, such as Gunton's magazine, *Social Economist*. See, for example, John Bates Clark, "Cost of Production as the Basis of Economic Movement," *Social Economist* 1 (July 1891): 287–94.

54. Indeed, the amount of labor necessary for producing a given object need have no relation at all to its final value. For example, argued Clark, the difference between iron and slag is not the amount of labor put into creating the two items but in their "utility." Though slag has no value despite the labor put into creating it, "a chance chemical discovery might reveal uses for the slags in their present forms, and they would then become wealth; but they would have been a product of labor before they became wealth as well as after" (Clark, *Philosophy*, 24–25).

55. Adams, *Outline*, 35, 36.

56. Clark, *Philosophy*, 78.

57. Maurice Dobb points out that this formulation of marginal utility theory "leaves the question: What fixes the position of the margin itself? To this the answer is that it is fixed by the available supply; which in turn raises the further question: What determines the limitation of supply?" For postbellum economists, the answer in large part was social preference. Production on a grand scale was now a reality—consumption depended on demand, and demand, Clark insisted, was based on socially constructed desire. If *value* is defined as the measure of utility, then Clark saw market value as "the measure of utility made by society considered as one great isolated being." Price reflected the social estimate of that value reflected in dollars. See Maurice Dobb, *Political Economy and Capitalism* (New York: International, 1945), 159–60; Clark, *Philosophy*, 82. See also Ronald L. Meek, *Studies in the Labour Theory of Value* (New York: Monthly Review Press, 1956); Dorfman, *Economic Mind*, 160–284; James Livingston, "The Social Analysis of Economic History and Theory: Conjectures on Late Nineteenth-Century American Development," *American Historical Review* 92 (February 1987): 88; Furner, *Advocacy and Objectivity*, 187.

58. Or, as Gunton would argue, the volume of products sold set wages (Clark, *Philosophy*, 126, 128–29).

59. F. H. Giddings, "The Concepts of Utility, Value, and Cost," *Publications of the American Economic Association* 6 (January–March 1891): 41–42. Giddings believed that those he saw as more racially advanced were better at estimating future utility, and his emphasis on the role of race in economic progress distinguished him from other economists, especially Clark, who did not share his sometime collaborator's views on that subject.

60. Clark, "Ultimate Standard," 85–87.

61. Franklin H. Giddings, "The Idea and Definition of Value," *Publications of the American Economic Association* 8 (January 1893): 88–89.

62. Arthur Twining Hadley, *Economics: An Account of the Relations between Private Property and Public Welfare* (New York: Putnam, 1896), 320.

63. Clark, *Distribution*, 17, 45–46; see also 48–49. As Henry has argued, "This in-

dividualist, Robinson Crusoe method is further developed in his argument that the universal laws of diminishing marginal utility and diminishing returns determine consumption, production, and distribution in not just modern propertied societies but in the fictitious world of the isolated individual" (*John Bates Clark*, 79).

64. While Clark's theoretical work moved toward neoclassical economics, however, he did not abandon his hope for a more democratic world in general and for a more just distribution of wealth specifically. Even as he held that these goals could best be achieved by letting natural law run its course, he actively supported political reforms such as the referendum, worked tirelessly for the Carnegie Endowment for International Peace, worked to establish the Federal Trade Commission, served as part of the committee that investigated malfeasance on the New York Stock Exchange, and taught courses at Columbia University on social reform. See Henry, *John Bates Clark*, 5; Dorfman, *Economic Mind*, 320, 205. For an especially eloquent argument that marginalism emphasized individual choice at the expense of a larger social vision, see Regenia Gagnier, *The Insatiability of Human Wants: Economics and Aesthetics in Market Society* (Chicago: University of Chicago Press, 2000).

65. Edwin R. A. Seligman, "Social Elements in the Theory of Value," *Quarterly Journal of Economics* 15 (May 1901): 337, 340.

66. Clark, *Distribution*, 52, 44–51; Henry, *John Bates Clark*, 53; Dorfman, *Economic Mind*, 201–2.

67. Seligman, "Social Elements," 323, 327, 324. For more on Seligman, Clark, and economics at Columbia, see Gerald Friedman, "Columbia and the Great Empirical Tradition of American Economics," in *Living Legacies: Columbia University after 250 Years*, ed. W. T. DeBary (New York: Columbia University Press, 2006), 414–25, esp. 417–19.

68. Seligman, "Social Elements," 336–37.

69. Edwin R. A. Seligman, "Social Aspects of Economic Law," *Publications of the American Economic Association*, 3rd ser., 5 (February 1904): 53, 57.

70. Indeed, at a memorial to Patten held at the 1923 AEA meeting, J. P. Lichtenberger noted that despite Patten's rejection of sociology, "no one more persistently and intentionally disregarded what he considered the artificial delimitations of the several fields of social science" ("Memorial to Former President Simon N. Patten," 270).

71. Ely, "Founding and Early History," 149.

72. "Memorial to Former President Simon N. Patten," 273. Patten was by all accounts a beloved figure, known for his generosity of spirit, his "ungainly figure and his genial, kindly, homely face" as well as for what Ely called his "tragic" "lack of flexibility [that] too often kept him from that closeness of personal companionship and intellectual cooperation that he desired" (273, 259).

73. Simon Nelson Patten, *The New Basis of Civilization*, ed. Daniel M. Fox (Cambridge: Belknap Press of Harvard University Press, 1968), 6, 12.

74. Ibid., 11, 14–15, 25, 71, 33–34, 150.

75. For Patten's assessment of Malthus, see Simon N. Patten, "Malthus and Ricardo," *Publications of the American Economic Association* 4 (September 1889): 9–34.

76. Patten, *New Basis*, 34, 188.

77. Jackson Lears, *Fables of Abundance: A Cultural History of Advertising in America* (New York: Basic Books, 1994), 116; Patten, *New Basis*, 141.

78. Daniel Horowitz, "Consumption and Its Discontents: Simon N. Patten, Thorstein Veblen, and George Gunton," *Journal of American History* 67 (September 1980): 306. See also Simon Nelson Patten, *Product and Climax* (New York: Macmillan, 1901), 42–53. Kelley made similar claims for leisure, which she, too, saw as a social right, in *Some Ethical Gains through Legislation* (New York: Macmillan, 1905), esp. 105–26. On the "new social rights," see Maureen A. Flanagan, *America Reformed: Progressives and Progressivisms, 1890s–1920s* (New York: Oxford University Press, 2007), 64–69.

79. "Memorial to Former President Simon N. Patten," 269.

80. Patten's reliance on racialism was most notable in his discussion of the right to a home. He worried that forced racial and ethnic mixing would lead to unnecessary competition and disruption. "Every race," he said, "should be given security and prosperity where they belong, but should not be allowed to disturb the orderly development of regions for which they are not fit" (Simon Nelson Patten, *The Theory of Prosperity* [New York: Macmillan, 1902], 223).

81. He also saw leisure as Americans' one opportunity for personal regeneration and the only bulwark against "degeneration," which he understood simultaneously in racial and economic terms, for anxieties about the "decline" of "American stock" were never far from Patten's mind (*Theory of Prosperity*, 224–25).

82. Ibid., 224.

83. "Memorial to Former President Simon N. Patten," 264. As Ely pointed out, however, Patten did not naively assume that consumption alone would promote "greater human happiness than the old economy of the English." Consumption had to be accompanied by decrease in commodity cost, for "the prosperity of the country is measured by its surplus utility, which is the difference between cost and the utilities of goods." Only as the cost (or social pain or sacrifice) decreased and incomes increased, through technological innovation, wise consumption, or governmental manipulations such as indirect taxation, could the social surplus increase ("Memorial to Former President Simon N. Patten," 266).

84. David Montgomery, *Workers' Control in America* (Cambridge: Cambridge University Press, 1980); Lears, *Fables*, 115.

85. The most influential statement of the shift from and conflict between character and personality is Warren Susman, *Culture as History: The Transformation of American Society in the Twentieth Century* (New York: Pantheon, 1984), 271–86. For a recent similar assessment of the social economists and Patten in particular, see Jeffrey Sklansky, *The Soul's Economy: Market Society and Selfhood in American Thought, 1820–1920* (Chapel Hill: University of North Carolina Press, 2002), 171–91, 225–32.

86. Patten, *Theory of Prosperity*, 244.

Four. "Labor Wants More!"

1. Samuel Gompers to editor, *Cigar Maker's Journal,* October 30, 1895, in *The Samuel Gompers Papers,* vol. 4, *A National Labor Movement Takes Shape, 1895–1898,* ed. Stuart B. Kaufman, Peter J. Albert, and Grace Palladino (Urbana: University of Illinois Press, 1991), 74.

2. "Eight Hours on Government Work: Extracts from Statement by President Samuel Gompers," *American Federationist* 11 (March 1904): 308.

3. Although Gompers's "pure and simple unionism" dominated the AFL throughout the 1890s and early 1900s, substantial differences of opinion often arose between the AFL's national leaders and local unions as well as within the AFL's upper echelons, as the struggles over the AFL platform in the mid-1890s demonstrated. For more on differences within the AFL and on the continuing presence of producerism, see, for example, Elizabeth Fones-Wolf and Kenneth Fones-Wolf, "Voluntarism and Factional Disputes in the AFL: The Painters' Split in 1894–1900," *Industrial and Labor Relations Review* 35 (October 1981): 58–69; Michael Kazin, *Barons of Labor: The San Francisco Building Trades and Union Power in the Progressive Era* (Urbana: University of Illinois Press, 1987); Michael Pierce, "The Populist President of the American Federation of Labor: The Career of John McBride, 1880–1895," *Labor History* 41 (February 2000): 5–24; Lawrence M. Lipin, *Workers and the Wild: Conservation, Consumerism, and Labor in Oregon, 1910–1930* (Urbana: University of Illinois Press, 2007).

4. See, for example, "Annual Report to the A.F. of L. Convention, Detroit, Michigan, December 1890"; "Annual Report to the A.F. of L. Convention, Kansas City, Missouri, December 1898"; "Annual Report to the A.F. of L. Convention, Atlanta, Georgia, 1911," all in Samuel Gompers, *Labor and the Common Welfare,* comp. and ed. Hayes Robbins (New York: Dutton, 1919), 2, 8, 20.

5. Samuel Gompers, "Organized Labor in the Campaign," *North American Review,* July 1892, in *The Samuel Gompers Papers,* vol. 3, *Unrest and Depression, 1891–1894,* ed. Stuart B. Kaufman and Peter J. Albert (Urbana: University of Illinois Press, 1989), 203.

6. On the demand for more and AFL ideology, see Lawrence Glickman, *A Living Wage: American Workers and the Making of Consumer Society* (Ithaca: Cornell University Press, 1997). Glickman's work opened the door for a serious reassessment of the ideas of the AFL and Gompers among labor historians, reviving and building on the arguments of Stuart B. Kaufman. For Glickman, the AFL's politics of more represented not an "abandonment of labor's oppositional position" but an effort to link economic demands both with the moral demands of labor republicanism and with labor republicanism's vision of a robust, engaged citizenry (156). Gompers's language, however, read in the context of the larger public debates regarding the economy and the labor question, suggests a subtle readjustment of Glickman's argument. Economic demands no longer had to be linked to political and social demands. By the late nineteenth century, Gompers echoed the historical economists in his belief that it had become impossible to untangle the economic from the social or political. As

such, the economic citizenship expressed by more represented an alternative to both the classical republican citizenship stressed by artisans and journeymen in the early nineteenth century and the liberal individualism of the mid–nineteenth century. See William R. Sutton, *Journeymen for Jesus: Evangelical Artisans Confront Capitalism in Jacksonian Baltimore* (University Park: Pennsylvania State University Press, 1998).

7. In other words, it did not emerge suddenly in response to the successful legal attacks on labor in the 1890s (particularly following the crushing blow to labor in *In re Debs* [1895]). Both Victoria Hattam and William Forbath have argued that the limited and limiting approaches of pure and simple unionism and volunteerism were among labor's few alternatives following this legal assault on organized labor. Pure and simple unionism's ideological origins, however, are visible in the 1870s and were clearly articulated by Gompers, Strasser, and others before the grim 1890s. See Victoria Hattam, *Labor Visions and State Power: The Origins of Business Unionism in the United States* (Princeton: Princeton University Press, 1993); William E. Forbath, *Law and the Shaping of the American Labor Movement* (Cambridge: Harvard University Press, 1991). See also David Ray Papke, *The Pullman Case: The Clash of Labor and Capital in Industrial America* (Lawrence: University Press of Kansas, 1999).

8. The AFL did not even begin to represent most workers in the United States, nor did Samuel Gompers represent the views of all members of the AFL, but by the turn of the century, the AFL increasingly served as the public voice of labor and Gompers as its single-most-visible representative. See David Montgomery, *The Fall of the House of Labor: Workplace, the State, and American Labor Activism, 1865–1925* (New York: Cambridge University Press, 1987); Julie Greene, *Pure and Simple Politics: The American Federation of Labor and Political Activism, 1881–1917* (New York: Cambridge University Press, 1998), esp. 9–12.

9. Samuel Gompers, *Seventy Years of Life and Labor* (New York: Dutton, 1925), 1:1–25; Harold C. Livesay, *Samuel Gompers and Organized Labor in America* (Boston: Little, Brown, 1978), 8–12.

10. Gompers, *Seventy Years,* 1:18.

11. Ibid., 75.

12. Carl Hillman, "Practical Suggestions for Emancipation" (1873), in *The Samuel Gompers Papers,* vol. 1, *The Making of a Union Leader, 1850–1886,* ed. Stuart B. Kaufman (Urbana: University of Illinois Press, 1986), 28.

13. Gompers, *Seventy Years,* 1:90, 77.

14. Ibid., 10, 26–47, 56.

15. Ibid., 93, 102, 55.

16. Historians have clearly pointed out the limitations of Gompers's reliance on trade unionism rather than more inclusive forms of worker organization. By their nature, trade unions excluded unskilled workers, meaning that most workers—and certainly most female and African American workers—had no place in unions. For a comprehensive exploration of the limitations of trade unionism, see Montgomery, *Fall;* Bruce Laurie, *Artisans into Workers: Labor in Nineteenth-Century America* (New

York: Hill and Wang, 1989). David Roediger and Philip Foner have suggested that the AFL's "tactical conservatism" also reflected anxiety about immigrant laborers who might easily be pressured into working longer hours for lower wages. This was certainly reflected in the AFL's attitude toward Chinese immigrants. See David R. Roediger and Philip S. Foner, *Our Own Time: A History of American Labor and the Working Day* (London: Verso, 1989), 151–52.

17. Gompers, *Seventy Years*, 1:47, 50. Gompers understood this push for practical achievement as a reflection of the particularities of the American circumstance: unlike their European counterparts, American workers had most political and legal rights but lacked significant economic power, both in and out of the workplace (60).

18. Samuel Gompers, "Speech Delivered by President Gompers before Meeting Civil Federation New York at the Banquet April 25th, 1905," *American Federationist* 12 (August 1905): 4.

19. For an assessment of the Knights' ideology in relation to understandings of citizenship, see Kim Voss, *The Making of American Exceptionalism: The Knights of Labor and Class Formation in the Nineteenth Century* (Ithaca: Cornell University Press, 1993), 82.

20. *Report of Proceedings of Seventeenth Annual Convention of the AFL* (n.p.: American Federation of Labor, 1897), 19.

21. Richard Schneirov, *Labor and Urban Politics: Class Conflict and the Origins of Modern Liberalism in Chicago, 1864–1897* (Urbana: University of Illinois Press, 1998), 186–91.

22. U.S. Congress, Senate, Committee on Education and Labor, *Report of the Committee of the Senate upon the Relations between Labor and Capital,* 48th Cong., 2nd sess. (Washington, D.C.: U.S. Government Printing Office, 1885), 1:294.

23. "Extempore Statement," *American Federationist* 7 (June 1900): 166.

24. Frank K. Foster, "Side-Lights on the Shorter Workday Demand," *American Federationist* 7 (November 1900): 341.

25. Say's Law made sense only in an economy defined by potential scarcity; in an economy characterized by large-scale, consistent, and increasing production, supply had to follow demand (Martin J. Sklar, *The Corporate Reconstruction of American Capitalism, 1890–1916* [New York: Cambridge University Press, 1988], 54; Donald Winch, *Riches and Poverty: An Intellectual History of Political Economy in Britain, 1750–1834* [New York: Cambridge University Press, 1996], 358–59).

26. Richard Theodore Ely, "Hard Times," Richard Theodore Ely Papers, Ms 411, Teaching and Research Notes, Box 5, Folder 3, Wisconsin Historical Society, Madison.

27. Samuel Gompers to Auguste Keufer, August 16, 1893, in *Samuel Gompers Papers,* 3:388. Keufer was general secretary of France's typographical union. See also "Ducey and Gompers," *New York World,* August 28, 1893, in *Samuel Gompers Papers,* 3:387.

28. On Steward, consumption, and labor politics, see Lawrence Glickman, "Workers of the World, Consume: Ira Steward and the Origins of Labor Consumerism,"

International Labor and Working Class History 52 (Fall 1997): 72–86. Glickman notes that Steward "understood consumerism less as the pursuit of amusement than as a potential locus of working-class power. His goal was not therapeutic but political" (75).

29. Stuart B. Kaufman, *Samuel Gompers and the Origins of the American Federation of Labor, 1848–1896* (Westport, Conn.: Greenwood, 1973), 177–78.

30. George Gunton, *Wealth and Progress: A Critical Examination of the Labor Problem* (New York: Appleton, 1887), 21–22.

31. *Constitution and Rules of Order of the Iron Molders' Union of North America* (Cincinnati: Press of the Ohio Valley, 1890), 6.

32. Schneirov, *Labor and Urban Politics*, 187.

33. "President Gompers' Address," *Louisville (Kentucky) Courier-Journal,* May 2, 1890, in *The Samuel Gompers Papers,* vol. 2, *The Early Years of the American Federation of Labor, 1887–1890,* ed. Stuart B. Kaufman (Urbana: University of Illinois Press, 1987), 311.

34. "Labor's Hard Lot," *Patterson (New Jersey) Labor Standard,* November 21, 1896.

35. Jonathan B. Harrison, *Certain Dangerous Tendencies in American Life* (1880) and Hamilton W. Mabie, *Essays on Work and Culture* (1902), quoted in Daniel Rodgers, *The Work Ethic in Industrial America, 1850–1920* (Chicago: University of Chicago Press, 1974), 10, 13.

36. "Barnum Sammy," *New York People,* October 13, 1895, in *Samuel Gompers Papers,* 4:68, 67.

37. "Labor," *Minneapolis Tribune,* October 27, 1895, in *Samuel Gompers Papers,* 4:71–72.

38. Thorstein Veblen, *The Theory of the Leisure Class,* ed. and intro. Martha Banta (1899; New York: Oxford University Press, 2007), 15–16; Kathleen Donohue, *Freedom from Want: American Liberalism and the Idea of the Consumer* (Baltimore: Johns Hopkins University Press, 2003), 35–37.

39. Paul Krause, *The Battle for Homestead, 1880–1892: Politics, Culture, and Steel* (Pittsburgh: University of Pittsburgh Press, 1992), 9, 252–66.

40. H. C. Daniels, *Capital, Labor, Unionism* (Hartford, Conn.: Daniels, 1906), n.p.

41. Gompers, "Speech," 4.

42. "On the Attitude of Organized Labor toward Organized Charity," *American Federationist* 6 (March 1899): 82.

43. *Constitution, By-Laws, Rules of Order, and Order of Business of the Brotherhood of Clothing Cutters and Trimmers* (Rochester, N.Y.: Spinning, 1894), 12.

44. The differences between Gompers's more and Booker T. Washington's call for African American economic self-sufficiency are instructive. Washington hoped that "material progress by blacks would foment white admiration," and he equated increased property holdings with progress toward racial equality, to the deep dismay

of many observers. Gompers rather pointedly imagined more as a demand for power and agency, not admiration. See David W. Blight, *Race and Reunion: The Civil War in American Memory* (Cambridge: Harvard University Press, 2002), 332.

45. Lizzie M. Holmes, "Economy That Proved Disastrous," *American Federationist* 8 (October 1901): 471.

46. In "On Wages," David Ricardo explained that "the natural price of Labour is that price which is necessary to enable the labourers, one with another, to subsist and to perpetuate their race, without either increase or diminution" (*The Principles of Political Economy and Taxation*, in *The Works and Correspondence of David Ricardo*, ed. Piero Sraffa [Cambridge: Cambridge University Press, 1953], 1:92).

47. The town's refusal to spend money constitutes hoarding, not saving, and thus represents, suggests Walter Benn Michaels, the fetishization of money as object rather than thrift, much like Trina McTeague's determination to always keep her gold "in hand" in Frank Norris's novel, *McTeague*. See Walter Benn Michaels, *The Gold Standard and the Logic of Naturalism* (Berkeley: University of California Press, 1987), 140–41.

48. "Testimony before the Industrial Commission, Washington, D.C., April 18, 1899," in Samuel Gompers, *Labor and the Employer,* comp. and ed. Hayes Robbins (New York: Dutton, 1920), 62.

49. Gunton, *Wealth and Progress,* 207. As Wilbur Aldrich put it in the same journal, "The growth of [women's] economic independence will lead to the attainment of political equality" ("The Economic Woman," *Social Economist* 5 [October 1893]: 234). See also Carroll D. Wright, "Why Women Are Paid Less than Men," *Forum* 13 (March–August 1898): 629; "Women Wage Earners," *New Orleans Times-Democrat,* May 23, 1895, in *Samuel Gompers Papers,* 4:32.

50. Florence Kelley Wischnewetzky to Richard Theodore Ely, April 23, 1891, Ely Papers, Correspondence, Box 3, Folder 11.

51. Charlotte Perkins Gilman, *Women and Economics: A Study of the Economic Relation between Men and Women as a Factor in Social Evolution* (1898; Berkeley: University of California Press, 1998), 58, 120, 63; see also 144, 215, 338.

52. "Social Questions in Magazine Literature," *Social Economist* 1 (June 1892): 236–37.

53. "President Gompers' Address," in *Samuel Gompers Papers,* 2:311.

54. The rhetoric of the family wage itself helped ensure that men remained, as Sue Porter Benson has pointed out, "more autonomous" than wage-earning women throughout the interwar period, both as consumers and as social actors ("Gender, Generation, and Consumption in the United States: Working-Class Families in the Interwar Period," in *Getting and Spending: European and American Consumer Societies in the Twentieth Century,* ed. Susan Strasser, Charles McGovern, and Matthias Judt [New York: Cambridge University Press, 1998], 240). Nonetheless, the disassociation of property ownership, self-employment, and social independence up the possibility of previously marginalized people laying claim to "economic liberty."

For further discussion of the possibilities for new conceptions of independence for women within proletarianization, see Ellen Carol DuBois, "Radicalism and the Women's Suffrage Movement," in *Feminism and Equality*, ed. Anne Phillips (New York: New York University Press, 1987), 127–38; Joan Wallach Scott, *Gender and the Politics of History* (New York: Columbia University Press, 1988), 53–67; James Livingston, *Pragmatism, Feminism, and Democracy: Rethinking the Politics of American History* (New York: Routledge, 2001).

55. Many historians have more firmly positioned the emergence of economic liberty in the Progressive Era. See, for example, Eric Foner, *The Story of American Freedom* (New York: Norton, 1998), 139–62. Foner sees the economic freedom stressed in the Progressive Era as a precursor to the economic freedom described by John Dewey in *Liberalism and State Action* (New York: Putnam, 1935). Mary O. Furner, conversely, locates that commitment to economic freedom in the early years of the "long progressive era" beginning in the 1880s. Democratic statists such as Ely and Henry Carter Adams, she argues, "proposed extending the claims of citizenship, including entitlements and protections against the pernicious insecurity of industrial modernism, among a new class of rights" ("The Republican Tradition and the New Liberalism," in *The State and Social Investigation in Britain and the United States*, ed. Michael J. Lacey and Mary O. Furner [Cambridge: Woodrow Wilson Center Press and University of Cambridge Press, 1993], 194–95). Similar arguments had already begun within the AFL.

56. Arthur Twining Hadley, *Economics: An Account of the Relations between Private Property and Public Welfare* (New York: Putnam, 1896), 371–72.

57. Clarence Darrow, "The Workingman and the Courts," Clarence Darrow Papers, MSRR, Box 11, Library of Congress, Washington, D.C. See also "Is It Ever to Be Thus?" *American Federationist* 3 (October 1896): 160.

58. "Sound Economics in Congress," *Social Economist* 6 (March 1894): 129, 130, 132, 131, 136.

59. "Economics of Dynamic Society," *Social Economist* 5 (December 1893): 339.

60. Not all writers in the *Social Economist* were as sanguine about mechanization. Edward Thimme, for example, was convinced that mechanization spurred unemployment ("Our Labor Outlook," *Social Economist* 5 [August 1893]: 171–72).

61. "The Economy of High Wages," *Social Economist* 6 (April 1894): 197.

62. Carroll D. Wright, "Hand and Machine Labor," *Gunton's Magazine* 18 (March 1900): 210, 209.

63. See, for example, David R. Roediger, "Ira Steward and the Anti-Slavery Origins of the Eight-Hour Day," *Labor History* 27 (Spring 1986): 412.

64. "A Shorter Working Year," *Social Economist* 5 (August 1893): 106.

65. "How Is Wealth Distributing Itself?" *Social Economist* 5 (November 1893): 267.

66. Edward Atkinson, "The Progress of the Nation," *Forum* 6 (October 1888): 126.

67. John Bates Clark, Carroll D. Wright, and Edwin R. A. Seligman were involved in the *Social Economist,* and Seligman's connections with Gunton are particularly notable. Seligman had positively reviewed Gunton's 1887 *Wealth and Progress* for *Political Science Quarterly.* When Gunton moved to New York to found the Institute for Social Economics and the *Social Economist*, the two met, and Seligman supported the institute. See Joseph Dorfman, *The Economic Mind in American Civilization,* vol. 3, *1865–1918* (New York: Viking, 1949), 47; Jack Blicksilver, "George Gunton: Pioneer Spokesman for a Labor–Big Business Entente," *Business History Review* 31 (Spring 1957): 2–6; "Prof. George Gunton Dead," *New York Times*, September 13, 1919.

68. "Economics of Dynamic Society," 339.

69. Gail Bederman, *Manliness and Civilization: A Cultural History of Gender and Race in the United States, 1880–1917* (Chicago: University of Chicago Press, 1995), 23–44.

70. W. E. Hart, "Wages as a Criterion of Civilization," *Social Economist* 1 (May 1891): 175, 174, 173.

71. Ellis Meriam, "The Economics of Luxury," *Social Economist* 1 (June 1891): 233.

72. For more on the role of desire in Gunton's thought, see Glickman, *Living Wage,* 76.

73. S. M. Jelley, *The Voice of Labor: Plain Talk by Men of Intellect on Labor's Rights, Wrongs, Remedies, and Prospects* (New York: Franklin, 1888), 168.

74. Rev. W. S. Harris, *Capital and Labor* (Harrisburg, Pa.: Minter, 1907), 121.

75. *Constitution of the General Assembly . . . of the Order of the Knights of Labor of America* (Philadelphia: General Assembly of the Knights of Labor, 1888), 5. As Schneirov has shown for Chicago, the Knights saw cooperatives as "an attempt to abolish and socialize personal property within the confines of existing property laws and market relations—in order to sustain and revive the Republic" (*Labor and Urban Politics,* 239). Though the Knights shared Gompers's belief that the "political rights of the people are not more sacred than their economic rights," they saw the abolishment of the wage system as the ultimate goal, even when they combined trade unionist and republican thought, as they often did in the 1880s.

76. *Constitution of the United Hatters of North America* (New York?: Hatters, 1898), 28. The 1903 constitution expressed similar concerns but did so even more stridently.

77. Quoted in Glickman, *Living Wage,* 31.

78. Schneirov, *Labor and Urban Politics,* 301, 316, 307. Sociologist Jason Kaufman has also pointed out that after the decline of the Knights, "former Knights flocked to (and founded) dozens of new lodges and unions, particularly those which better represented their interests by pursuing less ornate and more reasonable goals" ("Rise and Fall of a Nation of Joiners: The Knights of Labor Revisited," *Journal of Interdisciplinary History* 31 [Spring 2001]: 557).

79. *Report on the Chicago Strike of June–July, 1894, by the United States Strike Commission* (Washington, D.C.: U.S. Government Printing Office, 1895), 602, quoted

in Carl Smith, *Urban Disorder and the Shape of Belief: The Great Chicago Fire, the Haymarket Bomb, and the Model Town of Pullman* (Chicago: University of Chicago Press, 1995), 243.

80. Nick Salvatore, *Eugene V. Debs: Citizen and Socialist* (Urbana: University of Illinois Press, 1982), 60–69, 154. The term *vernacular socialism* comes from Rodgers, *Work Ethic*, 117–18. See also Smith, *Urban Disorder*, 238–52.

81. The AFL's political possibilities were limited, as historians have noted, by the organization's policies (on immigration, for example), by the structures of electoral politics, and by court rulings against labor, most notably *In re Debs* (1895), *Lochner v. New York* (1905), and the Danbury Hatters' Case (1908). See, for example, Gwendolyn Mink, *Old Labor and New Immigrants in American Political Development: Union, Party, and State, 1875–1920* (Ithaca: Cornell University Press, 1986); Elizabeth Sanders, *Roots of Reform: Farmers, Workers, and the American State, 1877–1917* (Chicago: University of Chicago Press, 1999); Forbath, *Law*. Nonetheless, the AFL had no interest in forming a political party, and its later entrée into politics was, as Julie Greene has shown, largely intended to ensure the passage of labor-friendly legislation; Gompers, in particular, remained stridently nonpartisan. As Greene points out, locals' enthusiasm for political action often made Gompers somewhat uncomfortable, and the AFL's structure meant that locals often followed their own interests quite aggressively (*Pure and Simple Politics*, 1–16, 107–43).

82. Philip S. Foner, *History of the Labor Movement in the United States*, vol. 1, *From Colonial Times to the Founding of the American Federation of Labor*, 4th ed. (New York: International, 1972), 517. For a particularly well-stated version of Foner's argument on the limitations of the AFL's and Gompers's programs, see Sarah Lyons Watts, *Order against Chaos: Business Culture and Labor Ideology in America, 1880–1915* (Westport, Conn.: Greenwood, 1991). Watts argues that Gompers's and the AFL's emergence "as the leading spokesmen for the American labor movement paved the way for the triumph of capital's new definition of labor. The AFL defined workers in narrowly economic terms," in marked contrast to the "broader definitions put forward by the Knights of Labor or, later, by Eugene V. Debs," which held "that workers were citizens with broad social obligations and political responsibilities. The AFL focused on institutional collective bargaining based on contracts and thus relegated itself to a functional role within the corporate structure" (xi).

83. That characterization of the IWW comes from Foster Rhea Dulles and Melvyn Dubofsky, *Labor in America: A History*, 6th ed. (Arlington Heights, Ill.: Harlan Davidson, 2004), 195–209.

84. Kim Moody, *An Injury to All: The Decline of American Unionism* (London: Verso, 1988), 56. Moody goes on to claim that "Gompers was rhapsodic on the subject" of capitalism.

85. For a particularly scathing indictment of the AFL in general and Gompers in particular, see Paul Buhle, *Taking Care of Business: Samuel Gompers, George Meany, Lane Kirkland, and the Tragedy of American Labor* (New York: Monthly Review Press,

1999). The exclusionary nature of AFL unions, especially in relation to nonwhite and female labor, should not be understated. The AFL and Gompers in particular were theoretically committed to including African American workers (but not Asian workers) in trade unions but only rarely insisted on their inclusion. And while the AFL argued that women workers deserved a full wage for their work, both the organization and many of its members were committed to the idea of a family wage. For more on male workers' resistance to women's work, see Eileen Boris, "'A Man's Dwelling House Is His Castle': Tenement House Cigarmaking and the Judicial Imperative," in *Work Engendered: Toward a New History of American Labor,* ed. Ava Baron (Ithaca: Cornell University Press, 1991), 114–41. At the same time, as Michael Kazin notes, the AFL was never as "unimaginative" as the standard narrative suggests. In 1910, the AFL had two million members, including waitresses, immigrants, African Americans, coal miners, and Socialists (*The Populist Persuasion: An American History* [New York: Basic Books, 1995], 53).

86. See, for example, Sean Wilentz, *Chants Democratic: New York City and the Rise of the American Working Class* (New York: Oxford University Press, 1984); Ronald Schultz, *The Republic of Labor: Philadelphia Artisans and the Politics of Class, 1720– 1830* (New York: Oxford University Press, 1993). Richard Stott has suggested that studies of labor republicanism in antebellum America focus disproportionately on artisans and journeymen; looking at less skilled workers might well decenter labor republicanism ("Artisans and Capitalist Development," in *The Wages of Independence: Capitalism in the Early American Republic,* ed. Paul Gilje [Madison, Wis.: Madison House, 1997], 101–16).

87. David Montgomery, "Labor and the Republic in Industrial America, 1860– 1920," *Le Mouvement Social* 111 (April–June 1980): 211. Montgomery notes that "counter currents" existed in the form of the IWW and Socialist Party but that they were consistently "less powerful and less heard." See also Shelton Stromquist, *Reinventing "The People": The Progressive Movement, the Class Problem, and the Origins of Modern Liberalism* (Urbana: University of Illinois Press, 2006), 5; Leon Fink, "New Labor History and the Powers of Historical Pessimism: Consensus, Hegemony, and the Case of the Knights of Labor," *Journal of American History* 75 (June 1988): 119.

88. As both David Brody and Richard Oestreicher have noted, much of the New Labor History focuses on the question of "when we lost," and that question itself structures the discussion of both labor republicanism and the AFL. See Richard Oestreicher, "Urban Working-Class Political Behavior and Theories of American Electoral Politics, 1870–1940," *Journal of American History* 74 (March 1988): 1264–65; David Brody, "Reconciling the Old Labor History and the New," *Pacific Historical Review* 62 (February 1993): 12. As a result, much labor history has retained what Gerald Friedman has described as a "strong antiquarian bias" rooted in nostalgia for past times and lost opportunities (review of *Perspectives on American Labor History: The Problem of Synthesis,* ed. J. Carroll Moody and Alice Kessler-Harris, *Journal of Economic History* 50 [September 1990]: 761–62). Some recent assessments of pro-

ducerism in general and Populism in particular have avoided that sense of nostalgia. Charles Postel's study, for example, shows California's Populists as resolutely modern, antinostalgic, and applying producerist ideals to modern society rather than using them to attempt to reassert a past social order (*The Populist Vision* [New York: Oxford University Press, 2007]).

89. As Haywood told a crowd of "effete" New Yorkers in 1912, "I despise the law and am not a law-abiding citizen. And more than that, no Socialist can be a law-abiding citizen. When we come together . . . to overthrow the capitalist system, we become conspirators then against the United States government." Salvatore suggests that by 1912, Haywood may have "come to believe too many of his own press clippings" (*Eugene V. Debs,* 253). Other members of the Socialist Party did not, however. In 1912, Haywood was pushed out of any leadership position in the party, and his original union, the Western Federation of Miners, voted to reaffiliate with the AFL.

90. John Spargo, *Applied Socialism: A Study of the Application of Socialistic Principles to the State* (New York: Huebsch, 1912), 182, 190. Spargo roundly attacked "ill-informed Socialists" for misreading Marx and placing far too much emphasis on the idea that "all wealth is produced by labor and, therefore, ought to belong to the laborers." Marx "was never guilty of that error. Nowhere does he attempt to base an argument for Socialism upon the 'right of labor' to the whole product of industry." Spargo continued, "As a matter of fact, Marx's theory of value has no more to do with the method of distribution in the Socialist State than with the length and breadth of the canals of Mars" (184–85). For more on Spargo's thought in contrast to vernacular socialism, see Rodgers, *Work Ethic,* 217–18.

91. Mark Pittenger, *American Socialists and Evolutionary Thought, 1870–1920* (Madison: University of Wisconsin Press, 1993), 128–29, 101. Debs was less insistent on the revolution, but he, too, felt that individual, "small" reforms of the existing system (such as worker's compensation laws, shorter days, and adequate municipal sanitation) did little more "than eas[e] the difficulties laborers faced in a capitalist world" (John P. Enyeart, "Revolution or Evolution: The Socialist Party, Western Workers, and Law in the Progressive Era," *Journal of the Gilded Age and Progressive Era* 2 [October 2003]: 395).

92. Enyeart, "Revolution or Evolution," 396.

93. On the flexibility of the AFL's program within the context of the postbellum economy, see, for example, Stuart B. Kaufman, *Samuel Gompers;* Glickman, *Living Wage;* Schneirov, *Labor and Urban Politics;* Dorothy Sue Cobble, "American Labor Politics, AFL Style," *Labor History* 40 (Spring 1999): 192–96. For a similar assessment of the AFL in the twentieth century, see Kevin Boyle, *The UAW and the Heyday of American Liberalism, 1945–1968* (Ithaca: Cornell University Press, 1995). For a discussion of the links between economic opportunity and social citizenship, see William E. Forbath, "The New Deal Constitution in Exile," *Duke Law Journal* 51 (October 2001): esp. 217–22.

94. "Our Labor Outlook," 242.

95. U.S. Congress, Senate, Committee on Education and Labor, *Report*, 1:460; Gabriel Edmonston, "When We Declared for Eight Hours," *American Federationist* 8 (October 1901): 406.

96. "Curious Relation of Labor to Labor," *Patterson (New Jersey) Labor Standard*, November 21, 1896.

97. "Economy of High Wages," 194.

98. "Individualism," *Social Economist* 1 (April 1891): 75, 76, 78.

99. James Duncan, "Labor Day Thoughts: For Economic Independence," *American Federationist* 9 (September 1904): 915–16.

100. Stuart B. Kaufman, *Samuel Gompers*, 197; John Turner, "A Peculiar Policy," *American Federationist* 3 (July 1896): 81. Turner served as president of the United Shop Assistants' Union in England; during 1896, he traveled extensively in America.

101. "President Gompers' Address," *Louisville (Kentucky) Courier-Journal*, May 2, 1890, in *Samuel Gompers Papers*, 2:313–14.

102. "On the Attitude of Organized Labor," 82. For just several of many other similar demands for more, see Samuel Gompers to editor, *Chicagoer Arbeiter-Zeitung*, May 4, 1896, in *Samuel Gompers Papers*, 4:161–62; "The Trades Unions Conference," *Manchester Guardian*, September 6, 1895, in *Samuel Gompers Papers*, 4:60.

103. Calls for more might well form the basis for demanding economic and social equality, as Gunton argued, but did not evade the question of real inequality of power or wealth. As Glickman has shown, demands for a living wage translated into very specific labor programs that did not sidestep questions of class or class inequality (*Living Wage*, esp. 147–62). Similarly, work remained at the center of consumerist politics in the twentieth century and continues to do so in contemporary America. It is impossible to read reports of decreased consumer spending aside from reports of declining real wages.

104. "A Social Agent in Factories," *Syracuse Standard*, September 27, 1902, Cyrus McCormick Jr. Papers, Series 2C, Box 42, McCormick–International Harvester Collection, Wisconsin Historical Society.

105. Industrial Betterment Report of J. H. Williams Company, Brooklyn, New York, December 20, 1905, on letterhead of American Institute of Social Service, McCormick Papers, Series 2C, Box 41.

106. C. E. Woods to F. A. Flather, August 18, 1904, McCormick Papers, Series 2C, Box 4. Box 134 contains numerous clippings on Haymarket. The events of 1886 clearly weighed on the minds of International Harvester's leaders.

107. *Chicago Post*, September 24, 1902, clipping in McCormick Papers, Series 2C, Box 42. Despite International Harvester's push to improve conditions in some plants, the *New York Times* reported continued abuses of women workers in 1912 at company mills in Auburn, New York. Then state senator Robert F. Wagner commented that the workers were "worn and pale, and their clothes, faces and hands were covered with oil and hemp cloth" ("Finds Women Driven by Harvester Trust," *New York Times*, August 1912, McCormick Papers, Series 2C, Box 42).

108. Samuel Gompers, "Labor Standards after the War," *Annals of the American Academy,* December 1919, in Gompers, *Labor and the Employer,* 31; Samuel Gompers to August Belmont, July 6, 1918, in Gompers, *Labor and the Employer,* 78.

109. Alice Kessler-Harris, *In Pursuit of Equity: Women, Men, and the Quest for Economic Citizenship in Twentieth-Century America* (New York: Oxford University Press, 2001), esp. 64–169. Political scientist Judith N. Shklar has similarly linked wage earning and full citizenship in twentieth-century America (*American Citizenship: The Quest for Inclusion* [Cambridge: Harvard University Press, 1991], 98).

110. On the exclusionary implications of naturalized rights, see, for example, Wendy Brown, *States of Injury: Power and Freedom in Late Modernity* (Princeton: Princeton University Press, 1995), 60–61.

111. For a view of how poor women of color used the language of economic citizenship for their own purposes, see Felicia Kornbluh, *The Battle for Welfare Rights: Politics and Poverty in Modern America* (Philadelphia: University of Pennsylvania Press, 2007).

112. Meg Jacobs has described twentieth-century economic citizenship a bit more broadly, as the "powerful dialectic" between "'concrete economic daily experience'" (in Caroline Ware's words) and "economic policy making," between "popular politics and elite policymaking" (*Pocketbook Politics: Economic Citizenship in Twentieth-Century America* [Princeton: Princeton University Press, 2005], 2–11). Like Kessler-Harris, Jacobs shows economic citizenship to be bound up with and enacted through the state, politics, and policy.

113. Roberto Alejandro, *Hermeneutics, Citizenship, and the Public Sphere* (Albany: State University of New York Press, 1993), 2; Linda K. Kerber, "The Meanings of Citizenship," *Journal of American History* 84 (December 1997): 833–54.

114. "On the Attitude," 82; "President Gompers' Address," *Louisville (Kentucky) Courier-Journal,* May 2, 1890, in *Samuel Gompers Papers,* 2:313–14; Stuart B. Kaufman, *Samuel Gompers,* 178. See also "The Labor Question," *Denver Rocky Mountain News,* February 10, 1888, in *Samuel Gompers Papers,* 2:82; "To the Officer and Members of the New York Stereotypers Association," ca. February 23–27, 1888, in *Samuel Gompers Papers,* 2:91.

115. Jacobs, *Pocketbook Politics,* 7. Such demands pushed policy makers, legislatures, and private enterprise to take into account consumers' needs and desires; the demands made consumers political actors. At the same time, explains Jacobs, the cross-class coalitions were fragile at best and often disintegrated under conflicting pressures for higher wages and lower prices.

Five. The End of the Labor Question

1. Jane Addams, *Twenty Years at Hull-House* (New York: Macmillan, 1910), 262, 267–69, 274, 276–77.

2. Ibid., 282–309.

3. Henry Steele Commager, *The American Mind: An Interpretation of American Thought and Character since the 1880s* (New Haven: Yale University Press, 1950), 53.

4. Addams, *Twenty Years,* 125.

5. Richard Schneirov, *Labor and Urban Politics: Class Conflict and the Origins of Modern Liberalism in Chicago, 1864–1897* (Urbana: University of Illinois Press, 1998), 10.

6. Charles Hoffmann, "The Depression of the Nineties," *Journal of Economic History* 16 (June 1956): 138; Douglas Steeples and David O. Whitten, *Democracy in Desperation: The Depression of 1893* (Westport, Conn.: Greenwood, 1998), 27–65. On the crisis of the 1890s generally, see Richard Schneirov, Shelton Stromquist, and Nick Salvatore, eds., *The Pullman Strike and the Crisis of the 1890s* (Urbana: University of Illinois Press, 1999).

7. Christina Romer, "Spurious Volatility in Historical Unemployment Data," *Journal of Political Economy* 94 (February 1986): 31.

8. Samuel Rezneck, "Unemployment, Unrest, and Relief in the United States during the Depression of 1893–1897," *Journal of Political Economy* 61 (August 1953): 324–28, 334–35.

9. Nick Salvatore, *Eugene V. Debs: Citizen and Socialist* (Urbana: University of Illinois Press, 1982), 119–22.

10. Debs quoted in Carl Smith, *Urban Disorder and the Shape of Belief: The Great Chicago Fire, the Haymarket Bomb, and the Model Town of Pullman* (Chicago: University of Chicago Press, 1995), 242.

11. Paul Krause, *The Battle for Homestead, 1880–1892: Politics, Culture, and Steel* (Pittsburgh: University of Pittsburgh Press, 1992).

12. Shelton Stromquist, "The Crisis of 1894 and the Legacies of Producerism," in *Pullman Strike,* ed. Schneirov, Stromquist, and Salvatore, 197. For a discussion of the decline but not disappearance of producerism within the labor movement, see David Montgomery, *The Fall of the House of Labor: Workplace, the State, and American Labor Activism, 1865–1925* (New York: Cambridge University Press, 1987); Leon Fink, *Workingmen's Democracy: The Knights of Labor and American Politics* (Urbana: University of Illinois Press, 1983); William E. Forbath, *Law and the Shaping of the American Labor Movement* (Cambridge: Harvard University Press, 1991); Schneirov, *Labor and Urban Politics;* Shelton Stromquist, *Reinventing "The People": The Progressive Movement, the Class Problem, and the Origins of Modern Liberalism* (Urbana: University of Illinois Press, 2006). For discussions of the decline of producerism in economic and social thought, see John L. Thomas, *Alternative America: Henry George, Edward Bellamy, Henry Demarest Lloyd, and the Adversary Tradition* (Cambridge: Harvard University Press, 1983); Eric Rauchway, "The High Cost of Living in the Progressives' Economy," *Journal of American History* 88 (December 2001): 899–924; Nancy Cohen, *The Reconstruction of American Liberalism, 1865–1914* (Chapel Hill: University of North Carolina Press, 2002); Kathleen G. Donohue, *Freedom from*

Want: American Liberalism and the Idea of the Consumer (Baltimore: Johns Hopkins University Press, 2003). On the persistence of producerism, see, for example, David Horowitz, *Vance Packard and American Social Criticism* (Chapel Hill: University of North Carolina Press, 1994); Michael Kazin, *The Populist Persuasion: An American History* (New York: Basic Books, 1995); Lawrence M. Lipin, *Workers and the Wild: Conservation, Consumerism, and Labor in Oregon, 1910–1930* (Urbana: University of Illinois Press, 2007); Daniel Scroop, "The Anti–Chain Store Movement and the Politics of Consumption," *American Quarterly* 60 (December 2008): 225–49.

13. Thomas J. Craughwell, *Stealing Lincoln's Body* (Cambridge: Belknap Press of Harvard University Press, 2007), 194.

14. Walter S. Logan, *An Argument for an Eight-Hour Law: An Address Delivered before the Manhattan Liberal Club, New York, December 22, 1892* (New York: Knickerbocker, 1894), 5–11.

15. Smith, *Urban Disorder,* 250–55; David Ray Papke, *The Pullman Case: The Clash of Labor and Capital in Industrial America* (Lawrence: University Press of Kansas, 1999).

16. Jane Addams, *Democracy and Social Ethics* (New York: Macmillan, 1902), 143, 139.

17. Ibid., 148, 151–53.

18. Daniel Rodgers, *Atlantic Crossings: Social Politics in a Progressive Age* (Cambridge: Belknap Press of Harvard University Press, 2000), 105–6. See also Joseph Dorfman, *The Economic Mind in American Civilization,* vol. 3, *1865–1918* (New York: Viking, 1949), 258–64. Dorothy Ross argues that Hadley shared few larger aims with Clark, Ely, Adams, and E. R. A. Seligman (*The Origins of American Social Science* [New York: Cambridge University Press, 1991], 111).

19. Arthur Twining Hadley, *Economics: An Account of the Relations between Private Property and Public Welfare* (New York: Putnam, 1896), 360.

20. "Dr. Ely Addresses Twilight Club," *Fond du Lac (Wisconsin) Daily Commonwealth,* March 16, 1905, Box 5, Additions, Ms 411, Richard Theodore Ely Papers, Wisconsin Historical Society, Madison.

21. Carroll Davidson Wright, "Are the Rich Growing Richer and the Poor Poorer?" *Atlantic Monthly,* September 1897, 307.

22. James Livingston, *Origins of the Federal Reserve System: Money, Class, and Corporate Capitalism* (Ithaca: Cornell University Press, 1986), 56–57. The number of mergers increased exponentially after 1893. In 1895, four mergers took place; that number grew to sixteen in 1898 and to sixty-three just one year later. Seventy-two of the ninety-three consolidations Naomi Lamoreaux analyzed controlled 40 percent or more of their industries, while forty-two firms controlled 70 percent or more. Within at most eight years, corporate capitalism had come to define not only economic life but also daily life (*The Great Merger Movement in American Business, 1895–1904* [Cambridge: Cambridge University Press, 1985], 1–2).

23. On the increase in distribution of goods, see Alfred Chandler, *The Visible Hand:*

The Managerial Revolution in American Business (Cambridge: Harvard University Press, 1977), 209–39; William Cronon, *Nature's Metropolis: Chicago and the Great West* (New York: Norton, 1991), 55–93, 207–59.

24. Jeffrey G. Williamson, *Late Nineteenth-Century American Development: A General Equilibrium History* (Cambridge: Cambridge University Press, 1974), 93–118; James Livingston, "The Social Analysis of Economic History and Theory: Conjectures on Late Nineteenth-Century Development," *American Historical Review* 92 (February 1987): 69–95.

25. George Gunton noted in 1889, for example, that capital's profit was "nowhere one-fourth as large as wages. Where the profits are highest, wages are 337 per cent greater than profits, and where they are lowest, wages are 1000 per cent greater than profits" ("The Economic Basis of Socialism," *Political Science Quarterly* 4 [December 1889]: 590–91). Gunton obtained the railroad figures from Henry Carter Adams's *First Annual Report on the Statistics of Railways in the United States to the Interstate Commerce Commission* (Washington, D.C.: U.S. Government Printing Office, 1889), 21. On rising real wages, see Carroll D. Wright, "Cheaper Living and the Rise of Wages," *Forum* 16 (October 1893): 221–28; Republican National Committee, *Republican Campaign Textbook 1896* (Washington, D.C.: Hartman and Cadick, 1896), 186–88.

26. David Montgomery, *Workers' Control in America: Studies in the History of Work, Technology, and Labor Struggles* (Cambridge: Cambridge University Press, 1980), 9–31; Livingston, "Social Analysis," 79–82.

27. Technological innovation cannot account for the reversal, as Williamson explains, since such developments did not begin significantly to raise productivity until after 1907 (*Late Nineteenth-Century American Development,* 118, 96). And although the United States continued to respond to international financial trends, Great Britain, which suffered a similar period of retardation, did not emerge from its slump until World War I.

28. Livingston, "Social Analysis," 82–87.

29. Hadley, *Economics,* 4, 9.

30. Arthur T. Hadley, "Jay Gould and Socialism," *Forum* 14 (January 1893): 686, 688, 687, 689–90.

31. Henry Carter Adams to E. R. A. Seligman, June 20, 1904, in Joseph Dorfman, ed., "The Seligman Correspondence II," *Political Science Quarterly* 56 (June 1941): 275.

32. Franklin MacVeagh, "The Responsibility of Wealth," n.d., Franklin MacVeagh Papers, Box 43, Manuscript Division, Library of Congress, Washington, D.C.

33. Schneirov, *Labor and Urban Politics,* 58–59, 262, 264–68. Schneirov also cites the importance of personal experience for Clarence Darrow, Jane Addams, Lyman Gage, and John Peter Altgeld.

34. Mary O. Furner, "The Republican Tradition and the New Liberalism: Social Investigation, State Building, and Social Learning in the Gilded Age," in *The State and Social Investigation in Britain and the United States,* ed. Michael J. Lacey and

Mary O. Furner (Washington, D.C.: Woodrow Wilson Center Press and Cambridge University Press, 1993), 171–241, esp. 174–75; Schneirov, *Labor and Urban Politics,* 270, 329–64.

35. Franklin MacVeagh, Speech on the "Chicago Plan," n.d., MacVeagh Papers, Box 43.

36. Franklin MacVeagh, "Labor Unions," 1905, MacVeagh Papers, Box 29. MacVeagh read this speech to the Commercial Clubs of Cincinnati, St. Louis, and Chicago in Cincinnati on May 27, 1905.

37. MacVeagh, Speech on the "Chicago Plan."

38. MacVeagh, "Responsibility of Wealth"; MacVeagh, Speech on the "Chicago Plan."

39. MacVeagh, "Responsibility of Wealth"; MacVeagh, Speech on the "Chicago Plan"; Karl Marx, *Grundrisse: Foundations of the Critique of Political Economy* (1953; London: Penguin, 1973), 706; George Herbert Mead, *Movements of Thought in the Nineteenth Century* (Chicago: University of Chicago Press, 1936), 382, 405–6. For Dewey, see, for example, his classic "My Pedagogic Creed," *School Journal* 54 (January 1897): 77–80. On the social self and incorporation, see James Livingston, *Pragmatism, Feminism, and Democracy: Rethinking the Politics of American History* (New York: Routledge, 2000), 9–11; Jeffrey Sklansky, *The Soul's Economy: Market Society and Selfhood in American Thought, 1820–1920* (Chapel Hill: University of North Carolina Press, 2002), 205–24; Wilfred M. McClay, *The Masterless: Self and Society in Modern America* (Chapel Hill: University of North Carolina Press, 1994).

40. Jane Addams, "A New Impulse to an Old Gospel," *Forum* 14 (November 1892): 345–46.

41. Addams, *Twenty Years,* 91.

42. Dorfman, *Economic Mind,* 47; Jack Blicksilver, "George Gunton: Pioneer Spokesman for a Labor–Big Business Entente," *Business History Review* 31 (Spring 1957), 2–6; "Prof. George Gunton Dead," *New York Times,* September 13, 1919.

43. David Montgomery, *Beyond Equality: Labor and the Radical Republicans, 1862–1872* (Urbana: University of Illinois Press, 1967), 230–60; Lawrence Glickman, *A Living Wage: American Workers and the Making of Consumer Society* (Ithaca: Cornell University Press, 1997), 99–128; Dorothy Douglas, "Ira Steward on Consumption and Unemployment," *Journal of Political Economy* 40 (August 1932): 532–43.

44. David R. Roediger and Philip S. Foner, *Our Own Time: A History of American Labor and the Working Day* (London: Verso, 1989), 85; Lawrence Glickman, "Workers of the World, Consume: Ira Steward and the Origins of Labor Consumerism," *International Labor and Working Class History* 52 (Fall 1997): 74–75.

45. Ira Steward, *The Eight Hour Movement: A Reduction of Hours Is an Increase of Wages* (Boston: Boston Labor Reform Association, 1865), 4–5, 19.

46. Ibid., 21, 23, 12.

47. Eric Foner, *Reconstruction: America's Unfinished Revolution, 1863–1877* (New York: Harper and Row, 1988), 478.

48. William D. Kelley, *Speeches, Addresses, and Letters on Industrial and Financial Questions: To Which Is Added an Introduction, Together with Copious Notes and an Index* (Philadelphia: Baird, 1872), 279.

49. Gompers argued in 1903 that the continuing belief that "every man should stand upon his own bottom and erect" rested on the assumption that "in what was termed 'the good old days, men owned the tools with which they worked." Now, however, "we have great machines of labor," and "the working man of today has lost his individuality" within the great "beehives of industry" ("President Gompers' Labor Day Address," typescript copy of article from the *Indianapolis Union*, September 12, 1903, 117A/11A, American Federation of Labor Papers, Box 46, Wisconsin Historical Society).

50. George Gunton, *The Economic and Social Importance of the Eight-Hour Movement,* 2nd ed. (Washington, D.C.: American Federation of Labor, 1889), 4–5.

51. "Individualism," *Social Economist* 1 (April 1891): 78; George Gunton, *Wealth and Progress: A Critical Examination of the Labor Problem,* 7th ed. (New York: Appleton, 1897), 206; "Sound Economics in Congress," *Social Economist* 6 (March 1894): 132.

52. David R. Roediger, "Ira Steward and the Anti-Slavery Origins of American Eight-Hour Theory," *Labor History* 27 (Spring 1986): 412; David Horowitz, *The Morality of Spending: Attitudes towards the Consumer Society in America, 1875–1940* (Baltimore: Johns Hopkins University Press, 1985).

53. Addams, *Democracy and Social Ethics,* 34–35.

54. Kathy Peiss, *Cheap Amusements: Working Women and Leisure in Turn-of-the-Century New York* (Philadelphia: Temple University Press, 1986); Nan Enstad, *Ladies of Leisure, Girls of Adventure: Working Women, Popular Culture, and Labor Politics at the Turn of the Twentieth Century* (New York: Columbia University Press, 1999).

55. Addams, *Democracy and Social Ethics,* 36–38. Weyl's and Addams's understandings of "democratic" were not as abstract as what Sklansky has called Cooley's "democracy of the psyche," for both Weyl and Addams were profoundly dubious of democratic ideals that did not address material concerns (*Soul's Economy,* 202–22).

56. Christopher Lasch, *The New Radicalism in America, 1889–1963: The Intellectual as Social Type* (New York: Norton, 1965), xiv; Christopher Lasch, *The True and Only Heaven: Progress and Its Critics* (New York: Norton, 1992), 342–44.

57. Walter Weyl, *The New Democracy: An Essay on Certain Political and Economic Tendencies in the United States* (1912; New Brunswick, N.J.: Transaction, 2005), 164, 161. For a discussion of Weyl's understanding of the consumer in relation to specifically formal politics, see Donohue, *Freedom from Want,* 115–50.

58. Martin J. Sklar, *The United States as a Developing Country: Studies in U.S. History in the Progressive Era and the 1920s* (Cambridge: Cambridge University Press, 1992), 143–96; James Livingston, *Pragmatism and the Political Economy of Cultural Revolution* (Chapel Hill: University of North Carolina Press, 1994), 3–50, esp. 3–23. I focus on these historians precisely because they are historians rather than economists and because Sklar first proposed the idea in 1969, extrapolated from Marx, of

disaccumulation. For a clear use of Sklar's ideas in relation to the periodization of the Gilded Age, see Richard Schneirov, "Thoughts on Periodizing the Gilded Age: Capital Accumulation, Society, and Politics, 1873–1898," *Journal of Gilded Age and Progressive Era* 5 (July 2006), http://www.historycooperative.org.proxy.queensu.ca/journals/jga/5.3/schneirov.html (July 7, 2008).

59. Livingston, *Pragmatism and the Political Economy,* 22.

60. Schneirov, "Thoughts."

61. Quoted in Livingston, *Pragmatism and the Political Economy,* 18.

62. This inversion is usually dated from 1907 or 1910 and seen as accelerating after 1919, but, as Sklar points out, it is possible to see that "the period from the turn of the century through the 1920s (and up to the present time) possesses a unitary character, not merely in an abstract sense of impersonal 'objective conditions,' but also in the sense that central developments in the sociopolitical history and in the cultural and intellectual history of the nation were significantly related to the emerging phase of disaccumulation." Thus, following Weyl's reasoning in particular, I suggest that we look at the whole period as defined by gradual process of disaccumulation (Sklar, *United States as a Developing Country,* 161).

63. Ibid., 157.

64. Weyl, *New Democracy,* 191, 192, 193–94, 196; Donohue, *Freedom from Want,* 128–43. Weyl took the idea of a social surplus from his adviser, Simon Nelson Patten.

65. Weyl, *New Democracy,* 217.

66. Ibid., 213.

67. Ibid., 200, 197, 188, 200.

68. Weyl was not the only scholar of the time to insist on the broadly political significance of material life. As observers of the New South since Ida B. Wells have shown, white southerners also understood the links between economic and consumer agency and political power. They enacted Jim Crow laws to exclude African Americans from the polity by systematically curtailing black participation in social and economic life, even as African Americans worked to claim membership in the new democracy through participation in leisure and consumer society. Middle-class African Americans' efforts to assert economic and social power by insisting on buying and using first-class rail tickets were likely to result in especially violent confrontations. Whites saw such behavior as particularly dangerous precisely because such ticket purchases were the highly visible sign of the social meanings of economic participation. See Andrew W. Kahrl, "'The Slightest Semblance of Unruliness': Steamboat Excursions, Pleasure Resorts, and the Emergence of Segregation Culture on the Potomac River," *Journal of American History* 94 (March 2008): 1108–36; Barbara Young Welke, *Recasting American Liberty: Gender, Race, Law, and the Railroad Revolution, 1865–1920* (Cambridge: Cambridge University Press, 2001), 280–322.

69. Frances Fenton Bernard, review of *The New Democracy,* by Walter Weyl, *American Journal of Sociology* 18 (September 1912): 262–63.

70. Weyl, *New Democracy,* 202, 194.

71. Ibid., 158; James T. Kloppenberg, *Uncertain Victory: Social Democracy and Progressivism in European and American Thought, 1870–1920* (New York: Oxford University Press, 1986), 277–97, 410–15.

72. On the expansiveness of Progressive Era reforms, see Linda Gordon, "If the Progressives Were Advising Us Today, Should We Listen?" *Journal of the Gilded Age and Progressive Era* 1 (April 2002): 109–21; Robert Johnston, *The Radical Middle Class: Populist Democracy and the Question of Capitalism in Progressive Era Portland, Oregon* (Princeton: Princeton University Press, 2006); Elisabeth Clemens, *The People's Lobby: Organizational Innovation and the Rise of Interest Group Politics in the United States, 1870–1925* (Chicago: University of Chicago Press, 1997); Rodgers, *Atlantic Crossings.*

73. "A Latter-Day Crusoe: Dick Bassett, the Hermit of Grand Traverse Bay," *New York Times,* July 19, 1891; "Michigan's Robinson Crusoe," *Chicago Herald,* August 23, 1890; "Dick's an Odd Hermit," *Chicago Herald,* July 11, 1891.

74. Nelson A. Miles, "The Lesson of the Recent Strike," *North American Review* 159 (August 1894): 184.

75. The closing of the frontier and growing urban centers were only part of Miles's diagnosis of modern ills. He also lambasted the cupidity of the railroads, which had foolishly overexpanded and then been unable to pay interest on their bonds and stocks. And he attacked the "vast hordes of cheap and degraded labor unloaded on our Atlantic coast" for driving down the wages of American workingmen ("Lesson," 181–82, 188).

76. Nelson A. Miles to Adjutant General, July 18, 1894, John McAllister Schofield Papers, Box 72, Manuscript Division, Library of Congress.

77. Leon Fink, "The New Labor History and the Powers of Historical Pessimism: Consensus, Hegemony, and the Case of the Knights of Labor," *Journal of American History* 75 (June 1988): 115–36.

78. Irving Bacheller, *Eben Holden: A Tale of the North Country* (Boston: Lothrop, 1910), 429, v–vi.

79. Owen Wister, *The Virginian: A Horseman of the Plains* (New York: Macmillan, 1902), viii, ix, 502.

80. While some scholars have argued that the Progressive Era courts were less committed to laissez-faire constitutionalism than is frequently assumed, Daniel Ernst has contended that in cases involving protective labor legislation, judges made "quite forceful assertions of middle-class assumptions about the moral value of work, the essential identity between the right to work and the right to manage, and the private nature of the labor contract" ("Free Labor, the Consumer Interest, and the Law of Industrial Disputes, 1885–1909," *American Journal of Legal History* 36 [January 1992]: 19). In an article in the 1904 *Columbia Law Review,* for example, Clarence D. Ashley noted with some dismay that the courts were increasingly willing to limit freedom of contract but still invoked it to strike down legislation regulating labor ("Should There Be Freedom of Contract?" *Columbia Law Review* 4 [June 1904]: 423–27). It makes sense, then, to see the *Lochner*-era decisions as efforts to answer the labor

question through the reassertion of old ideals of independence cast in new light. The courts' decisions thus appear no less unfavorable to labor but can be seen as actively participating in ongoing debates about the basis of citizenship and the nature of democracy in industrial America.

81. Daniel Ernst, *Lawyers against Labor: From Individual Rights to Corporate Liberalism* (Urbana: University of Illinois Press, 1995).

82. Paul Gilje, *Rioting in America* (Bloomington: Indiana University Press, 1996), 122; "The Great Strike in Brooklyn," *Harper's Weekly,* February 2, 1895.

83. A. J. F. Behrends, *Sermon on the Brooklyn Strike, Preached Sunday Morning, February 10, 1895, in the Central Congregational Church in Brooklyn, N.Y.* (Park Row, N.Y.: Christian Work, 1895); originally published in the *Brooklyn Daily Eagle,* February 14, 1895.

84. "A Tribute to Rev. A. J. F. Behrends, D.D.," *American Missionary* 54 (July 1900): 118–19; Amy Dru Stanley, *From Bondage to Contract: Wage Labor, Marriage, and the Market in the Age of Slave Emancipation* (Cambridge: Cambridge University Press, 1998), 36–37; Foner, *Reconstruction,* 166–70.

85. *Godcharles v. Wigeman,* 113 Pa. 431, 6 A. 354 (1886), 444; Charles W. McCurdy, "The Roots of 'Liberty of Contract' Reconsidered: Major Premises in the Law of Employment, 1867–1937," *Supreme Court Historical Society Yearbook* (1984): 24. Nine years later, Gordon similarly upheld an individual's right to contract in *Commonwealth v. Isenberg,* 4 Pa. Dist. 579 (1895).

86. *Ritchie v. People,* 155 Ill. 106 (1895), 112, 105. In general, judges did not follow Magruder's logic about women's rights as citizens. Between 1895 and 1908, the year of the *Muller* decision, in only two other instances did state courts overturn protective legislation for women: *Burcher v. People,* 41 Colo. 495 (1907); *People v. Williams,* 189 N.Y. 131 (1907). For further discussion, see Howard Gillman, *The Constitution Besieged: The Rise and Demise of Lochner Era Police Powers Jurisprudence* (Durham: Duke University Press, 1995), 242 n. 87.

87. *Ritchie v. People,* 108.

88. Ibid., 112, 105.

89. *Allgeyer v. Louisiana,* 165 U.S. 578 (1897), 589.

90. Ibid., 590.

91. Starr Hoyt Nichols, "Another View of the Union Label," *North American Review* 165 (October 1897): 432, 434, 436, 441.

92. Edward F. McClennen, "Some of the Rights of Traders and Laborers," *Harvard Law Review* 16 (February 1903): 253–54.

93. On free labor ideology, see Eric Foner, *Free Soil, Free Labor, Free Men: The Ideology of the Republican Party before the Civil War* (New York: Oxford University Press, 1970). On the relationships among abolition, self-ownership, and liberty of contract, see William E. Nelson, *The Roots of American Bureaucracy, 1830–1900* (Cambridge: Harvard University Press, 1982). For a discussion of Nelson's views on liberty

of contract in comparison with those of Elizabeth Mensch and Lawrence Friedman, see McCurdy, "Roots of 'Liberty of Contract' Reconsidered," 20–33.

94. *Lochner v. New York,* 198 U.S. 45 (1905), 57.

95. While the Court acknowledged that "the proprietors of these [mines] and their operatives do not stand upon an equality, and that their interests are, to a certain extent, conflicting," the physical weakness of the miners rather than the material inequality between operator and laborer ultimately justified the law. At the end of the decision, the miners emerge frail and emasculated, rendered incapable of choosing the terms of their labor by the conditions of their work; their physical weakness prevented them from exercising "private judgment." As Gillman has argued, the majority opinion was seen not as overturning previous support for liberty of contract in the workplace but as "an explanation for why these issues were not resolved by the workers themselves" (*Constitution Besieged,* 123).

96. John Marshall Harlan's dissent in *Lochner* strongly echoed Henry Brown's majority opinion in *Holden,* arguing that particular circumstances of work could limit the choice of contract. In general, Harlan was a strong supporter of freedom of contract, as his opinion in *Adair v. U.S.* shows (208 U.S. 161 [1908], 175, 174).

97. *Muller v. Oregon,* 208 U.S. 412 (1908); Sybil Lipschultz, "Hours and Wages: The Gendering of Labor Standards in America," *Journal of Women's History* 8 (Spring 1996): 126.

98. F. J. Stimson, "The Ethics of Democracy—Liberty," *Scribner's Magazine,* January–June 1894, 649, 652, 656.

99. A. B. Farquhar, "Speech to Congress over Hours Bill HR 3076," Folder 4, Box 4, National Civic Federation Papers, Division of Rare Books and Manuscripts, New York Public Library, New York.

100. James Gordley, "Contract Property and the Will—The Civil Law and Common Law Tradition," in *The State and Freedom of Contract,* ed. Harry N. Scheiber (Stanford: Stanford University Press, 1998), 86–87. On Hurst, see William J. Novak, "Law, Capitalism, and the Liberal State: The Historical Sociology of James Willard Hurst," *Law and History Review* 18 (Spring 2000): 118–19.

101. Wai-Chee Dimock, *Residues of Justice: Literature, Law, and Philosophy* (Berkeley: University of California Press, 1996), 210.

Afterword. Residues of the Labor Question

1. Selig Perlman, *A Theory of the Labor Movement* (New York: Kelley, 1949), 6–7.

2. Gabriel Kolko, *The Triumph of Conservatism: A Re-Interpretation of American History, 1900–1916* (Glencoe, Ill.: Free Press, 1963); J. David Greenstone, *Labor in American Politics* (New York: Knopf, 1968); David Montgomery, *Workers' Control in America* (Cambridge: Cambridge University Press, 1980); Shelton Stromquist, *Reinventing "The People": The Progressive Movement, the Class Problem, and the Origins of Modern Liberalism* (Urbana: University of Illinois Press, 2006).

3. David Steigerwald, "All Hail the Republic of Choice: Consumer History as Contemporary Thought," *Journal of American History* 93 (September 2006): 399.

4. Doug Rossinow has argued that "historians at times gave the impression that rebellions in U.S. history . . . were authentic and inspiring only to the extent that they were free from any taint of liberal ideology." One historiographical consequence has been the installation of the "Knights . . . to heroic status in the annals of Gilded Age America," "exempted . . . from the moral stains of narrow self-interest, elitism and racism that have marked the reputation of the American Federation of Labor's craft unionists" (*Visions of Progress: The Left-Liberal Tradition in America* [Philadelphia: University of Pennsylvania Press, 2008], 2, 18).

5. Thomas Frank, *What's the Matter with Kansas? How Conservatives Won the Heart of America* (New York: Metropolitan, 2004.)

6. Steven Greenhouse, *The Big Squeeze: Tough Times for the American Worker* (New York: Knopf, 2008), 4–5. See also "Little Change in Workers' Poverty Level," *Los Angeles Times*, June 30, 2000; "Hourly Pay in U.S. Not Keeping Pace with Price Rises," *New York Times*, July 18, 2004; "Real Wages Fail to Match a Rise in Productivity," *New York Times*, August 28, 2006; "Answers about Fighting Poverty in New York," *New York Times*, May 28, 2008; "Low Income Working Families under Strain," *New York Times*, October 14, 2008; Working Poor Families Project, "Still Working Hard and Still Falling Short," http://www.workingpoorfamilies.org/pdfs/NatReport08.pdf (May 7, 2010). The number of Americans officially living in poverty has increased even as the poverty line itself, adjusted for inflation, has been lowered.

7. Steven Greenhouse, "Americans' International Lead in Hours Worked Grew in 90's, Report Shows," *New York Times*, September 1, 2001.

8. The arguments for understanding class as reducible to the means of production often suggest an ontological or transhistorical understanding of class. But as Christopher Clark, among many others, has pointed out, class was defined much more broadly in the late eighteenth and early nineteenth centuries and was as much "an ideological claim" as a relationship to productive property ("Comment on the Symposium on Class in the Early Republic," *Journal of the Early Republic* 25 [Winter 2005]: 559; see also Jennifer L. Goloby, "The Early American Middle Class," *Journal of the Early Republic* 25 [Winter 2005]: 537–45).

9. On the continuing importance of work and the workplace for economic democracy, see William E. Forbath, "Caste, Class, and Equal Citizenship," in *Moral Problems in American Life: New Perspectives on Cultural History*, ed. Karen Halttunen and Lewis Perry (Ithaca: Cornell University Press, 1998), 167–200; Nancy K. MacLean, *Freedom Is Not Enough: The Opening of the American Workplace* (Cambridge: Harvard University Press, 2008).

10. Joseph A. McCartin, *Labor's Great War: The Struggle for Industrial Democracy and the Origins of Modern American Labor Relations, 1912–1927* (Chapel Hill: University of North Carolina Press, 1997). McCartin notes that although many workers

understood industrial democracy to include workplace control, that battle had, by and large, already been lost (7).

11. Michael Kazin and Steven J. Ross, "America's Labor Day: The Dilemma of a Workers' Celebration," *Journal of American History* 78 (March 1992): 1307.

12. "On the Attitude of Organized Labor toward Organized Charity," *American Federationist* 6 (March 1899): 82. Democracy might well include, as it did in many places, the tools of direct democracy such as the initiative, the referendum, and the recall. But out of the debates over the labor question emerged a consensus that in an industrial society marked by mass production, democracy had economic and cultural aspects as well. On the expansion of cultural politics, see, for example, Sarah Jo Peterson, "Voting for Play: The Democratic Potential of Progressive Era Playgrounds," *Journal of the Gilded Age and Progressive Era* 3 (April 2004): 145–75; James Livingston, *Pragmatism, Feminism, and Democracy: Rethinking the Politics of American History* (New York: Routledge, 2001).

13. Martin J. Sklar, *The United States as a Developing Country: Studies in U.S. History in the Progressive Era and the 1920s* (Cambridge: Cambridge University Press, 1992), 157. For less technical but very similar argument, see Richard Hofstadter, *The Age of Reform: From Bryan to F.D.R.* (New York: Vintage, 1955), 315–16.

14. Walter Weyl, *The New Democracy: An Essay on Certain Political and Economic Tendencies in the United States* (1914; New Brunswick, N.J.: Transaction, 2005), 174–77. As Paul Douglas (who was strongly influenced by both John Bates Clark and the Quaker reform tradition) showed in his impressive 1930 work on real wages, non-union payroll workers saw their hourly rate of pay increase much more rapidly than did union workers (usually skilled workers) in the first two decades of the twentieth century. At the same time, the number of hours each worker labored declined throughout the same period, so real annual income did not increase with the same alacrity as it had in previous decades, and most of the increase was found in the historically lower paid and less skilled echelons of the working class. Stanley Lebergott's and Albert Rees's modifications of Douglas's statistics demonstrated that all manufacturing workers saw an increase in real wages throughout the period (though unevenly by industry) and that most of that increase came from rising wage rages on a particular job rather than from occupational mobility. However, Rees also showed that in keeping with capitalists' efforts to wrest control and profit from skilled workers via mechanization, output per man-hour increased far more rapidly than did real hourly wages. Wage earners' share of total manufacturing output, therefore, fell. See Paul Douglas, *Real Wages in the United States, 1890–1926* (1930; New York: Kelley, 1966); Stanley Lebergott, "Earnings of Nonfarm Employees in the U.S., 1890–1946," *Journal of the American Statistical Association* 43 (March 1948): 74–93; Albert Rees, *Real Wages in Manufacturing, 1890–1914* (Princeton: Princeton University Press, 1961), 124–27; Albert Rees, "Douglas on Wages and the Supply of Labor," *Journal of Political Economy* 87 (October 1979): 915–22; Mary O. Furner, "Knowing Capitalism:

Public Investigation and the Labor Question in the Long Progressive Era," in *The State and Economic Knowledge: The American and British Experiences,* ed. Mary O. Furner and Barry Supple (Cambridge: Cambridge University Press, 1990), 263–68.

15. Michael J. Sandel, *Democracy's Discontent: America in Search of a Public Philosophy* (Cambridge: Belknap Press of Harvard University Press, 1996), 225–26; Warren Susman, *Culture as History: The Transformation of American Society in the Twentieth Century* (New York: Pantheon, 1984), 271–86.

16. Weyl, *New Democracy,* 164, 1, 209, 197.

17. Consumers and consumerist movements have not used the language of producerist class politics, but that omission does not mean they have been blind to social distinctions and differences of power. Rather, it suggests that social distinctions are played out, articulated, and understood outside the workplace and separate from control or ownership of productive property. Nor are consumers or consumerist actions inherently apolitical. Consumer boycotts sought to harness the public power of purchasers for specifically social aims; consumer and mass culture have served as means of forging and solidifying collective social identities; consumer action has helped forge both social and political change. See Lawrence B. Glickman, "The Strike in the Temple of Consumption: Consumer Activism and Twentieth-Century American Political Culture," *Journal of American History* 88 (June 2001): 99–128; Lawrence Levine, "The Folklore of Industrial Society: Popular Culture and Its Audiences," *American Historical Review* 97 (December 1992): 1369–99; Lizabeth Cohen, "Encountering Mass Culture at the Grassroots: The Experience of Chicago Workers in the 1920s," *American Quarterly* 41 (March 1989): 6–33; Kathleen Donohue, *Freedom from Want: American Liberalism and the Idea of the Consumer* (Baltimore: Johns Hopkins University Press, 2003); Meg Jacobs, *Pocketbook Politics: Economic Citizenship in Twentieth-Century America* (Princeton: Princeton University Press, 2004).

18. On the role of economic democracy in the civil rights movement, see, for example, Risa L. Goluboff, *The Lost Promise of Civil Rights* (Cambridge: Harvard University Press, 2007); MacLean, *Freedom Is Not Enough.*

19. Matt Miller, "Is Labor Out in Front on Health Care?" *New York Times,* February 13, 2005; Keith Bradsher, "Fiercest Fight on Taxes, Health Care for Miners," *New York Times,* March 15, 1992.

20. Jane Addams, *Democracy and Social Ethics* (New York: Macmillan, 1902), 6.

Index

ROSANNE CURRARINO is an associate professor of history at Queen's University in Kingston, Ontario, Canada.

The University of Illinois Press
is a founding member of the
Association of American University Presses.

Composed in 10.5/13 Adobe Minion Pro
by Celia Shapland
at the University of Illinois Press
Manufactured by Cushing-Malloy, Inc.
University of Illinois Press

1325 South Oak Street
Champaign, IL 61820-6903
www.press.uillinois.edu